THE FORMATION OF SCHOLARS

THE FORMATION OF SCHOLARS

SCHOLARS

Rethinking Doctoral Education for the Twenty-First Century

George E. Walker, Chris M. Golde, Laura Jones,

Andrea Conklin Bueschel, Pat Hutchings

o

Foreword by

Lee S. Shulman

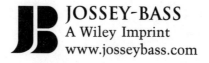

JOSSEY-BASS
A Wiley Imprint
www.josseybass.com

THE CARNEGIE FOUNDATION FOR THE ADVANCEMENT OF TEACHING

Published by Jossey-Bass
A Wiley Imprint
989 Market Street, San Francisco, CA 94103-1741—www.josseybass.com

Jossey-Bass books and products are available through most bookstores. To contact Jossey-Bass directly call our Customer Care Department within the U.S. at 800-956-7739, outside the U.S. at 317-572-3986, or fax 317-572-4002.

Jossey-Bass also publishes its books in a variety of electronic formats. Some content that appears in print may not be available in electronic books.

Library of Congress Cataloging-in-Publication Data

The formation of scholars : rethinking doctoral education for the twenty-first century / George E. Walker . . . [et al.]; foreword by Lee S. Shulman.—1st ed.
    p. cm.
    "Carnegie Foundation for the Advancement of Teaching."
    Includes bibliographical references and indexes.
    ISBN 978-0-470-19743-1 (cloth : alk. paper)
    1. Doctor of philosophy degree. 2. Universities and colleges—United States—Graduate work. I. Walker, George E.
  LB2386.F67 2008
  378.24—dc22
                                              2007035493

Printed in the United States of America
FIRST EDITION
HB Printing   10 9 8 7 6 5 4 3 2

THE CARNEGIE FOUNDATION FOR THE ADVANCEMENT OF TEACHING

Founded by Andrew Carnegie in 1905 and chartered in 1906 by an Act of Congress, The Carnegie Foundation for the Advancement of Teaching is an independent policy and research center whose charge is "to do and perform all things necessary to encourage, uphold, and dignify the profession of the teacher and the cause of higher education."

The Foundation is a major national and international center for research and policy studies about teaching. Its mission is to address the hardest problems faced in teaching in public schools, colleges, and universities—that is, how to succeed in the classroom, how best to achieve lasting student learning, and how to assess the impact of teaching on students.

CONTENTS

FOREWORD

Academics are very careful with words. The title of this book, *The Formation of Scholars,* embodies two key terms that call for explanation and interpretation. Why *formation?* Why *scholars?* The answer is that the juxtaposition of these two ideas captures the essential character of the work reported in this volume. Doctoral education prepares scholars who both understand what is known and discover what is yet unknown. They conserve the most valued knowledge of the past even as they examine it critically. They invent new forms of understanding as they move their fields ahead. Yet the more they understand, the heavier their moral obligation to use their knowledge and skill with integrity, responsibility, and generosity. They are thinkers and actors, intellectual adventurers and moral agents. The idea of formation, borrowed from religious educators, refers to the kind of education that leads to an integration of mind and moral virtue that we often call character or integrity.

When I first began working in teacher education, I was admonished by insiders never to use the phrase "teacher *training.*" Training implied mindless, routine practice more appropriate to an assembly line than to a classroom. It also reinforced the rampant behaviorism that dominated the fields of teacher preparation and teacher evaluation. The correct term was "teacher *education,*" which more aptly captured the fundamentally intellectual, strategic, and thoughtful functions associated with teaching. I took this instruction to heart. Indeed, when I delivered my presidential address to the American Educational Research Association in 1984, I concluded my remarks with a revision of Shaw's "Those who can, do; those who cannot, teach," changing it to "Those who can, do. Those who *understand,* teach." Teaching must be understood as an intentional act of mind for which a rich educational experience is necessary. Yet this move may not be enough.

In recent years, my colleagues and I at The Carnegie Foundation for the Advancement of Teaching undertook our comparative studies of education across the "learned professions" of law, engineering, the clergy, teaching, medicine, and nursing. In parallel, we initiated the study of doctoral education that is described and analyzed in this book. We recognized early on that doctoral education could be examined as a form of professional preparation. Those with PhDs are prepared both to know and to do. Holders of the PhD are prepared to profess their disciplines and their fields of study, not only to understand them deeply but also to take upon themselves the moral responsibility to protect the integrity of their field and its proper use in the service of humanity. We found the term *formation*—used extensively in the field of religious education and the preparation of clergy—to be particularly appropriate for describing this integration of the intellectual and the moral in preparing for the many roles of the scholar—discovery and synthesis, teaching and service. Thus we had evolved from training to education and from education to formation.

The PhD is the monarch of the academic community. It is the very highest accomplishment that can be sought by students. It signals that its recipient is now ready, eligible, indeed obligated, to make the most dramatic shift in roles: from student to teacher, from apprentice to master, from novice or intern to independent scholar and leader. The PhD marks its holder as one charged to serve as a steward of the discipline and profession. If this language sounds mildly ecclesiastical, it is no accident. We do not choose the language of "formation" or "stewardship" capriciously. The doctorate carries with it both a sense of intellectual mastery and of moral responsibility. That the entire process concludes with all members of the community dressed in religious robes and engaged in an act of ordination of the novice by the master with a priestly hood is no accident.

So is the PhD to be understood as just one more learned profession, the academic parallel to engineering, law, or medicine? Not really. I remember my surprise at the scheduling of commencements at my alma mater. When completing graduate study at the University of Chicago, I saw that the undergraduate commencement was to be held on Friday, when all of the baccalaureate degrees would be awarded—including the degrees of MD and JD. The graduate commencement for recipients of master's degrees and PhDs was scheduled for the following day. When I expressed my confusion over this placement of the medical and law degrees, I was informed that both of these degrees were inherently "undergraduate." Indeed, we regularly refer to the four years of medical school as "undergraduate medical education." Outside the United States, the first medical degree has traditionally been the Bachelor of Medicine; only recently has the first law degree changed from an LLB to a JD, without any alteration in curriculum requirements or standards. These degrees did not prepare their recipients for lives of scholarship and teaching. True graduate degrees are special.

What accounts for the mystique of the PhD? It is the academy's own means of reproduction. In a Darwinian sense, the academy invests most heavily in its own means of reproduction and sustainability. The denouement of the doctorate, the dissertation, is not only a piece of original research intended to set its writer apart from all who preceded her. It is also a celebration of the scores of scholars on whose shoulders any piece of individual scholarship rests. Even as the candidate writes the dissertation—the contribution to knowledge, the evidence of scholarly innovation and invention—the text is peppered with footnotes and references, citations and bibliographies, acknowledgments and attributions. Each of these bears witness to every scholar's debt to her predecessors in scholarship. References and footnotes also acknowledge the work of contemporaries who live in the same professional and disciplinary community as the candidate, or in a closely neighboring field of study. Scholarship is a social and communal activity. Thus candidates give recognition to the continuing presence of their extended intellectual community as the scaffold that supports and sustains their research work, whether present in the teachers and colleagues of one's own program, or ever helpful in the whispers, hints, proof texts, and challenges of scholars long dead but still audible through their published work. It is also why, we argue in this volume, nothing is more critical to the quality of a doctoral program than the character of the intellectual community created by its teachers and students.

We at the Carnegie Foundation elected to devote five years to the study of the PhD and its possible futures because we felt strongly that the academic profession bridges past and future in the context of each individual doctoral program. The doctorate as an institution provides the stability and tradition that renders scholarship a human activity that transcends generations, cultures, and contexts. It is both a paragon of innovation and a defender of the faith. The doctorate is both transformation and impediment; it preserves what is enduring, but can also paralyze— hardening categories and freezing traditions into empty rituals. The best doctoral programs attempt to discover the "sweet spot" between conservation and change by teaching skepticism and respect for earlier traditions and sources while encouraging strikingly new ideas and courageous leaps forward. As readers of the late Thomas Kuhn can aver, scholars are evaluated and rewarded by how faithfully they labor within the existing paradigms, but they are celebrated and venerated for scientific revolutions that shatter old paradigms and create new ones.

Also decided, unlike most previous studies of the doctorate, to treat doctoral education as domain- and field-specific, not as a generic activity at the all-university level. Both scholarship and teaching in any field reflect the character of inquiry, the nature of community, and the ways in which research and teaching are conducted in that particular discipline or disciplinary intersection. We therefore elected to distribute our efforts across a set of fields selected to represent the full extent of the academic enterprise.

This kind of work is complex and labor intensive. Working across six fields—chemistry, education, English, history, mathematics, and neuroscience—demanded the efforts of a remarkably diverse and multi-talented team. Since I write both to introduce the volume and, as president of the Foundation, to express my gratitude to my colleagues, the scholars who made this work possible, I conclude by turning to them and acknowledging their creative leadership.

Leading the team was George Walker, a theoretical physicist by training and scholarship, who served for many years as graduate dean and vice president for research at Indiana University. A national leader in graduate education, George has been an energetic and charismatic leader of this work. Coaxing him to leave Bloomington to come west and lead this project was no small challenge. Fortunately, he is a lifelong San Francisco Giants baseball fan, which made the "pitch" far easier than it might have been.

Chris Golde began her academic career at Stanford University with a pioneering dissertation study of the complexities of doctoral education and continued this work as a faculty member at the University of Wisconsin. As director of research for the Carnegie Initiative on the Doctorate (CID), she coordinated the several research functions associated with the effort and was a central figure in designing the many convenings that brought together participants both within and across disciplinary communities.

Laura Jones, trained as an anthropologist and archaeologist, joined the project to add strength to the research and convening programs of the CID. Andrea Conklin Bueschel, a higher education scholar with special interest in the unique role of community colleges, was a key member of the team.

Pat Hutchings, vice president of the Foundation, coordinated the final critical stages of writing this book, leading its transformation from a rich and varied array of insights and hypotheses into the tightly argued and gracefully presented monograph we have before us.

The project was counseled by a wise advisory committee chaired by Donald Kennedy, former president of Stanford University and editor-in-chief of *Science* during the entire period of the study.

I am particularly grateful to the hundreds of faculty members and doctoral students from more than forty institutions that participated in the work over its five-year lifetime. They were the engines of reform, the experimenters as well as the experimented-upon. If this work makes the future impact that we intend, it will be through their efforts, past and future.

Doctoral education is a set of experiences that incorporates training, education, and formation. It is a process led by faculty and brought to life by students. It is the key experience upon which the future of global higher education rests. We hope that this volume will support the many ways in which the formation of scholars can be effected through the transformation of graduate education.

Lee S. Shulman
Stanford, California

ACKNOWLEDGMENTS

The Carnegie Initiative on the Doctorate (CID) and this resulting volume are products of much hard work, commitment, and the dedication of many, many people. The CID team was particularly fortunate to have had the opportunity to work closely with and benefit from the talent of many staff members. Amita Chudgar and Kim Rapp were research assistants for the CID, contributing important ideas, analysis, and feedback. Sonia Gonzalez, Leslie Eustice, Ruby Kerawalla, Tasha Kalista, Emily Stewart, and Lydia Baldwin all provided invaluable administrative support to the project, not only ensuring that the trains ran on time, but doing so with good cheer and great skill.

The Carnegie Foundation is a highly collaborative setting and many additional colleagues played major roles in the work as well, providing support, critical feedback, generous collaboration, and contributions to everything from convenings to manuscript suggestions. In particular, Mary Taylor Huber, Gay Clyburn, and Sherry Hecht read drafts of this manuscript several times and gently guided its direction. And of course Lee Shulman's influence on the work was front and center throughout, as it is in all of the work of the Foundation.

We are also fortunate to have many colleagues beyond Carnegie who have influenced the work of the CID and therefore shaped this volume. The essayists who provided initial "grist for the mill" for each discipline helped provoke and encourage our participants—and us—to consider ideas and directions that were in many ways "unnatural acts." Their work, collected in *Envisioning the Future of Doctoral Education*, is an important foundation for this book. We have also benefited from the input of many people who contribute daily to graduate education, including graduate deans, staff members of disciplinary societies, interested observers who participated in our convenings, and funding agencies. We are also grateful to our anonymous external reviewers for their helpful comments.

The Atlantic Philanthropies was Carnegie's major financial partner in this work. We are grateful to them for several decades of support of graduate education and our work in particular.

In addition, our advisory committee offered crucial and thoughtful advice throughout the project. The committee was chaired by Donald Kennedy, president emeritus and Bing Professor of Environmental Science and Policy emeritus, Stanford University, and editor-in-chief of *Science* magazine. The other members were Bruce Alberts, former president of the National Academy of Sciences and professor of biochemistry and biophysics, University of California, San Francisco; David Damrosch, professor of English and comparative literature, Columbia University; Michael Feuer, executive director of the Division of Behavioral and Social Sciences and Education, National Research Council; Phillip Griffiths, professor of mathematics and former director of the Institute for Advanced Study, Princeton University; Dudley Herschbach, Baird Professor of Science in chemistry, Harvard University; Stanley Katz, professor of Public and International Affairs and director of the Center for Arts and Cultural Policy Studies at Princeton University; Joshua Lederberg, Sackler Foundation Scholar and professor emeritus, Rockefeller University; Kenneth Prewitt, Carnegie Professor of Public Affairs, Columbia University; Robert Rosenzweig, president emeritus of the Association of American Universities; Henry Rosovsky, Lewis P. and Linda L. Geyser University Professor emeritus, Harvard University; Lee S. Shulman, president of The Carnegie Foundation for the Advancement of Teaching; and Debra W. Stewart, president of the Council of Graduate Schools.

We are also grateful for the support of the disciplinary and professional societies that represent the six CID disciplines. They have provided multiple opportunities for us and our campus participants to share the work of the CID—at conferences, in newsletters and journals, and in meetings with leadership. In many ways, they are one of the keys to ensuring that the excellent work begun by campuses in the CID continues and becomes part of their regular discussions and activities.

- The American Chemical Society (ACS)
- The American Educational Research Association (AERA)
- The American Historical Association (AHA)
- The American Mathematical Society (AMS)
- The Association of Departments of English (ADE)
- The Association of Neuroscience Departments and Programs (ANDP)
- The Council of Graduate Schools (CGS)
- The Modern Language Association (MLA)
- The Society for Neuroscience (SfN)

Finally, none of the work of the CID would have been possible (or nearly as much fun) without the tremendous investment of time, energy, and imagination of our campus participants. The graduate students, faculty, and staff of the CID departments *were* the project. Their hard work was what made the CID successful. Their challenges, struggles, and successes taught us about what, in fact, is possible in doctoral education. Their collaborative spirit and willingness to take risks provided a valuable response to the many indictments of graduate education. Their commitment to improving the education and lives of doctoral students was the greatest reward. It is to them that this work is dedicated.

ABOUT THE AUTHORS

GEORGE E. WALKER is currently vice president for research and dean of the University Graduate School at Florida International University. From 2001 to 2006, he served as senior scholar and director of the Carnegie Initiative on the Doctorate at The Carnegie Foundation for the Advancement of Teaching. Dr. Walker is a theoretical nuclear physicist who obtained his undergraduate education at Wesleyan University, his graduate education at Case Western University, and his post-doctoral education at the Los Alamos National Laboratory and at Stanford University. Most of his scholarly career was at Indiana University, where he was vice president for research and dean of the Graduate School for many years. He was twice honored by physics graduate students with the "Outstanding Contributions to Graduate Education" award, and by his peers through election as a Fellow of the American Physical Society. He led the establishment of a Nuclear Theory Center at Indiana University. He is also chair of the Physics and Advanced Technology Directorate Advisory Committee, and chair of the Nuclear Division Advisory Committee, both at Lawrence Livermore National Laboratory. In addition, he is a member of the National Advisory Board of the Center for the Integration of Research, Teaching, and Learning (CIRTL). Among many other boards, Walker has served as president of the Association of Graduate Schools of the Association of American Universities, as chair of the Board of the Council of Graduate Schools, and as member of the National Advisory Board of the National Survey of Student Engagement. He is coeditor, with Chris M. Golde, of *Envisioning the Future of Doctoral Education: Preparing Stewards of the Discipline—Carnegie Essays on the Doctorate* (2006).

CHRIS M. GOLDE is associate vice provost for graduate education at Stanford University. From 2001 to 2006, she served as senior scholar and research director for the Carnegie Initiative on the Doctorate at The Carnegie Foundation for the Advancement of Teaching. Before joining Carnegie, she was a faculty member at the University of Wisconsin-Madison. Her research and writing have focused on doctoral education, particularly the experiences of doctoral students and doctoral student attrition. She is the lead author of *At Cross Purposes: What the Experiences of Today's Doctoral Students Reveal About Doctoral Education,* the 2001 report of a national survey funded by The Pew Charitable Trusts (www.phd-survey.org). She is coeditor, with George E. Walker, of *Envisioning the Future of Doctoral Education: Preparing Stewards of the Discipline—Carnegie Essays on the Doctorate* (2006). She holds a PhD in education from Stanford University.

LAURA JONES is an applied anthropologist practicing in the areas of archaeology, public history, heritage preservation, and community planning and outreach. Her geographical areas of research interest are California and Oceania. Currently she holds the position of director of Heritage Services and University Archaeologist at Stanford University. She was senior scholar and director of the Community Program at the Carnegie Foundation from 2000–2006. In addition to publications in anthropology, she is the author of an upcoming article giving a comparative view on educational practices in the sciences and the humanities, "Converging Paradigms for Doctoral Training in the Sciences and Humanities," to appear in *Changing Practices in Doctoral Education.* She holds a doctorate in anthropology from Stanford University.

ANDREA CONKLIN BUESCHEL is currently senior program officer with the Spencer Foundation. She formerly served as research scholar with the Carnegie Foundation, where she worked on the Carnegie Initiative on the Doctorate and the Strengthening Pre-collegiate Education in Community Colleges projects. She has conducted research and written on policy links and disjunctures between K–12 and higher education, with a focus on the high school to college transition, especially for students who hope to be the first in their families to attend postsecondary education. In addition, she has served as researcher and managing director for an educational consulting firm, and has held various administrative posts in higher education. She is coeditor of the forthcoming *New Directions for Community Colleges* volume *Policies and Practices to Improve Student Preparation and Success.* Dr. Bueschel has a PhD in education from Stanford University.

PAT HUTCHINGS is vice president of The Carnegie Foundation for the Advancement of Teaching, working closely with a wide range of programs and research initiatives. She has written widely on the investigation and documentation of teaching and learning, the peer collaboration and review of teaching, and the scholarship of teaching and learning. Recent publications, both drawing from Carnegie's work, include *Ethics of Inquiry: Issues in the Scholarship of Teaching and Learning* (2002) and *Opening*

Lines: Approaches to the Scholarship of Teaching and Learning (2000). Her most recent book, *The Advancement of Learning: Building the Teaching Commons* (2005), was coauthored with Mary Taylor Huber. She holds a doctorate in English from the University of Iowa and was chair of the English department at Alverno College from 1978 to 1987.

THE FORMATION OF SCHOLARS

MOVING DOCTORAL EDUCATION INTO THE FUTURE

Even if you are on the right track,
you'll get run over if you just sit there.

—Will Rogers[1]

AS YOU READ THESE WORDS, some 375,000 men and women are pursuing doctoral degrees in institutions of higher education in the United States. Most are young adults—many with family commitments, and some juggling careers as well—but PhD programs are also populated by the occasional octogenarian and precocious teen. Some are in their first semester of work; others have been toiling for twenty years. Over 43,000 will graduate this year from the 400-plus institutions that offer the degree.[2]

Many of those who receive PhD's will assume positions of leadership and responsibility in arenas that directly shape the lives we lead. A remarkable number of Nobel laureates from around the world received degrees at U.S. universities. Four of the ten most recent secretaries of state have been doctoral degree holders, as are five of the six current members of the Federal Reserve Board,[3] and numerous world leaders. PhD's develop life-saving medical interventions, shape social programs and policies, and turn their talents to entrepreneurial ventures in the global economy. Approximately one-half of those who receive doctorates this year will join the ranks of college and university faculty who educate today's undergraduates, some of whom will become teachers themselves, in the United States and beyond, shaping the futures of our children and grandchildren. And some will prepare new PhD's, so the effects of doctoral education ripple out across nations and generations.

The importance of doctoral education to this country's current and future prospects can hardly be overestimated. The questions are: What will it take to ensure that the United States continues to be, as many have observed, "the envy of the world"? What will it take to meet the challenges that doctoral education faces today and to make the changes those challenges require?

Some of the challenges are long standing and well known. About half of today's doctoral students are lost to attrition—and in some programs the numbers are higher yet. Those who persist often take a long time to finish and along the way find their passion for the field sadly diminished.[4] Many are ill-prepared for the full range of roles they must play, be they in academe or beyond, and often the experience is marred by a mismatch between the opportunities available to students as they complete their work and their expectations and training along the way. In most disciplines, women and ethnic minorities are still underrepresented among doctoral students. And what makes all of these challenges yet *more* challenging is that few processes for assessing effectiveness have been developed in graduate education, and it is difficult to muster ambition or urgency for doing better in the absence of information about what needs improvement. Thus, one finds attitudes of complacency ("Our application numbers are strong and so is our national ranking, so where's the problem?"), denial ("We don't have problems with gender or ethnic diversity here"), and blame ("Students these days just aren't willing to make the kinds of sacrifices we did to be successful").

Complicating matters is a set of newer challenges, many of them emerging as we write, and only partly recognized and understood. New technologies are altering and accelerating the way knowledge is shared and developed. And the marketplace for scholars and scholarship is now thoroughly global. Much of the most important, pathbreaking intellectual work going on today occurs in the borderlands between fields, blurring boundaries and challenging traditional disciplinary definitions. The need for firmer connections between academic work and the wider world of public life is increasingly clear, as well. And graduate education, like higher education more generally, faces shifting student demographics, new kinds of competition, growing pressures for accountability, and shrinking public investment. In short, expectations are escalating, and doctoral programs today face fundamental questions of purpose, vision, and quality. The Will Rogers quip that opens this chapter seems made to order: "Even if you are on the right track, you'll get run over if you just sit there."

The Carnegie Initiative on the Doctorate

The good news is that doctoral education is, by its nature, in the business of asking hard questions, pushing frontiers, and solving problems, and over the past several years the five of us have been privileged to work closely with faculty and students from doctoral programs that have made the decision to not "just sit there." The Carnegie Initiative on the Doctorate (CID) has involved eighty-four PhD-granting departments in six fields—chemistry, education, English, history, mathematics, and neuroscience (for the full list of departments, see Appendix B). Our emphasis in this book, and in the Carnegie Initiative on the Doctorate, was on the PhD, although many of our participating education departments also grant the EdD.[5] By concentrating on a limited number of disciplines and interdisciplines rather than on doctoral education in general, the CID aimed to go deep and to work very directly with faculty and graduate students from the ground up. Thus, although the support and assistance of administrators, graduate deans in particular, and disciplinary societies was vital, the work was done by departments on matters within the control of departments—which is, after all, where the action is in graduate education.

---
o

Over the five years of the program, participating departments made a commitment to examine their own purposes and effectiveness, to implement changes in response to their findings, and to monitor the impact of those changes. Many used their participation to continue plans and activities that were already begun but would benefit from the structure, prestige, and interaction provided by a national initiative. Our role, in turn, included visiting the departments, interviewing campus team members, and bringing project participants together (sometimes by discipline, sometimes by theme) to report on their progress, learn from one another, and help us make sense of their experiences in ways that others can build on. (See Appendix A for a summary of the CID project.) In addition, both faculty and students participated in projectwide surveys, the results of which served as rich grist for discussion and debate about the preparation of scholars in the broadest sense, whether they work in industry, government, or academe. (See Appendix C for an overview of the CID surveys.)

Certainly there was much to discuss. Not surprisingly, in a project sponsored by The Carnegie Foundation for the Advancement of Teaching, an organization whose mission is to "uphold and dignify the profession of the teacher," a recurring theme was the need for practices that will better prepare tomorrow's PhD's to be teachers, equipped with the knowledge and skills to convey their field's complex ideas to a variety of audiences, not only in the classroom, but in the many other settings in which doctorate holders work. This is an arena in which higher education has made notable progress over the past several decades. Many institutions today—and most of those participating in the CID—offer training programs for graduate teaching assistants, sometimes through a campus-wide teaching center, but often through special opportunities housed in the department as well. And fields in which opportunities to teach have traditionally been limited (for example, neuroscience graduate programs often have no corresponding undergraduate program) are now finding creative ways to provide experience in the classroom. But what the CID has made clear is the need for much greater attention to the sequencing of these opportunities and to the need not only for more teaching but for better, more systematic feedback and reflection that can turn pedagogical experience into pedagogical expertise.

The same diagnosis holds, we believe, when it comes to preparation for the research role. Ironically, this aspect of doctoral education—the sine qua non of the doctorate—has largely been taken for granted and therefore ignored in reports and recommendations on graduate education that have appeared in the past several decades. Our view, in contrast, is that what might be called "the pedagogy of research" (and its different embodiments in different fields) is badly in need of attention. Most graduate faculty care deeply that their students learn how to ask good questions, build on the work of others, formulate an effective and feasible research design, and communicate results in ways that matter. But these outcomes are often more hoped for and assumed than designed into instruction. Although education at other levels is being reshaped by new knowledge about how people learn, these same insights seem to have washed over graduate education with little effect. For instance, whereas undergraduate education now embraces a host of strategies to engage students in research, those approaches have received less attention in doctoral education settings—even though the same faculty members may teach both undergraduate and graduate students. As a consequence, the central tasks and assignments that doctoral students encounter on the long road to research expertise, and the model of apprenticeship that shapes their interactions with faculty, have gone pretty much unchanged from generation to generation, the product of long-standing arrangements and rites of passage that work well for some students but poorly for others.

Even more distressing, CID participants told us, the rationale for program requirements has often been lost in the mists of history: students may well not understand why certain elements are required or toward what end, and faculty, if pushed, will acknowledge that there is no unified vision underpinning many of the experiences students are expected to complete. Departmental deliberations undertaken as part of the CID often uncovered inconsistent and unclear expectations, uneven student access to important opportunities, poor communication between members of the program, and a general inattention to patterns of student progress and outcomes. More alarming, the pressures of funded research may work against the kinds of risk taking, creativity, and collaboration that are increasingly the hallmark of cutting-edge intellectual work in today's world. And worse yet, students may be treated as cheap labor in the service of an adviser's current project and personal advancement.

Both doctoral students and faculty suffer under these circumstances. The life of a tenured faculty member may appear to be one of privilege and intellectual reward, but many are torn by increasing and competing demands for scholarship, fund raising, teaching and mentoring, community engagement, and family life. Their doctoral students, in turn, often feel burdened by debt, exploited as lab technicians or low-paid instructors, and disillusioned by the disgruntlement of overworked faculty mentors. The passionate zeal with which many students begin their studies is unnecessarily eroded, a loss that faculty decry as much as students do. It is hard, in short, not to be disheartened by the waste of human talent and energy in activities whose purpose is poorly understood. Serious thinking about what works in doctoral education, and what no longer works, is an urgent matter.

In the chapters that follow we will have much more to say about these and other very real challenges to doctoral education, and the ways in which today's approaches fall short of what is needed as we move into the twenty-first century. But we will have much to say about creative solutions and approaches, as well, for we have had a marvelous perch for observing and learning through our work. What will be clear along the way is that no single set of best practices or models can fit the diverse settings that constitute the landscape of graduate education. What works in one field or on one campus may be quite wrong in another. What *does* work in all settings, we argue, and what is distinctly absent from most doctoral programs, are processes, tools, and occasions through which both faculty and graduate students can apply their habits and skills as scholars—their commitment to hard questions and robust evidence—to their purposes and practices as educators and learners.

Mirror, Mirror

The power of this process and its benefits are illustrated in the experience of Columbia University's English department, where graduate students and faculty have worked together to bring about a number of immediate improvements as well as a renewed sense of intellectual community in which future improvements can take shape and thrive.

Long considered a premier graduate program in the field, consistently ranked in the top ten and home to a number of high-profile faculty stars over the years, Columbia's Department of English and Comparative Literature is large and intellectually lively. Approximately eighteen new PhD students are admitted each year, all of them receiving five full years of funding. In addition to traditional areas within literary studies, graduate students can explore interdisciplinary interests through the Center for Comparative Literature and Society and the Institute on Women and Gender. Admission is highly competitive (around 5 percent) and the student-to-faculty ratio is an impressive five-to-one.

In August of 2001, Jonathan Arac, a member of the department during the 1980s, was invited to return from his position at the University of Pittsburgh to assume the role of chairperson. The department had undertaken a major overhaul of the graduate program a decade earlier, and when the opportunity arose to participate in the CID, Arac and his colleagues seized the moment. Though the doctoral program was in good health, a number of what Arac calls "stress points" had developed, including a sense that advising could be stronger and opportunities for graduate students to teach literature more abundant. As in many humanities departments, the "culture wars" of the 1980s and 1990s had taken a heavy toll, creating what the *New York Times* called "intellectual trench warfare" (Arenson, 2002, p. 1). A sustained focus on strengthening doctoral education was a welcome opportunity, Arac recalls, "to come together around substantive issues involving our work together" (J. Arac, interview with the authors, August 30, 2006).

As a participant in the Carnegie initiative, the department turned to its standing Committee on Guidance and Evaluation, which included David Damrosch, then director of Graduate Studies, several faculty members, and graduate students. Working in consultation with others in the department and with Arac, the committee created and administrated a survey of students, examined peer programs elsewhere, and eventually issued a report detailing fifty-four recommended changes in what Damrosch termed a "major review and overhaul of our graduate program's requirements" (D. Damrosch, e-mail to the authors, March 11, 2004).

Although some of the proposals and subsequent changes were fine tunings, others required substantial changes. Oral examinations were redesigned to provide "a stronger and clearer structure, so that students and faculty will have a better idea of what they are setting out to do" (Department of English and Comparative Literature, 2004, section 4-A). The roles of dissertation committees were also rethought. An ambitious set of procedures for advising "at every stage of the program" was put in place, aimed especially at improving time to degree (Damrosch, 2006, p. 43). And, in response to the "stress point" about teaching, new opportunities were created for graduate students to teach introductory literature courses.

At a more general level, the experience of careful self-study raised awareness of possibilities for greater collegiality and communication among faculty and graduate students. "For students who are committing themselves to our profession, we can surely do a better job of consultation as we seek a good meeting of our interests and their needs," the report declared (Department of English and Comparative Literature, 2004, section 3-J). In this spirit, the department launched a new seminar series that invites graduate students and faculty to question established notions of literary fields of study. The new structure creates a lively trading zone where senior faculty exemplify the traditions of scholarly discourse in the field, and up-and-coming junior faculty and graduate students can push the leading edge of new areas of inquiry.

But what was "truly memorable," according to Arac, and "will stand a good long time in the department memory as a beneficial fruit" of work with the CID, was the process of "live remolding" through which the resulting document was vetted and negotiated by the department as a whole during a series of four ninety-minute meetings over a number of weeks. "Given that one of the symptoms of the 'bad days' of the 1990s was that no one was willing to come to meetings," Arac notes, "the fact that these meetings were well attended and that their process was effectively interactive was quite extraordinary."

Columbia's experience is worth highlighting not because of the particular changes per se (although they are noteworthy), but as an illustration of the value of a process that is inevitably and necessarily ongoing. Indeed, this volume is less about specific innovations and practices than it is about the importance of asking questions, gathering information, and creating opportunities for shared deliberation about future directions and improvements. Efforts like Columbia's yield powerful lessons about what happens when departments ask hard questions about their purposes, their students, their effectiveness, and about the mechanisms for refining and improving what they do.

The Formation of Scholars

The PhD is a route to many destinations, and those holding the doctorate follow diverse career paths. Some seek out a life in academe, whether in a research university where one of their roles is to guide future generations of graduate students, or in institutions where the central mission is teaching undergraduates. Others—the majority in some fields—end up in business or industry, or in government or non-profit settings. All of these, we would argue, are *scholars,* for the work of scholarship is not a function of setting but of purpose and commitment. Thus, one might be a scholar of the politics of the Middle East at the U.S. Department of State, or at the state university; a physicist might conduct her investigations on campus or at a federal research laboratory—or in both places. Whatever the setting, the profession of the scholar, and doctoral preparation for that profession, requires specialized, even esoteric knowledge. But they also entail a larger set of obligations and commitments that are not only intellectual but moral.

In this sense, doctoral education is a complex process of *formation*—a term we borrow from Carnegie's work on preparation for the professions, and especially the study of clergy.[6] Graduate education clearly entails technical training (learning how to splice a gene or analyze Russian census records requires very particular kinds of knowledge and skills), and the language of training is widespread in the doctoral context. Formation, in contrast, points not only to the development of intellectual expertise but to the growth of "the personality, character, habits of heart and mind" and "the role that the given discipline is capable of and meant to play in academe and society at large" (Elkana, 2006, pp. 66, 80). What is formed, in short, is the scholar's professional identity in all its dimensions.

The concept of formation also brings into focus the essential role of the learner. Clearly there are aspects of graduate education that faculty must pass along to graduate students; transmission is fundamental to education. But the development of professional identity as a scholar is ultimately a process that students themselves must shape and direct.

Some of the most exhilarating findings from the CID point to what happens when students take more active roles, more responsibility for their own progress and development, whether by using new tools, such as portfolios, for documenting and reflecting on their progress; by serving as mentors to one another; by pursuing connections between research and teaching; or by participating in departmental deliberations about the structure and effectiveness of their own doctoral program—an experience that many of the graduate students participating in the CID found formative indeed. This conception of scholarly formation shapes the vision of doctoral education that readers will find in this volume.

Following from this vision of formation are several corollary themes. The first is the theme of **scholarly integration.** As many readers will know, the Carnegie Foundation has been a persistent voice for a more comprehensive conception of academic work. *Scholarship Reconsidered: Priorities of the Professoriate,* the 1990 report by then-president Ernest Boyer (1990), set in motion a series of reforms aimed at creating a more capacious view of scholarship, encompassing not only basic research but integrative and applied work, as well as the work of teaching. Of course, the notion that teaching and research should be more closely linked is an old theme, espoused by many over the years. Even so, it is a view that runs deeply counter to the practices of higher education, as illustrated by a story told by literary scholar Gerald Graff about having his teaching evaluated: "When my classroom was observed by a professor in the 'visitation' I was required to have as a teaching assistant (and again until I became a tenured professor, after which it was assumed that nothing could be done about me), the only suggestions my senior colleague offered were that I close the door to my classroom and speak a little louder. . . . Clearly, questions of teaching were not thought to be intellectually interesting the way, say, the structure of a metaphysical lyric or the history of ideas is interesting" (Graff, 2006, pp. 375–376).

But this sense that teaching and research are distinct and unequal arenas of work has begun to change, as many campuses have rewritten tenure and promotion policies to bring greater weight to teaching and to establish forms of evaluation and peer review that recognize the intellectual and scholarly aspects of faculty's work as educators.[7]

This more integrated view of scholarship has begun to be embraced in doctoral education settings as well. Consider, for example, the National Science Foundation–supported Center for the Integration of Research, Teaching, and Learning (CIRTL) at the University of Wisconsin-Madison. Working with graduate students (as well as post-docs and faculty) in science, technology, engineering, and mathematics (STEM) fields, CIRTL seeks to inculcate practices of "teaching-as-research: the deliberate, systematic, and reflective use of research methods by STEM instructors to develop and implement teaching practices that advance the learning experiences and outcomes of both students and teachers" (Center for the Integration of Research Teaching and Learning, n.d.). As the CIRTL mission suggests, there are gains to be made by looking at teaching through the lens of research (what many are calling "the scholarship of teaching") and at research through the lens of teaching (as we have done in the CID by focusing on "the pedagogy of research").[8] To use a phrase that took hold in the CID, "scholarship segregated is scholarship impoverished," and what is needed are deeper forms of integration and connectedness. With this vision in mind, we highlight doctoral education practices that foster this kind of integrated scholarly formation.

A second major theme is **intellectual community.** Doctoral education is perhaps most easily thought of as a series of milestones on the way to the PhD: course taking, comprehensive exams, approval of the dissertation prospectus, the research and writing of the dissertation, the final oral defense (to name some of the most common). At their best, these milestones and the requirements behind them allow students to develop the knowledge, skills, and dispositions to thrive as scholars in their chosen fields; many graduate programs today are looking for ways to make these elements more powerful and more clearly aligned with evolving purposes. But in our work with departments participating in the Carnegie Initiative, a clear lesson was the importance of the culture in which these program elements exist. In an essay written for the CID, historian Thomas Bender argues:

> Much more attention needs to be directed to the culture of the department: making it a safe place for all faculty and students; making intellectual and pedagogical discourse part of the department's public culture; making it a place of participatory governance, openness, and recognizably fair in the treatment of all members, with adequate grievance procedures. One might say that the long preceding sentence moves away from the curricular matter of doctoral training, but in fact I am convinced that the hidden curriculum embedded in the departmental culture is of enormous importance in the intellectual and professional formation of graduate students [Bender, 2006, pp. 304–305].

A culture of intellectual community is, in this sense, not simply a matter of potlucks and hallway conversation; it is "the hidden curriculum," sending powerful messages about purpose, commitment, and roles, and creating (or not) the conditions in which intellectual risk taking, creativity, and entrepreneurship are possible. In this volume, then, we have tried to present visions of academic life characterized by real partnerships between faculty and students, habits of respect for and interest in one another's work, and the lively exchange of ideas in which new knowledge is forged and transformed.

This focus on intellectual community underlines a basic truth about graduate education: that it is, ultimately, about learning. Learning is the central business, the core task, of both students and faculty—and the learning in question is often of a very special kind because it breaks new ground and builds new knowledge. Much of the debate about higher education over the last century has been about the tension between research and teaching, and how the former crowds out the latter (see for example, Cuban, 1999). Learning, and the intellectual community that nurtures learning by all members of the community, may just be the nexus where these two functions come together in more productive, integrative ways in doctoral education. And of course these are also the conditions in which the formation of scholars can occur most productively.

The third theme running through this volume is **stewardship.** Etymologically rooted in Old English, the word *steward* first referred to the person who regulated a household and supervised the table (Stimpson, 2006, p. 404). The term has ecclesiastical overtones as well. The Oxford English Dictionary defines stewardship as "the responsible use of resources, especially money, time and talents, in the service of God." One root is the parable of the talents, in which a man gave each of his three servants some coins to take care of in his absence. Two of the servants traded with the coins and doubled their holdings; the third was fearful of the master and buried the coins. Those who had taken risks and used the coins were rewarded; the one who had simply saved the money was punished. Here the emphasis is on investing, risk taking, and putting talents (whether coins or abilities) to work, not on hoarding and saving. A steward of the discipline or interdiscipline considers the applications, uses, and purposes of the field and favors wise and responsible applications.

The contemporary environmental movement has adopted the word *steward* by focusing on sustainable management that will make resources available for many generations to come. Here the emphasis is on people living in concert with the environment and on preservation with an eye toward the future. A steward, then, thinks about the continuing health of the discipline and how to preserve the best of the past for those who will follow. Stewards are concerned with how to foster renewal and creativity. Perhaps most important, a steward considers how to prepare and initiate the next generation of stewards.

In the Carnegie Initiative on the Doctorate, we adopted the notion of stewardship as encompassing a set of knowledge and skills, as well as a set of principles. The former ensures expertise and the latter provides the moral compass. A fully formed scholar should be capable of *generating* and critically evaluating new knowledge; of *conserving* the most important ideas and findings that are a legacy of past and current work; and of understanding how knowledge is *transforming* the world in which we live, and engaging in the transformational work of communicating their knowledge responsibly to others.[9]

The generative function points to the fact that the PhD is, at its heart, a research degree. It signifies that the recipient is able to ask interesting and important questions, formulate appropriate strategies for investigating these questions, conduct investigations with a high degree of competence, analyze and evaluate the results of the investigations, and communicate the results to others to advance the field. Conservation implies understanding the history and fundamental ideas of the discipline, but recognizes that stewards are aware of the shoulders on which they stand and must judge which ideas are worth keeping and which have outlived their usefulness. Conservation also entails understanding how the field fits into the larger, and changing, intellectual landscape. Transformation speaks of the importance of representing and communicating ideas effectively, and encompasses teaching in the broadest sense of the word—not simply as conveying information, that is, but as a dynamic process of transforming knowledge so that new learners can meaningfully engage with it. Such transformation requires that stewards understand other disciplines, the differences between disciplinary views of the world, and how to communicate across traditional boundaries. The application of knowledge, and its responsible use, is another facet of transformation.

By invoking the term *steward,* and by focusing on the formation of scholars who can indeed be good stewards, we intend to convey a sense of purpose for doctoral education that is larger than the individual and implies action. A scholar is a steward of the discipline, or the larger field, not simply the manager of her own career. By adopting the care of the discipline as a touchstone, and by understanding that she has been entrusted with that care by those in the field on behalf of those in and beyond it, the steward embraces a larger sense of purpose. The reach of that purpose is both temporally expansive (looking to the past and the future) and broad in scope (considering the entire discipline, as well as intellectual neighbors in related fields).

Predictably, perhaps, the language of stewardship travels well in some academic circles, and less well in others. But the concept, which is moral and ethical as well as intellectual and technical in its import, provides a provocative framework for raising issues about the purpose of doctoral education that may otherwise remain unspoken and unexamined.

Overview of the Volume

The themes of scholarly formation, integration, intellectual community, and stewardship introduced in this first chapter weave together and run through the entire volume. In Chapter Two, we turn to the big picture, tracing the contours of doctoral education as it has evolved over time. As even a compressed history makes clear, change has been a constant throughout that evolution, and many of the changes reflect shifts in the larger social, political, and economic context of the PhD. At the same time, the long view underlines the difficulty of change and suggests a set of strategies that have been enacted through the CID—the importance of starting with the disciplines, for instance, and with conceptions of the purpose and future of the field. Indeed, as many observers point out, the disciplines today are undergoing major transformations, making this a fruitful time to think carefully about the shape of doctoral education in the twenty-first century.

Chapter Three looks at how graduate programs can constructively grapple with questions about what they do, why, and with what success. This is hard work, with few tools or habits ready at hand, and one of the central aims of the CID has been to provide frameworks—such as the ideas of stewardship and formation—to guide such reflection and self-examination. In the process, we have learned a lot about the obstacles to this kind of stocktaking—how living with cross-purposes is sometimes easier than negotiating a common vision, for instance. But we have also found compelling "existence proofs" of how programs in a variety of fields can hold a mirror up to themselves and enact principles of what came to be called "PART" by CID participants: purposefulness, assessment, reflection, and transparency.

Chapter Four takes readers much closer to the ground to examine specific practices and elements in doctoral education and how they can be made more powerful. Though this volume is not a how-to manual, the principles of progressive development, integration, and collaboration around which this chapter is structured clearly have practical implications. And examples of new approaches to the pedagogy of research, the development of teaching expertise, the dissertation, and leadership development can, we believe, be learned from and adapted to many settings. Indeed, one of the most rewarding aspects of the CID was the energetic exchange of ideas that developed among different fields and campuses.

Chapter Five focuses on what might well be called the "signature pedagogy" of doctoral education, apprenticeship. The tradition of close work between a faculty "master" and student "apprentice" has its roots in medieval guild culture, which then took hold in the early university as well. This central relationship is not the only approach to graduate teaching and learning; there are courses, seminars and independent study. But apprenticeship remains a central experience. The question is whether it is serving the purposes most important to the formation of scholars in the twenty-first century, and our answer is that it is not—and that many students in many fields would greatly benefit from an alternative model of doctoral education in which apprenticeship is a shared function, and a reciprocal one, that fosters learning for both professor and student. This vision—and there are wonderful examples of how it might look on the ground in programs we have studied and worked with—is foundational to the concept of intellectual community that has been central to the CID.

Chapter Six then turns to the theme of intellectual community, which we see both as a condition for making the kinds of changes and improvements described elsewhere in this volume and as a consequence, or a product, of those improvements. It is not, certainly, a difficult goal to embrace (who could be opposed to a more humane, vibrant, open intellectual community?), but neither is it easily achieved. Indeed, many students report that the culture of their chosen program makes already daunting challenges even harder, and the difficulties are often felt most keenly by students of color and women, international students, and by those attending part-time. The goal, then, is to create environments in which all qualified students can succeed in the fullest way, becoming responsible stewards of their disciplines, academic citizens, and contributors to the larger society. The benefits of a thriving intellectual community, however, go beyond the important goal of nurturing individual scholars. It also fosters the development of new knowledge by encouraging scholarly debate and intellectual risk taking. Intellectual communities are not simply happier places to work; they are also more efficient engines of knowledge production than their dysfunctional, antisocial, or apathetic counterparts.

Finally, Chapter Seven pulls things together and returns once again to the urgent need for change. What is needed, we argue, is not simply deliberation, which is essential, but action. Thus we issue a challenge to students, faculty, university administrators, and external partners who must be involved in moving doctoral education successfully into the twenty-first century. This final chapter also sets forth an agenda for further study.

Throughout the volume, we have drawn primarily on our work with the eighty-four CID participating departments (a list of departments is in Appendix B) because we know them well and have worked with them to document their efforts in ways that can usefully be shared with others. (For electronic representations of departments' work, including many of the examples described throughout this volume, see the CID Gallery Web site at http://gallery.carnegiefoundation.org/cid).

Of course the CID-participant programs are only a subset of the world of doctoral education; important activity and new thinking is evident much more widely. The Council of Graduate Schools continues to be an important venue for grappling with new challenges and trading ideas (for example, Council of Graduate Schools, 2004, 2007), and the Association of American Universities has recently released several key reports on doctoral education (Association of American Universities, 1998a, 1998b, 2005; Mathae and Birzer, 2004).

In the disciplinary societies, as well, new energy and resources have been brought to bear on this work, for instance through the 2004 report from the American Historical Association on graduate education (Bender, Katz, Palmer, and Committee on Graduate Education of the American Historical Association, 2004). The National Science Foundation has been another important catalyst for new efforts, through a program to promote interdisciplinary doctoral programs, another linking graduate students with K–12 teachers and students, and a third prompting shifts in the culture of mathematics graduate programs.[10]

Lively deliberations about the future of doctoral education are taking place in other countries as well, and we have been privileged to participate in symposia with European Union countries and to visit with leaders from Chinese research universities about their plans. In the latter, for instance, a new government scholarship program will send 7,000 scholars (including doctoral students) to eighty countries to pursue advanced study.

We see and draw from this broader landscape as a context for our claims and recommendations. And of course we have drawn, too, on earlier studies and initiatives undertaken by others. Finally, we have drawn on our own personal experiences—as graduate students ourselves (some rather recently, some longer ago); as mentors working with graduate students in our various settings; as active scholars with our own areas of research and expertise; and (in one case) as a long-time graduate school dean who has lived with many of the issues we will explore in these pages.

Our hope is that this book will be a resource and an "owner's manual," to borrow a term from Henry Rosovky, former dean of the faculty of arts and sciences at Harvard and CID advisory committee member, for those who feel ready to ride the wave of change in doctoral education. It is not written as an educational research report, but as a tool for thinking, to provoke, inspire, and assist the community of scholars on the ground— and especially the students who are joining that community of scholars. We hope the ideas and examples we present will be a starting point for lively conversation and creative action among those who care about doctoral education.

ENDNOTES

1. The epigraph is widely attributed to Will Rogers, although there is no clear documentation of its source according to Steve Gragert, associate director of the Will Rogers Memorial Museum in Claremore, Oklahoma.

2. The figure of 375,000 enrolled doctoral students is an estimate. The National Postsecondary Student Aid Study data suggest a slightly higher number: 390,000, which is 14 percent of the 2.8 million enrolled graduate or first professional degree-seeking students (Choy, Cataldi, and Griffith, 2006). The Council of Graduate Schools institutional survey reports 340,000 (out of 1.5 million graduate students), which should be considered a lower bound because not all degree-granting institutions participate in the survey (D. Denecke, e-mail to the authors, June 5, 2006). Determining the number of doctoral students is further complicated by the fact that some doctoral students are counted as master's students in the early years of their studies.

   The total number of doctorates granted each year comes from the Survey of Earned Doctorates reports. In 2005 the total was 43,354, and has been climbing (Hoffer and others, 2006). The most recent Carnegie Classification recognizes 413 institutions in the various doctoral-granting categories (Carnegie Foundation for the Advancement of Teaching, 2006). Likewise, the most recent Survey of Earned Doctorates report, *Doctorate Recipients from United States Universities 2005,* lists 416 doctoral-granting universities (Hoffer and others, 2006).

3. Of the ten most recent secretaries of state, the following have held doctorates: Condoleezza Rice (University of Denver), Madeline Albright (Columbia University), George Schulz (MIT), and Henry Kissinger (Harvard University). The Federal Reserve Board has seven spots, six of which are filled as we write this note; five members have PhD's: Ben S. Bernanke, Chairman (MIT), Donald L. Kohn (University of Michigan), Susan

Schmidt Bies (Northwestern University), Randall S. Kroszner (Harvard University), and Fredrick Mishkin (MIT).

4. Predictably the numbers vary by discipline and setting. Attrition rates, insofar as they are known, are thought to average 40 to 50 percent (Golde, 2005; Lovitts, 2001). Estimates range from 20 percent to nearly 70 percent depending on discipline. According to data from the Survey of Earned Doctorates the average registered time to degree was 8.7 years in 2005, ranging from 5.7 years in chemistry to 9.7 years in history and 13.7 in education (Hoffer and others, 2006, Table A-3).

5. The field of education has long struggled with drawing clear distinctions between these two doctorates, the research doctorate and the doctorate of practice, and we are encouraged by renewed efforts to distinguish and invigorate both degrees (see Shulman, Golde, Bueschel, and Garabedian, 2006). We recognize the growing trend to develop new degrees, often referred to as "clinical doctorates," "professional doctorates," or "practice doctorates," but in the CID and in this volume our primary concern is research doctorates and the PhD.

6. The Carnegie Foundation for the Advancement of Teaching has a long history in the study of professional education, beginning with the Flexner report on medicine in 1910 and a study of legal education in the 1930s. This tradition continues today with comparative studies of law, engineering, clergy, nursing, medicine, and teacher education. The language of formation derives primarily from the study of the preparation of clergy, where the authors write, "A distinguishing feature of professional education is the emphasis on forming in students the dispositions, habits, knowledge, and skills that cohere in the professional identity and practice, commitments and integrity. The pedagogies that clergy educators use toward this purpose—formation—originate in the deepest intentions for professional service" (Foster, Dahill, Goleman, and Tolentino, 2006, p. 100).

7. In *Faculty Priorities Reconsidered* (2005), Kerry Ann O'Meara and Eugene Rice present findings from a campus survey, reporting that 35 percent of chief academic officers say that teaching now counts more than it did ten years earlier. That—for those who have sought greater recognition of the scholarly work of teaching—is the good news. The sobering counterweight is that, on 51 percent of campuses, research, too, counts more than it did ten years ago (O'Meara and Rice, 2005, p. 320). Clearly the ante is being raised on all fronts. Thus, in the CID and other Carnegie Foundation programs, we have been especially interested in forms of academic work in which teaching, research, and service are seen as an interconnected whole rather than three different pigeonholes to be filled.

8. The "scholarship of teaching and learning" may no longer need a special note; it has been a growing part of the higher education landscape for more than a decade now—the focus of a number of national initiatives, an animating agenda on hundreds of campuses, a topic on the program of many disciplinary and education conferences, a new thrust for a number of journals, and the theme of a long list of publications. In *The Advancement of Learning: Building the Teaching Commons,* Mary Taylor Huber and Pat Hutchings argue that "the scholarship of teaching and learning entails basic but important principles that can and should be in every professor's repertoire. It means viewing the work of the classroom as a site for inquiry, asking and answering questions about students' learning in ways that can improve one's own classroom and also advance the larger profession of teaching" (Huber and Hutchings, 2005, p. 1).

9. This formulation may recall the "vision of the research university of the twentieth century" as a "sheltered grove in which knowledge is propagated, created and applied" (Atkinson and Tuzin, 1992, p. 23).

10. The Integrative Graduate Education and Research Traineeship (IGERT) program was initiated in 1997 to establish innovative new models for graduate education and collaborative research that transcend traditional disciplinary boundaries. The Graduate Teaching Fellows in K–12 Education (GK–12) program funds graduate students in science, technology, engineering, and math (STEM) fields to work with teachers in K–12 schools. Both of those programs are NSF-wide and cross several directorates. The Division of Mathematical Sciences sponsored the Vertical Integration of Research and Education in the Mathematical Sciences (VIGRE) program from 1998–2002, aimed at "the development of a community of researchers and scholars in which there's interaction among all the members" (National Science Foundation, 1997, p. 1). Mathematics departments that received multi-year VIGRE grants were expected to "vertically integrate" their graduate traineeship program, an undergraduate research experience program, and a post-doctoral program.

2

SETTING THE STAGE
FOR CHANGE

*The genius of American graduate education is
that no one is in charge.*

—Kenneth Prewitt[1]

THE UNITED STATES IS A NEWCOMER ON THE DOCTORAL EDUCATION SCENE, relative to its European forebears, but its rise to international prominence has been meteoric. The first doctorate in the United States was awarded in 1861, and by 1900 a total of about 3,500 doctorates had been granted. At the start of the twentieth century, about 500 PhD's were awarded each year; by 1960 annual production exceeded 10,000. Now, as the twenty-first century begins, more than 40,000 doctoral degrees are awarded each year, adding to the more than 1.36 million doctorates granted by U.S. universities during the twentieth century.[2] The scope and scale of the enterprise has grown along other dimensions too. The number of universities granting doctorates swelled from forty-four in 1920 to over 400 today (see Table 2.1). New fields emerged, as well, many of them in recent decades. Along the way, the profile of the student body has changed dramatically, becoming more diverse in many ways, including by national origin. Whereas Americans once went to Europe for the doctoral degree, students now come from around the globe to study here.

This tale of continuous expansion, innovation, and diversification is one without an author. No one, as this chapter's epigraph observes, "is in charge." By almost any measure, it is a tale of success—and a typically American one at that, as early educational leaders both borrowed and departed from European models to fashion a new type of institution

Table 2.1. The Growth of Doctoral Education in the United States[1]

Year	Number of doctorates granted	Number of doctorate-granting universities	PhD's per thousand BA's granted
1900	382	25	9.1
1920	562	44	12.6
1940	3,277	90	17.6
1960	9,733	165	25.0
1980	31,020	320	35.1
2000	41,368	406	36.2

suited to the evolving needs of a young nation. Today, the U.S. model of graduate education is admired around the world.

But this prominence comes with a shadow side. As the reputation of American universities has climbed over the last fifty years, successful practices have become deeply ingrained traditions, and, just as fish take water for granted, those inside the system find it hard to see those traditions and practices clearly; they are taken for granted, invisible, rarely interrogated. This is true, certainly, of the most visible elements of PhD programs: the qualifying or comprehensive examinations, the dissertation, and other requirements that have taken shape in the various disciplines and interdisciplines that constitute doctoral education today. It is also true of the less visible features of the enterprise: the valuing of specialization over broader kinds of formation, the way research and teaching are segregated and often set in opposition to each other, the atomized habits of faculty life that work against community, and the patterns of faculty-student interaction (the apprenticeship tradition) that shape scholarly formation. To think creatively about the future of graduate education, it is useful, then, to look back, remember how today's realities came to be, reflect on the rhythms of change (and stasis), and draw from these, as we have tried to do, key principles for moving doctoral education into the future.

A Short History of Doctoral Education in America

Relative to undergraduate education, the history of graduate education has received little scholarly attention, but many readers will know of its German origins. In the 1800s American college graduates desiring advanced training traveled to Europe to get it; most chose to study in Germany. By one estimate some 10,000 Americans took German degrees during the nineteenth century (Berelson, 1960, p. 11). Not surprisingly, when graduate education took root in the United States—and there were several failed efforts to establish graduate study here—many features of the German model prevailed. Two notable characteristics were the emphasis on scientific inquiry and the expectation that faculty members would carry out research. The first PhD's—three of them—were granted by Yale in 1861, but the American model really gathered force when Johns Hopkins University opened in 1876. It pioneered research-oriented PhD degrees in the arts and sciences, and supported students with fellowships (Rudolph, 1962).

The climb to eminence over the next century and a quarter is a remarkable tale, to which we can hardly do justice here. But understanding the story of American graduate education allows us to consider how the current state of affairs developed and how further evolution can be fostered. This is a story of contradictions. On the one hand, growth and innovation are obvious hallmarks; indeed these are features that other countries seek to emulate. On the other hand, as colleges and universities have matured, they have developed traditions and administrative structures that may make current realities seem unalterable. Before we describe our theory of changing doctoral education, we tell an abbreviated history of American doctoral education as it grew and changed through four stages. The reader will see recurring tensions about the purpose of doctoral education, a theme we return to in Chapter Three.

Stage One: Establishment

What we now recognize as the American model of doctoral education emerged in the period from the 1880s to the 1930s. From the very beginning the enterprise was diverse and decentralized—a grafted hybrid of an undergraduate college (the English roots) and the graduate college (the German roots), with the same faculty teaching both groups of students. Because efforts to establish a single national university never got off the ground, this structure found a home on more and more campuses (Storr, 1973). And financially, especially in this stage, the graduate college was largely dependent on the undergraduate college—tuition and endowment funded the faculty, and teaching assistantships funded many of the students (Geiger, 1986, p. 219; Katz and Hartnett, 1976, p. 9).

Requirements for doctoral study were set by each university's "graduate faculty" (a subset of each campus's professoriate), under the leadership of a graduate dean who lacked budgetary or appointment power (Berelson, 1960, pp. 10–11). After completing an undergraduate degree, the prospective student applied for admission and entered a community devoted to research and scholarship; participated in graduate seminars (a format developed for graduate education) as well as more informal, individualized teaching arrangements; passed examinations in two foreign languages (usually French and German) as well as a comprehensive examination (which many students failed); and concluded his studies by submitting a written thesis for approval by a committee of faculty members. Upon receipt of the degree, PhD holders entered an academic career. In these early years, students completed doctoral study in about two years (Harvard University, n.d.; Mayhew and Ford, 1974, pp. 5–6; Rudolph, 1962, chaps. 13 and 16). Thus began the cycle of professional preparation we take for granted today, in which promising students are nurtured by faculty and then become faculty themselves, committed to bringing up the next generation (Thelin, 2004).

It was during the early decades of the century that disciplines, as separately delineated interest areas, and academic departments, as structures within the university, took hold. Fields of study proliferated, especially in the new scientific and applied disciplines. By 1905, fifteen learned societies and numerous scholarly journals had been established. The shift from scholar as polymath, able to range freely among fields and areas of interest, to scholar as specialist was well underway. In parallel, authority about matters of disciplinary expertise (curriculum and hiring) shifted from the president to departments (Geiger, 1986, pp. 16–40; Rudolph, 1962; Storr, 1973, p. 50).

Even in the midst of this initial burst of growth and invention, concerns about quality were never far from the surface. In February 1900, the presidents of fourteen universities came together to form the Association of American Universities (AAU) to consider "matters of common interest relating to graduate study" (Speicher, n.d.). In particular, they sought to address issues of quality and prestige. As historian Roger Geiger tells it, "The creation of the AAU was a declaration by the leading American universities of independence and equality with regard to European universities as well as an endeavor to guarantee the value of their product against 'cheaper' foreign and domestic competition" (1986, p. 19).

Questions of purpose were front and center during this establishment phase. For one, college faculty often resisted efforts to expand into graduate study, fearing a dilution of attention and resources. Harvard's president Charles Eliot responded to critics of the proposed Graduate Department: "It will strengthen the College. As long as the main duty of the faculty is to teach boys, professors need never pursue their subjects beyond a certain point. With graduate students to teach, they will regard their subjects as infinite, and will keep up that constant investigation which is so necessary for the best teaching" (Harvard University, n.d.). For another, the appropriate balance between research and teaching in university faculty life arose almost immediately. At the 1906 AAU meeting an entire session was devoted to the question "To what extent should the university investigator be relieved from teaching?" (Association of American Universities, 1906).

During the 1920s and 1930s the early sprouts became stronger seedlings. By the end of this era there were nearly 100 doctoral-granting institutions, and the AAU had grown to thirty-one members, two of them Canadian universities. Doctoral education, now an accepted and established segment of the larger higher education scene, was poised for unprecedented (and unplanned) explosive growth following World War II.

Stage Two: Expansion and Link with Funded Research

Sometimes characterized as the Golden Age of higher education, the decades of the 1940s through 1960s were a period of enormous growth. Following World War II, undergraduate education opened its doors to middle and working class students, largely because of the Servicemen's Readjustment Act of 1944 (also known as the G.I. Bill of Rights). State, federal, and foundation funding converged to expand the capacity to provide postsecondary education. Then, as the first of the baby boomers hit college in the 1960s, existing institutions continued to expand their enrollments, and new colleges were founded at the rate of one a week throughout the decade.

The expansion of undergraduate education was more than matched in doctoral education, which experienced even greater rates of growth (see Table 2.1). Here, too, federal funding set the stage. The Manhattan Project and Vannevar Bush's manifesto, *Science, the Endless Frontier* (1945), ushered in the era of federal funding for university research. Federal agencies like the National Science Foundation and the National Institutes of Health were established, channeling money into universities for faculty research that also supported graduate students. Federal funds also helped to develop university infrastructure, including buildings and equipment, and sought to democratize science education by developing the capacity for PhD production at "second-tier" institutions (National Board on Graduate Education, 1975b; Thelin, 2004, chapter 7).

This trend continued in the 1960s, when the post-Sputnik National Defense Education Act (NDEA) of 1957 released a flood of federal money to university campuses. Federally funded fellowships and traineeships grew.

In 1960 there were 5,500 graduate fellowships worth $24 million, and by 1970 the government funded 43,000 fellowships valued at $226 million (Mayhew and Ford, 1974, p. 149). Between 1960 and 1970 the number of doctorates granted tripled—from 10,000 to 30,000 per year—and the number of doctoral-granting institutions grew by nearly 50 percent, from 165 to 240 (Thurgood, Golladay, and Hill, 2006). In short, the 1960s proved to be a decade of explosive growth for doctoral education.

Many of the features of doctoral education that are now taken for granted took shape and settled (comfortably or otherwise) into place during these years. The strong link between federal research dollars, faculty research agendas, and graduate student research efforts was forged. Graduate faculty teaching loads were reduced to allow more time for research in the sciences, and, in the interests of equity, this privilege was extended to the social sciences and humanities as well. As a result, graduate students were given more explicit responsibilities as research and teaching assistants (Thelin, 2004, pp. 281–282), and time to degree rose, by this point, to about five years (Berelson, 1960, p. 158). The increased scale of graduate education and the sheer size of universities led inevitably to the delegation of authority for many aspects of doctoral education—admissions, fellowship allocation, curricular requirements—from the institution's graduate faculty as a whole to individual departments. At the same time, universities developed bureaucratic processes (which may feel ossified today) to handle the ballooning undergraduate and graduate student populations.

Tensions around purposes were never far from the surface. The continued postwar support of graduate education was largely due to the "realization that the nation's scientific and technological preeminence required a vast reservoir of highly educated manpower" (National Board on Graduate Education, 1972, pp. 1–2), but many wondered whether too many doctorates were being granted, resulting in a dilution of quality. But the demand was undeniable, and it was not just for researchers. The boom in undergraduate enrollment brought with it an unprecedented need for college teachers and early stirrings about the need for better ways to prepare those teachers.

Stage Three: Retrenchment and Innovation

Inevitably, though, the bubble burst. Often referred to at the time as "the new depression in higher education" (Breneman, 1975), the 1970s were a time of retrenchment as federal funding declined (cutbacks in R&D

funding began in 1969), the academic job market constricted, and military draft deferments ended in 1968. Even as recessions in 1970 and 1974 led to increased numbers of applications for graduate study, doctoral degree production flattened (National Board on Graduate Education, 1975a).

Not surprisingly, hard times prompted energetic conversation about the purposes of graduate education. In 1971 the National Board on Graduate Education was established to provide "unbiased, thorough analysis of graduate education today and its relation to American society in the future," and during its three-year life the organization issued six reports (National Board on Graduate Education, 1973, p. iii).[4] Change was, for better or worse, the central theme, as the board's reports stressed "the difficult process of adjustment to reduced growth rates in a less supportive environment" and urged that "changes in the scope or function of graduate education should reflect the graduate school's central role in maintaining and advancing scientific and humanistic culture which is not only the means to an end, but is an end in itself" (National Board on Graduate Education, 1972, pp. 2, 6).

More pointedly, the board recommended that "federal, state, and institutional policies should encourage more explicit differentiation of function among graduate programs than currently exists" (National Board on Graduate Education, 1975a, p. 49). Noting that most colleges added doctoral programs in an effort to garner the prestige "accorded [to] the traditional PhD program and the faculty members associated with it," the board urged that any newly founded programs serve part-time and older students with applied programs aimed at solving regional and national problems (National Board on Graduate Education, 1975a, p. 49). One promising response to the growing concern about the preparation of doctoral students for teaching was the design of a new degree, the doctorate of arts (DA), but the DA never spread widely.[5]

Meanwhile, students brought powerful voices to the table, raising concerns about the relevance of what they were studying. Student dissent contributed to the creation of new fields of study, including ethnic studies and gender studies. Students also critiqued the structure of doctoral programs; one survey found that up to a third of the best students in the program dropped out because they found requirements too constraining (Heiss, 1970, pp. 179–180). Criticisms helped change requirements, such as new forms and timing for comprehensive exams (Mayhew and Ford, 1974, p. 146). Ultimately, most departments removed even language requirements.

Even in politically tumultuous and financially challenging times, changes in doctoral education were measured and incremental, rather than revolutionary. Although some programs contracted slightly during the 1970s and early 1980s, new doctoral programs—many looking quite traditional—continued to open (Bowen and Rudenstine, 1992, pp. 57–62). The forces of aspiration and emulation seemed unstoppable.

Stage Four: Diversification and Fragmentation

The student population changed considerably in the 1980s and 1990s (see Table 2.2). Though numbers vary by field, it was during this period that doctoral education opened fully to women. About 40 percent of the doctorates awarded to women in the entire twentieth century were granted in the 1990s (Thurgood and others, 2006, p. 16). Currently half or more of the doctorates in psychology, biological sciences, the humanities, education, health sciences, and most social sciences go to women; the physical sciences (26.4 percent) and engineering (18.3 percent) remain less hospitable (Hoffer and others, 2006). U.S. doctoral study also became markedly more international at this time. Most international doctoral students are from Asia, and most of those hail from China. Twenty-four thousand doctorates were awarded by U.S. universities to students from the People's Republic of China in the 1990s (Thurgood and others, 2006, p. 18). Again, the distribution is not even across fields; over half the doctorates awarded in the latter half of the 1990s in agricultural sciences, mathematics and computer science, and engineering were granted to non-U.S. citizens.

These changes, in turn, made the failure of graduate education to diversify by race and ethnicity a glaring problem. In the last quarter of the twentieth century fewer than 10 percent of the doctorates granted were received by minority U.S. citizens: African Americans, 3 percent; Asian/Pacific Islanders, 2 percent; Hispanics, 2 percent; and American Indians/Alaska natives, 0.3 percent (Thurgood, and others, 2006, pp. 19–20). Shifting public priorities raise further questions about purpose in relation to larger social agendas.

Table 2.2. Demographic Distribution of Doctoral Recipients[6]

Year	Female	U.S. Racial and Ethnic Minority	International	Total Doctorates
1960	10.7%	—	12.7%	9,733
1970	13.5	—	15.5	29,498
1980	30.3	8.3%	18.7	31,020
1990	36.3	9.6	30.9	36,067
2000	43.8	16.1	32.6	41,368

Fields of study in doctoral education have also fragmented and diversified. New areas of study continue to emerge, and one sign that a field has "arrived" is when the doctorate is granted. The biological sciences have been particularly lively during this stage, with new areas of inquiry appearing and recombining, far outpacing the ability of taxonomies or university structures to keep up. In other areas as well—physical sciences, engineering, the arts—explicitly interdisciplinary efforts in research and, by extension, graduate education have come to the fore.

The 1990s were once again a time of increasing degree production, fueled in part by a prediction of imminent faculty retirements and a commensurate hiring boom. As it turned out, these forecasts were premature; increased fiscal pressures on universities created a reluctance to hire on the tenure track, and the removal of mandated retirement-age regulations resulted in fewer than predicted departures. Consequently universities moved towards contingent faculty labor (the so-called "adjunctification" of the professoriate) and, in the sciences, created a huge number of post-doctoral appointments (National Science Foundation, 2003, p. 13). These trends led to a diversification of career paths, as nonacademic employment for PhD's became common in many fields and, in some, the norm (Nerad and Cerny, 1999). Indeed, the range of responses to the rise of nonacademic careers—embraced in some fields and reviled in others—is one way in which disciplinary differences in the doctoral student experience became more pronounced in the last quarter of the twentieth century. As differences among fields in terms of structure, culture, governance, funding, career paths, and other features have become more pronounced, so too have questions about doctoral education's purpose and its ability to meet future needs.

A Fifth Stage: Waves of Reform

As even a short history makes clear, concerns about the purpose and quality of doctoral education are nothing new. The character of concerns has shifted, certainly, from an interest in distinguishing the American upstart from its much older European cousins, to competing on the global scientific stage, to addressing new social and political realities. As the enterprise has evolved, it has invented new approaches and structures to guide its work and future, locally and nationally—from the AAU, to the National Board on Graduate Education, to the Council of Graduate Schools (CGS). Indeed The Carnegie Foundation for the Advancement of Teaching has been a player in these efforts a number of times over the last century (see Exhibit 2.1). In recent years, the appetite for serious attention to doctoral education has grown; starting in the 1990s, a series of significant reform efforts have come into the picture. These projects preceded the CID and primed the environment.

---

o

Exhibit 2.1. The Carnegie Foundation's Involvement in the Study of Graduate Education

In 1927 Henry Suzzallo, who would shortly become president of the Carnegie Foundation, conducted an extensive review of the state of graduate education in an effort to outline a plan of research. Noting that "less objective study has been made of higher education on the graduate school situation than of any other of the important units," he identified five areas for research: the student population, the graduate teaching population, the alignment between preparation and career outcomes, the distinctions between the master's degree and doctorate, and "a careful analysis of the processes of instruction themselves" (Suzzallo, 1927, pp. 83, 87).

In October 1937 William S. Learned, Benjamin Wood, and others at the Foundation conducted the first administration of a newly developed test to "determine a student's fitness to undertake graduate study" at Columbia, Harvard, Princeton, and Yale. It quickly proved useful as a supplement to transcripts for admissions and for determining who should receive fellowships. The result, the Graduate Record Examination, was administered by the Foundation until 1947 when the Educational Testing Service was formed (Savage, 1953).

In 1939, the Foundation published an early history of three influential American universities, *Studies in Early Graduate Education: The Johns Hopkins, Clark University, the University of Chicago,* focusing on the characteristics that led to their success (Ryan, 1939). Its companion, *Studies in American Graduate Education,* delayed because of World War II, was a comprehensive summary of the state of U.S. graduate education, based on a statistical analysis of student enrollment records and site visits to twelve leading graduate universities between 1937 and 1939 (Edwards, 1944).

In 1983, the Foundation published a slim volume called *Scholarship and Its Survival: Questions on the Idea of Graduate Education,* by Jaroslav Pelikan, dean of the Yale graduate school from 1973 to 1978. Pelikan makes the case for "scholarship as a way of life," noting, "I have come to believe, reluctantly but ineluctably, the very survival of scholarship is at stake today" (1983, p. xviii). His concerns about the purposes of graduate education and the future of the humanistic disciplines served as the opening salvo for an invited colloquium on graduate education, sponsored by the Foundation and the Institute for Advanced Study in December 1983. Subsequently Pelikan wrote a longer volume, *The Idea of the University* (1992), which included many ideas that evolved from this earlier work on graduate education.

○

One prompt for these efforts was the publication in 1989 of Bowen and Sosa's *Prospects for Faculty in the Arts and Sciences*. Their forecast of a coming wave of faculty hiring failed to materialize, and a generation of would-be professors who had been encouraged to enroll in graduate school was stranded. This set in motion considerable attention to the connections between the career paths of doctoral recipients and the preparation they receive.

One response was to make more concerted efforts to prepare graduate students as teachers. Fueled by concerns about the quality of instruction provided by teaching assistants in undergraduate courses, the training of TAs became a highly visible reform agenda, and major research universities took turns hosting a national conference on the topic.

With these issues in view, the Preparing Future Faculty (PFF) initiative was launched in 1993 as a collaboration between CGS and the Association of American Colleges & Universities (AAC&U). The goal was to provide doctoral students with opportunities to observe and experience faculty roles at academic institutions with varying missions, diverse student bodies, and different expectations for faculty. Usually this involved partnerships between research universities and nearby two-year and four-year colleges. Over a decade of activity, formal programs were implemented at more than forty-five doctoral degree-granting universities and nearly 300 partner institutions in the United States (Preparing Future Faculty National Office, n.d.).

Building on PFF and other initiatives, a new project, called Re-Envisioning the PhD, synthesized the concerns of seven groups of stakeholders: research universities, K–12 schools, doctoral students, government agencies, industry, foundations, and educational associations. The project concluded with a conference in spring 2000 at which participants agreed on seven recommendations, including a need for "carefully planned, systematic collaborations" for change, more attention to preparation for teaching roles within and outside of academe, and the need to "make transparent to prospective doctoral students what doctoral education consists of and requires" (Nyquist and Woodford, 2000). Project staff also developed a Web-based clearinghouse of

Promising Practices for effective graduate education, which continues to expand and provide innovative ideas to the field (see http://www.grad. washington.edu/envision).

Drawing on the conference's recommendations, a further initiative was established. The Responsive PhD (2000–2005), housed at the Woodrow Wilson National Fellowship Foundation, took a broad approach, working at the campus level at twenty universities. Its leaders emphasized four themes, called "the four Ps": crafting new paradigms, exploring new practices, recruiting and retaining new people, and forming new partnerships (2005).

The 1990s were also marked by concern for the interrelated matters of high attrition rates and ever-lengthening time to degree, particularly troubling in the humanities. *In Pursuit of the Ph.D.* (Bowen and Rudenstine, 1992) drew national attention to those problems. In response, the Mellon Foundation created the Graduate Education Initiative (GEI), which included fifty-one departments at ten universities and explicitly tied graduate student funding to students' satisfactory and timely degree progress. In return for fellowship funds, departments clarified expectations and rationalized their programs (Ehrenberg and others, 2005). In the same vein, the CGS PhD Completion Project (2005–2010) is working to implement best practices for reducing doctoral student attrition.

Disciplinary societies have also become increasingly active agents of change. Their readiness to engage in serious reform has often been primed by self-studies of doctoral education and the future of the discipline.[7] Studies, in turn, have led to discipline-based reform activities. For example, in 2001 the American Chemical Society established an Office of Graduate Education and now publishes a newsletter for graduate students.

All of these predicate efforts set the stage for further efforts. The disciplines selected for the CID had all demonstrated concern about the future of doctoral education in their fields. And many of the CID participating universities had a history of involvement in prior reform efforts; some seem to have participated in all of them. In short, the CID did not start de novo; the Foundation planted seeds in soil that had been well prepared, and we trust that it, in turn, will set the stage for further work. Like scholarship, organizational change builds on efforts that come before.

This fifth stage in the history of graduate education has brought reforms that have already had significant impact. But the work is not done. And now is not the time to relax efforts at reform. With mounting pressure to change, graduate education must redouble its efforts to rethink the deep and surface structures for the formation of scholars in the twenty-first century.

Turning Resistance into Momentum

Looking back over more than a century of doctoral education and efforts toward reform, two stories emerge. On the one hand, the story is of change—gradual, yes, but ongoing and significant as PhD programs have evolved in response to new funding sources and incentives, more and different students, recalibrated purposes, and other changing circumstances both within and outside of the academy. On the other hand, the story is one of stasis—of structures and assumptions that have become increasingly difficult to budge. We took both stories into account as we developed our plan of action for the Carnegie Initiative on the Doctorate.

The details of what we did are described in Appendix A, but our plan of action must be understood as reflecting four larger ideas about doctoral education and what it takes to change it. We highlight these four because they offer different ways to think about seemingly stubborn obstacles to reform.

The (Partial) Myth of Money

In any conversation about how doctoral education can be improved, the theme of money comes up early and often. Unfortunately, it is often a conversation stopper. As history makes clear, funding patterns and incentives can radically reshape academic passions and pursuits. The availability of external funding, especially federal research funding, which began in the middle of the last century, has created a dynamic of competition and striving that makes attention to other matters (such as undergraduate teaching, or engagement with the community) a continuing struggle in many settings. The operative principles seem to be that more money leads to higher quality, and that nothing can be accomplished without the inducement of financial reward. This, in turn, supports a belief that positive change cannot take place in the context of the tight or diminishing resources faced by many public universities today, and that even affluent programs cannot afford to invest time and resources in improving their programs without additional funding.

We do not intend to downplay the significance of the financial challenges facing higher education. But Carnegie's work with a wide variety of doctoral programs suggests a different way to think about funding and

the incentives it creates. For one thing, it bears noting that a good deal of
money gets spent on ineffective practices. For another, money can induce
temporary change but not necessarily improvement or lasting impact.
Even more, funding can be seen not only as a condition for change but as
its consequence. The CID did not provide funding to participating departments, but a number of them have made improvements that have, in turn,
led to a new source of funds. For example, the University of Texas's history department, working closely with the dean of Liberal Arts, developed
a set of reforms that improved its graduate program, allowing the department to better compete nationally for new students. As a result, the
administration has begun to deliver substantial annual increases that allow
the history department, for the first time, to offer a significant number of
multi-year support packages. It has also increased discretionary funds that
will be used to support recruitment, research, and placement efforts
(R. Abzug, e-mail to the authors, September 6, 2006, and November 9,
2006). At the University of Nebraska, efforts to bring more women into
the study of mathematics, and to create a more supportive culture for students who might otherwise not thrive in the field, have brought significant
federal (and institutional) funds to the program over the past decade.

And of course not all the "goods" come immediately in the form of
funds. In the University of Michigan chemistry department, new opportunities for graduate students to explore educational issues (for instance,
through a partnership with the College of Education entitled Chemical
Sciences at the Interface of Education) have attracted outstanding appli-
cants to the doctoral program. According to Professor Brian Coppola,
"A number of excellent students have selected our PhD program over
departments ranked higher than ours because we openly embrace future
faculty development" (Hutchings and Clarke, 2004, p. 169). Over time
(in the classic chicken-and-egg dynamic of academic reputation-making)
better students help attract and retain more prestigious faculty, who bring
in more grant support and more cutting edge research, which brings in
more outstanding students. . . . This, then, is the cycle that drives
improvement: good ideas and good faith leading to rewards that are
invested in developing more good ideas.

The Power of the Disciplines

One of the themes in the history of graduate education, and in attempts
to change it, is the increasing power of the disciplines and the departments that house them on university campuses. Though the need for work
that crosses disciplinary boundaries is increasingly on the institutional

agenda, and many universities are creating new incentives to encourage such work, doctoral education remains a locally controlled process: admissions, curriculum, and quality standards are all controlled by the department's graduate faculty. As any graduate dean will testify, disciplines and departments rule the day when it comes to shaping the experience of doctoral candidates. In short, departments have tremendous power and are deeply resistant to external pressures for change; they are, if you will, part of the stasis side of the story.

But the disciplines can also be engines of change, and that is very much how we have seen them in the CID. In contrast to a number of previous efforts to reform graduate education, the CID chose to go deep rather than broad, working in a small number of fields rather than across the full spectrum of graduate education.

This strategy reflects a basic recognition that the cornerstone of the faculty member's identity is her disciplinary affiliation. Thus, a vision of doctoral education in the service of preparing stewards of the discipline is one that appeals to faculty "where they live" and calls on them to make common cause with others who share their passion for the field and its future. Over and over, we found that ensuring the good of the discipline is a special responsibility that scholars take very seriously. Seen in this way, a department is not a silo or fortress barricading itself against the outside world, but rather a home base from which good ideas can travel. That is, effective practices and new ideas can be carried by faculty and students who teach and study at several universities over the course of their careers. Allegiance to the discipline, and a commitment to ensuring its health into the future, makes it possible—even for departments that compete (as of course they do) for students, faculty, or grants—to collaborate on building and advancing the field in the name of a higher good. In these ways the disciplines open new routes into the future of doctoral education.

Moreover, honoring the disciplines opens new doors to conversations among disciplines. Too often cross-disciplinary conversations about graduate education devolve into comparisons between those seen as "haves" and the apparent "have-nots." But, in fact, one of the clear lessons of our work has been the value of mixing it up, allowing departments and fields that do not typically interact to share what they do (and what they worry about) in ways that prompt powerful learning and change across settings. This was most apparent in the cross-disciplinary convenings we held the summer of 2006, which were organized by theme. Mathematicians, historians, and neuroscientists alike struggle with how to foster creativity and how to help students ask important questions. And they were intrigued to learn how differently things are sometimes done in other settings. For instance, CID participants eagerly traded different models of qualifying exams—grant proposals, portfolios, and take-home exams.

The Double-Edged Sword of Decentralization

The fact that "no one is in charge," as noted in the epigraph of this chapter, may seem to be a recipe for undercutting the effectiveness of any reform effort. Unlike Europe, where control of graduate (and all of post-secondary) education has been much more centralized and top-down, in the United States local decision making and diversity are features of higher education.

On the one hand, this highly decentralized structure makes American graduate education at once messy and unruly, and at the same time highly resistant to systemic change. In this sense, it is an element of stasis, a condition that makes widespread reform much more difficult than it might otherwise be. But we would argue that the decentralized nature of U.S. graduate education may also promote change because it means there are many more places from which good ideas and innovative practices can emerge. As one observer of higher education quipped in the 1950s, "They can do things at Kansas now that used to be done only at Harvard" (Berelson, 1960, p. 108). We would go further today, asserting that sometimes "they can do things at Kansas" that *cannot* be done at Harvard. In short, the U.S. system is perfectly designed for spawning local experiments; what is needed are more occasions, more channels, for making this work visible and available for others to build upon.

With this in mind, the CID has involved a wide range of institutions, diverse in a variety of ways that matter in education, and at different points on the aspirational pecking order that, for better or worse, command attention in higher education. And we strongly emphasized the importance of making local experiments and innovations public. Reports to the field, rather than reports to the Carnegie Foundation, were the expectation. And departments responded admirably, putting on panels at national meetings and writing about their work. Useful accounts can be found in, among other places, the Spring 2004 issue of *Peer Review*, a featured article in *Chemical and Engineering News* (Everts, 2006), and the electronic representations of departments' CID work at http://gallery. carnegiefoundation.org/cid. Through this commitment to public exchange, reformers and innovators can be, in the words of neuroscientist Zach Hall, "vectors of information, skills, and ideas not only within programs but also across them" (Hall Z. W., 2006, p. 216).

Students as Agents of Change and Improvement

If anyone is in charge of graduate education, the general agreement is that it is the faculty. And clearly faculty are necessary actors in any meaningful reform. But one of the most powerful lessons of Carnegie's work over the past five years is that students may well be the secret weapon for change. Enlisting them as partners in this work may not be a move that comes easily to faculty members; in general doctoral students (like students at other levels) have been seen not as agents, but as the products—or, more cynically, as "byproducts" (Bousquet, 2002)—of the educational process. But when unleashed upon an agenda as important as the quality of the educational experience, students bring staggering imagination and energy to bear.

Anticipating that this might be the case, we asked every participating CID department to include doctoral students in their work from the outset—as participants in the process of self-study, deliberation, and creative problem solving. Students also attended and actively participated in project convenings at the Carnegie Foundation, where their perspectives were crucial in shaping deliberations; indeed, the convenings became a sort of microcosm of the sort of intellectual community that many of the departments were also seeking to strengthen at home. Over and over, faculty gave testimony to their newfound respect for students as agents of change. Many cited this as the single most transformative insight emerging from the CID.

Along the way, students who participated in the process of reflection and change found themselves thinking differently about their own learning, becoming more intentional, more purposeful, more able to shape their own experiences—all habits that will give them a firm foundation in the shifting landscape of scholarly and professional life in the future. Clearly the formation of these students was influenced by participating in the CID in ways that promise to shape their work as future scholars in whatever settings they enter.

Back to the Future

The history of graduate education is in large part a history of shifting and competing purposes. At the broad national level, enduring debates about purpose have centered on two sets of questions.

First, what is the degree for? How "pure" should it be? Is it preparation for a particular career or vocation, or is it education in the quest for knowledge and understanding? Back in 1912, Princeton's founding dean of the graduate school, Andrew Fleming West, complained, "The most sordid and dangerous thing just now in our graduate schools [is that they are] attracting . . . men, not because they must be scholars but because they want a job" (Berelson, 1960, p. 19). These questions of purpose continue to be vexing today. Are students' vocational aspirations and concerns trumping their passion for knowledge and inquiry? When PhD chemists work in university or industrial settings, are these equally laudable outcomes? Do they demand different preparation?

Second, for whom is the degree? Should any student who desires a PhD be allowed to try for one? A recurring concern has been that too many universities are granting doctorates to too many students, resulting in dilution of quality. Concern about the proliferation of "sham graduate schools" was raised by the AAUP in the early 1900s (Berelson, 1960, p. 20). At mid-century the question still remained: "Some leaders of graduate education were worried about the impact of numbers upon quality when the system produced 500, 1,000, 3,000 doctorates a year; what would they say today about the production of 9,000?" (Berelson, 1960, p. 32). And what would they say about today's production of over 40,000, one might ask? Indeed, the entry of for-profit and online universities into doctoral study has raised many eyebrows, as has the large number of the EdD's granted by schools of education. And although it is unlikely that anyone would now question whether women or African Americans are constitutionally or intellectually able, there is resistance in many quarters to adopting policies or practices to deliberately and systematically diversify the student population.

These tensions about purpose are arguably intrinsic to the very enterprise of graduate education. Throughout the last 125 years there have been many competing opinions, and certainly no lasting resolution. As new challenges appear, questions of purpose return with new force.

The question, then, is about the particular challenges facing doctoral education today and in the coming decades. What are the larger social and intellectual developments that cannot be ignored if doctoral education is to move successfully into the twenty-first century? Many observers point to globalization, new market forces, and changing patterns of funding as circumstances demanding urgent response. We agree. But perhaps even more influential will be shifts in the way knowledge itself is generated and exchanged, potentially redefining the core work of the fields around which doctoral education has traditionally been organized.

Early on in the work of the CID, we commissioned essays by scholars in each of the six participating fields, inviting them to reflect on their disciplines and how doctoral students should be prepared as stewards. In addition, we asked several scholars to read through the full set of essays and tell us what they saw. (The entire collection was published in 2006 as *Envisioning the Future of Doctoral Education* [Golde and Walker].) Their answers converged on a number of trends: a move toward greater interdisciplinarity and interaction with neighboring disciplines; growing commitment to team work—even in disciplines traditionally marked by solitary scholarship—with more collaboration in both research and teaching; and greater purposefulness in reaching out to partners and audiences outside of academe in ways that connect academic work with the larger social context. Many of the authors talk as well about the need for breadth of preparation to complement in-depth specialization, and the need for more flexible, integrated conceptions of scholarly work, whether in the laboratory, the library, the classroom, or the community. Taken together, these trends provide an urgent motive for change. And, says David Damrosch, they "reveal nothing less than an emerging pedagogical 'consilience,' to use Edward Wilson's term, which suggests the outlines of a substantial shift in the goals and methods of graduate education" (2006, p. 34).

We share Damrosch's sense that graduate education faces significant shifts in the ways doctoral students are prepared, and some of those shifts are well underway. As intractable as questions of purpose are from a system-level perspective, they can nevertheless be the subject of fruitful deliberation within a department or program. Agreeing upon the purpose of particular requirements—what is the role of the dissertation?—can result in significant improvement in the educational effectiveness and intellectual climate of the department.

But we know, too, that change is not easy, and it certainly is not automatic. There are few habits or processes at the graduate level that prompt programs to take stock, agree on goals, and design better ways of achieving those goals. The assessment movement, for example, which raises questions about goals and effectiveness, has focused almost exclusively on undergraduate education.[8] And in some cases, "assessment" has brought with it bureaucratic baggage that does not play well in graduate programs. The need, then, is for a way for faculty and students to step back and examine what they do and why—not as a process imposed from the outside but as a commitment to inquiry and improvement reflecting their own high standards for the discipline and its students. This is our topic in the next chapter.

ENDNOTES

1. Prewitt is the Carnegie Professor of Public Affairs, School of International and Public Affairs at Columbia University—and also a member of the National Advisory Committee for the Carnegie Initiative on the Doctorate.

The epigraph comes from his essay *Who Should Do What? Implications for Institutional and National Leaders,* one of the commentaries on the collection of disciplinary essays commissioned at the start of the CID (2006, p. 23).

2. The U.S. Office of Education has taken responsibility for tallying the number of degrees ever since the early years, although researchers have more confidence in the data once the Office's statistical field service was established in 1923. Walter Crosby Eells conducted an exhaustive analysis of alumni directories and other historical data and his most generous count of doctorates totals 3,553 granted by 1900 (Eells, 1956). However, others found that about a third of these were awarded by universities lacking legitimate doctoral programs or adequate facilities, and another 8–10 percent were honorary (Thurgood, Golladay, and Hill, 2006, p. 3). More detailed information about doctoral recipients became available with the advent of the Survey of Earned Doctorates, tabulated annually since 1957, and collected by means of a survey administered to all new PhD's shortly before graduation. The 2006 NSF report *US Doctorates in the 20th Century* provides a wealth of historical data (Thurgood and others, 2006).

3. The number of doctoral-granting institutions and the number of doctorates awarded come from Figures 2.1 and 2.4 the 2006 *US Doctorates in the 20th Century* (Thurgood and others, 2006), with the exception of the year 2000, which come from the Survey of Earned Doctorate report, *Doctorate Recipients from United States Universities: Summary Report 2004* (Hoffer and others, 2005, Tables 1 & 2, pp. 39–40). The ratio of doctorates to bachelor's degrees is based on a table in Bowen and Rudenstine (1992, p. 21), with data for 1900 computed from Berelson who uses 250 PhD's for 1900 (1960, p. 26), and for 2000 from the *Digest of Educational Statistics: 2005,* Table 251 (National Center for Education Statistics, 2005).

4. The National Board on Graduate Education (NBGE) was established in 1971 by the Conference Board of Associated Research Councils. It had a three-year term, from June 1972 until June 1975. During that time, the organization issued six reports: (1) *Graduate Education: Purposes, Problems, and Potential;* (2) *Doctorate Manpower Forecasts and Policy;* (3) *Federal Policy Alternatives Toward Graduate Education;* (4) *Science Development, University Development, and the Federal Government;* (5) *Minority Group Participation in Graduate Education;* (6) *Outlook and Opportunities for Graduate Education* (National Board on Graduate Education, 1972, 1973, 1974, 1975a, 1975b, 1976). The NBGE also issued five technical reports.

5. The first Doctor of Arts (DA) degree was adopted at Carnegie Mellon University in the fields of English, fine arts, history, and mathematics in 1967,

although the DA was first proposed in 1932. It was envisioned as a preparation for college teaching in each of the disciplines, rather than for a career
in research. Four powerful advocacy groups—the Carnegie Commission
on Higher Education, the Carnegie Corporation, professional associations,
and state higher education coordinating boards—encouraged the adoption
of the degree. The development of the DA was largely a top-down process,
aided by planning grants and fellowship support from the Carnegie Corporation, which invested $3.2 million in the effort (Glazer, 1993).

Between 1967 and 1990 the DA was adopted at thirty-one institutions
in eighty-eight departments in forty-four fields, most popularly English
(thirteen), mathematics (eight), and history (eight). During those twenty-
three years 1,943 DA degrees were awarded (Glazer, 1993). By 1991, only
twenty-one universities were still granting the DA, a number which has
shrunk to twelve as we write this volume. The DA degree never spread nor
found the success that its proponents had imagined. Glazer attributes this
to a combination of factors: competitive pressures that emphasize research
over teaching for faculty and students, the collapse of the academic job
market, and the proliferation of other specialized doctorates including
music, business, fine arts, and many of the professions. We would argue
that it failed to spread widely because the PhD was still being used for all
career paths in most fields, and as long as one could earn a PhD, the DA
was no competition.

6. The data are from the Survey of Earned Doctorates (Hoffer and others,
2001, Tables 7, 8, and 11; Thurgood and others, 2006). The first U.S. doctorate awarded to an African American was to physicist Edward Alexander
Bouchet in 1876 from Yale. However, data on the race and ethnicity of doctoral recipients were not systematically collected until 1975. The propor-
tions by race and ethnicity are computed from a total of those U.S. citizens
who reported their ethnicity. The first American woman to earn a doctorate
from a U.S. university was Helen Magill, in 1877 from Boston University,
in Greek. The 1978 National Research Council's *A Century of Doctorates*
reported gender data in five-year averages. From 1900 to 1904, 8.8 percent of U.S. PhD's were women, in 1920–1924 this rose to 15.1 percent,
for 1940–1944 it was 13.5 percent, and it dropped to 10.8 percent in the
1960–1964 period (Harmon, 1978, p. 17). This same report notes that
the proportion of international students was a stable 7–9 percent until the
1960s, when the upward trend began (p. 47).

7. The most comprehensive recent disciplinary study of doctoral education
comes from the field of history (Bender and others, 2004). The American
Chemical Society regularly surveys its membership, which comprises most

doctorate-holding chemists regardless of whether they work in academia or industry. A set of survey reports can be found on the American Chemical Society Web page (American Chemical Society, 2002). The Modern Language Association regularly collects and publishes data about graduate education as well, particularly related to the job market and career paths, and has sponsored conferences and other publications (for example, Laurence, 1998, 2002; Lunsford, Moglen, and Slevin, 1989; MLA Committee on the Status of Graduate Students in the Profession, 2001; MLA Executive Council Task Force on Graduate Education, 1999; Modern Language Association, 1998, 2003). The mathematics community was galvanized by several reports sponsored by the federal government (Board on Mathematical Sciences, 1990; Board on Mathematical Sciences of the National Research Council, 1992; National Research Council, 1984; Odom, 1998); and since 1965 the AMS, MAA, ASA, and IMS have co-sponsored the Annual Survey of Mathematical Sciences. This reflects only some of the activities in disciplines represented in the CID, and other disciplinary societies have also been very active.

8. Two recent exceptions are worth noting. The 2006 edited volume *The Assessment of Doctoral Education* (Maki and Borkowski, 2006), includes numerous models and case studies. A publication by the Responsive PhD project highlights promising practices and how they were assessed (Woodrow Wilson National Fellowship Foundation, 2005).

3

TALKING ABOUT PURPOSE

MIRRORS, LENSES, AND WINDOWS

One of the most powerful motivations for change is looking in the mirror.

—Lee S. Shulman[1]

ONE OF THE MOST COMMON YET MYSTIFYING MILESTONES on the road to the PhD is the qualifying (or, as it is known in some quarters, comprehensive, general, or candidacy) examination. A long-standing, often-dreaded element of doctoral education, the experience that results in advancement to candidacy takes a variety of forms.[2] In some cases "quals" are summative and backward looking, serving to assess whether a student has acquired sufficient content knowledge. In other cases they look forward and provide a roadmap for work to come, focusing on a student's ability to generate new insights, ask questions, make connections, and focus on a special area of expertise. And of course some look both back and forward. Candidacy exams often serve educational goals as well as gatekeeping functions; the process of preparing for and taking the exam, in whatever form, provides an important learning opportunity in and of itself.

Or so one would hope. As our work with students and faculty in the CID reminded us, qualifying exams can also be a source of profoundly mixed messages and cross-purposes. The educational purpose of the exam is often unclear to students. Although a majority of students surveyed in the CID said that expectations about the exams were conveyed to them, their responses suggest considerable confusion in such comments as: "we are left drifting," "in the dark," "terrifyingly nebulous," "hazy," "opaque," and "just stumbling through."[3] Students may see the importance of mastering certain material in principle, but the actual steps toward that mastery are much less clear.

Students also say that their understanding of the exams often comes from informal sources, usually more veteran students. The formal channels—including faculty, administrators, handbooks, and Web sites—are often contradictory or outdated in their information. Changing requirements, even when they are for the better, may actually increase confusion. As a history student said, "I think that morale would be improved and the results would be better if the faculty explained to the graduate students what they were supposed to get out of the exam process, besides ulcers and migraines."

This opacity contributes to anxiety on the part of students who often over-prepare and delay taking their exams for months and years. And since it is often the case that no student fails the exam, some may conclude that the entire ordeal is largely a sham. Equally troubling are departments in which students fail the exam, but feel blindsided because all the feedback they had received until that moment had been positive. These frustrations are amplified when students see tremendous variation in the standards faculty members in the same department use to evaluate exams.

Sadly, faculty members may be nearly as confused as students, since many of them are administering an exam designed by others and inherited from the past. When the CID faculty survey asked, "To what extent do faculty in your department have a shared understanding of the educational purpose of the qualifying exam?" we learned that such understanding was far from universal (see Table 3.1). The responses were similar for a second question, "To what extent do faculty have a shared understanding of what constitutes an acceptable level of student performance on the qualifying exam?"

Our point here is not that qualifying and comprehensive exams are irretrievably broken; no doubt they work very well in many settings. The confusion of purpose that sometimes swirls around such experiences does, however, indicate a more general imperative for doctoral programs: to step back, take stock, grapple with, and clarify the purposes behind their practices. What are the central goals for student learning? What vision of the field and its future drives the design of the program? Is there a design, or is the program simply an accretion of elements inherited from the past, unexamined in the light of current and coming realities?

Table 3.1. Extent to Which Faculty Perceive a Shared Understanding of
the Educational Purpose of the Departmental Qualifying Exam[4]

	Understanding shared by all faculty	Neutral	Not shared (Individually determined)
Education	55%	25%	20%
Neuroscience	55	31	14
Mathematics	53	34	13
Chemistry	49	40	11
History	44	29	27
English	35	32	33

Source: *Carnegie Graduate Faculty Survey*

In this chapter we look at the need for serious deliberation about purposes, why such deliberation is often so difficult, and consider some of the processes and tools that can help move doctoral programs toward the capacity for ongoing improvement—which, we believe, is the single best strategy for meeting future needs and challenges.

The metaphor in the title of the chapter deserves some explanation. Mirrors, lenses, and windows improve vision—and thus understanding and motivation to change—by providing new views. Mirrors allow us to see ourselves. Sometimes the reflection is unflattering, but mirrors reveal images that "for the most part have been inaccessible or invisible" (Shulman, 2002). Lenses enhance the ability to see by sharpening focus and magnifying detail in one area. With "new ways of looking, new vantage points," Shulman says, "we can now compare that improved view with our visions of the possible and desirable, and thereby be motivated and directed toward change." Windows provide the opportunity to gaze at the work done by our neighbors. Windows also offer our neighbors the reciprocal opportunity to take a long hard look at our own professional practice. Leaning over the windowsill and talking is in the scholarly spirit of exchange and shared learning. "These comparative peeks through the window offer another dimension of both motivation and direction toward change for educators," he concluded.

Difficult Dialogues

Most would agree that it is laudable for faculty and graduate students to grapple with issues of purpose, program design, and effective practices. But the reality is that time and financial resources are in short supply for everyone involved. In the absence of an immediate crisis or difficulty (say, a major student uprising, or an unexpected shortfall in funding), serious deliberation about purposes and their achievement is a significant challenge.

This point came home to us early in the work of the Carnegie Initiative on the Doctorate, when we first convened discipline-based teams from participating departments. Each team was invited to make a presentation about the goals of its program, and the presentations were thoughtful and incisive, generating lively discussion. But participants were also clear in saying that "purpose" and "goals" were not everyday topics of conversation back home in the department.

Why not? First, there are few occasions that prompt such reflection and self-examination. Accreditation, which (for better or worse, depending on whom you ask) requires evidence of student learning, has focused almost exclusively on undergraduate education. Most graduate programs undergo periodic external reviews, and these can be helpful, certainly. But such exercises are sometimes viewed as a charade, triggered by administrative agendas rather than by internal needs and interests. Sometimes, too, earlier reviews have taught faculty members unfortunate lessons: that reviews are an exercise that can be gamed, that they are done to please others, that nothing will change. Such lessons breed cynicism and inertia. Worse yet, candid analyses of shortcomings may be viewed as leading to negative outcomes, such as reduced budgets or fractured departments, rather than resulting in support for new directions and the solution of thorny problems.

In addition, the task of "visioning" and setting goals may smack of corporate thinking or calls for educational accountability that are perceived by faculty as efforts to curb academic autonomy. Tactics used in the business world do not fit easily into the culture of academe. Even when undertaken with an open mind, such tasks can rapidly degenerate into endless wordsmithing, yielding only bland clichés. "The goal of our department is to help all students reach their potential as future researchers and scholars" is a worthy but not very meaningful goal.

Perhaps, however, the greatest obstacle to serious, substantive deliberation about purpose, as a number of department leaders told us, is that some differences are better not discussed. Not talking about purposes, that is, helps maintain a precarious peace, and, according to literary scholar Gerald Graff, some faculty are very good at keeping that peace. To avoid "having to confront and (heaven forbid!) debate their disagreements in public," Graff reports, English faculty developed an elaborate "system of negotiated compromises. . . . Under this system, which had grown up in the climate of expansion and affluence that universities had enjoyed for most of the twentieth century, intellectual turf wars were neutralized by the simple device of adding a new component in order to appease the feuding parties and preserve peaceful coexistence" (Graff, 2006, p. 374).

This kind of compromise is not restricted to the humanities. According to historian of science Yehuda Elkana (2006), there is "more fundamental controversy within the sciences than its practitioners are willing to confront," and, as graduate education has become more sharply specialized, the need to understand and grapple with inconsistencies, contradictions, and competing paradigms has been diminished in ways that impoverish scientific thinking (p. 65).

Conflict avoidance has heavy costs for both faculty and students "not only in being deprived of the climate of debate that scholars need to avoid going brain dead . . . but in the confusion and disorientation about 'the profession' that results from curricular mixed messages" (Graff, 2006, p. 374).[5] Students need to learn to debate ideas and develop their own judgment about their relative merits. Ultimately this is how disciplines grow and develop. And respectful debate—especially when the stakes are high—is a hallmark of a healthy intellectual community.

With such impediments, how can graduate programs grapple fruitfully with who they are and what they do? How can the subject of change and improvement even be broached?

Reflections on Purpose

During our work with CID departments, we persistently encouraged faculty and students to ask and answer three sets of foundational questions:

1. What is the **purpose** of the doctoral program? What does it mean to develop students as stewards? What are the desired outcomes of the program?

2. What is the **rationale and educational purpose of each element** of the doctoral program? Which elements of the program should be affirmed and retained? Which elements could usefully be changed or eliminated?

3. How do you know? What **evidence** aids in answering those questions? What evidence can be collected to determine whether changes serve the desired outcomes?

Our expectation was not that programs would march neatly through these questions, one by one. The goal, rather, was to help to establish a kind of substrate, a frame of reference, for a wide variety of activities, tasks, and conversations. The questions served, one might say, as a kind of mirror, reflecting reality back to the department. And though not all programs made great breakthroughs, and none, we suspect, would say that their work was complete at the end of the CID, opening the conversation about purpose allowed important steps forward for many programs.

Consider, for example, the University of Nebraska-Lincoln department of mathematics. With more than a hundred years of history, the program has naturally had ups and downs, but since the end of the 1980s—thanks in large part to leadership from former chair James Lewis—the fortunes of the graduate program have been steadily on the rise: more and better doctoral students, a national award for successful recruitment and graduation of women, federal money to run several programs to bring women into the profession, and demonstrable success in creating a nationally recognized department.[6] "We did all this," says current chair John Meakin, "without lowering standards or changing requirements. It was a matter of creating a positive, supportive environment, and accepting only qualified people we knew would succeed" (J. Meakin, interview with the authors, July 24, 2006). Graduate students are actively engaged in the intellectual community of the department, treated as junior colleagues, involved in ongoing work on the undergraduate curriculum and in hiring. Meakin says, "We're kind of pleased with the way the graduate program has gone."

Even so, something was missing. "One of the purposes of getting involved in the CID was to think through the purposes of doctoral education, and one of the challenges was to create a document that actually reflects what we believe," Meakin asserts.

Though the process for creating such a document was fairly straightforward, "it wasn't easy, actually." The first step was "a sort of looking around, asking what kinds of students we're trying to create, and what they do when they complete the program." What this initial scan revealed was that the program was producing three kinds of students: one group going on to post-docs in PhD-granting institutions and then to research careers; another group moving to positions in four-year colleges where research is also expected; and a third going to places like the National Security Agency, industry, and government. Faculty asked themselves what each group needs to know and what qualities students need to develop.

As chair, Meakin put his hand to a first draft of those qualities ("learning outcomes," to use the current educational jargon), shared it with the department's CID committee, and then with the entire faculty and graduate students. "We didn't have meetings and meetings and meetings about it," Meakin says, "but we had a lot of input." Although there was none of the rancor described by Graff, there were "some issues" about whether the department could do "a good job in all three areas, or should focus on just one." At end of day, the faculty opted for the complete trio since all three reflect what department members see as stewardship of the discipline. This may seem like the kind of compromise by accretion that Graff argues against, but the point is that hard questions of purpose were *debated* at Nebraska, rather than avoided.

The result is a statement that fits on two sides of a sheet of paper: a description of the three possible career paths, and a list of eight goals (see Exhibit 3.1). It is not, Meakin is quick to add, "something that everyone should adopt." The focus is local, reflecting local discussion and agreement, "a wish list, really, a set of milestones we can use for guidelines and evaluation purposes as we think about our program." In the language of this chapter's title, the document is both a mirror—reflecting the program's own vision of itself—and a set of lenses for examining whether it is achieving that vision.

Exactly how this document will be used over time remains to be seen, but already a number of lens-like uses have taken shape, many of them aimed at strengthening the sense of intellectual community and supportive culture that the program has worked hard to create over the last several decades. All incoming graduate students are given a copy of the statement during orientation, with the understanding that their first homework assignment is to read and critique it. Then, as students leave the program, with or without completing the degree, they are interviewed. The program document serves as a template for that interview, where they are invited to reflect on "whether we are delivering the kind of educational experience that the document promises." In the future, the statement may be incorporated into a survey of program alumni, as well.

In conclusion, Meakin says that developing the statement "was a useful thing for the faculty to think through, and useful to put up front for the students so they can see what we're shooting for." He doesn't claim that the statement is perfect, and doesn't know what directions it might take in the future, or what uses will turn out to be most worthwhile. The bottom line, as we see it, is that it is a rare thing for program participants to step back, take a measured, careful look in the mirror, and force themselves to articulate in the clearest language they can what they collectively seek for students. Such an accomplishment is a powerful first step toward further improvements.

○

Exhibit 3.1. Purpose of the Doctoral Program in Mathematics at the University of Nebraska-Lincoln

The purpose of doctoral education in mathematics is to produce the next generation of mathematicians who will advance mathematical research and maintain the integrity and vitality of the discipline. Doctoral graduates in mathematics should become stewards of the discipline, people who are entrusted with preserving and developing the mathematical literature and with communicating mathematical knowledge to others.

A doctoral graduate in mathematics should have a deep, active knowledge of some area of mathematics, and should have made a significant contribution to the literature in that area. In addition, doctoral graduates in mathematics should possess the following:

- A broad knowledge of the mathematical literature, its historical development, and how diverse parts of mathematics relate to each other

- A general understanding of the centrality of mathematics in society, and the interrelations between mathematics and other disciplines

- Preparation and skill to teach mathematics at different levels

- An understanding of and commitment to the ethical principles that underlie professional work in the discipline of mathematics

- A sense of membership in the community of current and former mathematical scholars, and an understanding of the historical roots of this community

- A commitment to the profession, engaging in professional service, both within the graduate's immediate community, and within the broader community of mathematical scholars

- The ability to communicate the beauty and power of mathematical ideas to diverse audiences

- The ability to help others learn to combine creativity and imagination with the rigor, logic, and precision of mathematics

(For the full statement and further information about the department's work in the CID, see the University of Nebraska-Lincoln mathematics department's Web page, CID Work, at http://gallery.carnegiefoundation.org/cid.)

○

Data Lenses and Windows

Serious engagement with questions of purpose needs serious fuel, and some of the best fuel comes in the form of information. To use the terms in the title of this chapter, one needs not only mirrors but lenses that allow for a variety of new perspectives on what is being examined. Often in educational settings the need for data and evidence of effectiveness is seen as something required by others (and such requirements are on the rise), but some of the most forward-looking, purposeful graduate programs have begun to create and analyze their own evidence, motivated by questions they want to answer. In doing so, they turn their research lenses and skills on themselves.

The story we tell about the Columbia University English department in Chapter One is about the power of serious reflection on the program's future: its purposes and elements, its central practices, and the intellectual community in which it can flourish. It is also a story about the power of data to catalyze conversation and action. During the 2003–2004 academic year, the department engaged in an extended process of self-study, beginning with a survey of current students that covered "every facet of the program and its requirements." The responses provided "a wealth of statistical information and many thoughtful, creative ideas for change, many of which made their way into a final package of reforms." David Damrosch, then director of Graduate Studies, notes particularly how many surprises came to light in the process, especially for "tenured faculty [who] may have little awareness of what the system's disadvantages may have been for the unlucky few—in fact, the many—who have dropped out along the way or who have failed to find a job they like." Among the revelations was "how many hours a week the students in our 'fully funded' PhD program were working off-campus just to make ends meet." Damrosch concludes, "There is no better way to begin studying a program than with a survey of this sort" (Damrosch, 2006, pp. 41–42, 36).

The chemistry department at Duke University might well concur. As part of the program's participation in the CID, a survey of graduate students was conducted in 2003; results were presented and discussed at a town hall meeting open to all members of the department, faculty and students alike. Many of the findings were positive and affirming; students were pleased with the preparation they receive as teaching assistants, for example, and they were unanimous about the success with which faculty "communicate their excitement for their research." But, as at Columbia, there were surprises. A significant proportion of students (four to one) indicated that they would like to take more courses outside the department, a finding that calls "for thinking on our [the faculty's] part concerning what courses we could enthusiastically recommend" (Pirrung, 2003, p. 2). Around the issue of affiliation—the process through which students select a primary research adviser—the survey revealed that there was "significant interest" by students in the concept of research rotations, or working in the labs of several potential advisers before making their final selection. Another surprise: only one in ten students indicated that "the level at which graduate courses are taught is too high." This response prompted discussion among the faculty as to the appropriate expectations for introductory graduate coursework. The survey also brought to light a number of intriguing differences among subfields. These are issues that the department probed because they are well-known tension points in the field of chemistry. Indeed, most departments face questions about the appropriate emphasis on coursework in research-intensive degree programs, adviser-student matching, and taking courses outside of the department.

Perhaps, however, the most broadly significant finding was that students need clearer explanations of what the program requires of them. Clarifying "not only the 'whats' but the 'whys' of our requirements" is high on the list of recommendations following from the survey process, as it was, in fact, for many of the programs that used surveys to provide more focused views of their work. Surveys have a number of limitations, but they also offer powerful lenses for seeing the program in new ways. Surveying students and alumni on a regular basis can provide a longitudinal perspective on the effectiveness of the doctoral program.

Other kinds of information may also provide useful lenses. For example, in 2004–2005, as part of an ongoing commitment to an iterative process of data collection and collaborative deliberation, the English department at the University of Pittsburgh pioneered a seminar series consisting of three events attended by several dozen faculty and graduate students. Each event focused on one of the three departmental program areas: literature, film studies, and composition and rhetoric. At each seminar, a panel of faculty members presented evidence about the types of intellectual work that had been fostered in the doctoral program since the early 1990s (documented by data such as dissertation titles), how this work was carried out (courses by area, and faculty advising on doctoral committees), and the specific outcomes of this work (job placement). Director of Graduate Studies Eric Clarke also reported on the areas of interest listed in applications for admissions, reflecting perceived departmental strengths. The presentations allowed faculty members and students to discuss issues informed by evidence about the program, and to move forward with a number of improvements in each program area: renaming one program area to reflect changes in faculty hiring and expertise, proposing changes to the graduate curriculum committee, and redesigning the departmental Web site to make purposes and requirements clearer and more explicit to students and other users.[7]

Our point here is about the power of data as a lens, but the metaphor of windows is relevant as well. When programs examine themselves and gather systematic information about what they do and how it works, and then share that information with those elsewhere, they not only have new lenses but they also open up windows that allow for learning across sites. We take this kind of sharing for granted in the world of scholarly research. Data are to be shared, not kept secret. They are to be built upon, not hidden.

Thus far, there are few tools for systematic cross-program comparisons in graduate education.[8] But a step in this direction emerged in a creative data-gathering effort undertaken in the neuroscience program at The Ohio State University. In a poster presented at the 2005 Society for Neuroscience meeting, the program explained its intent as follows: "We are engaged in a self-evaluation . . . that uses special representations of neuroscience and related disciplines ('maps') to examine the scope and content of neuroscience at OSU and to compare our program to others in the CID and across the country. We will present maps and graphs generated by quantitative metrics of our program" (Pyter and others, 2005).

The products of this effort include five different maps derived from data on the disciplinary heritage of students (degree fields of students and their scientific "parents"), publication patterns, sources of funding, primary departmental affiliation of faculty and students, and topographic maps of students' research foci. (This fifth map is shown in Exhibit 3.2.) The mapping exercise provided powerful lenses for faculty and students from the OSU program to improve local practices; they used program maps to generate a "flow diagram" for describing the program on the Web site, and also to revise the student handbook. But what was also important about the process was its potential for opening windows and inviting useful comparisons: "Our maps allow visual comparisons between the research and scholarly 'landscape' of individual faculty and students, at OSU and other universities, and in the future they will be used as metrics to chart the technical and conceptual development of neuroscience graduate students as they move from matriculation to graduation" (Pyter and others, 2005). By putting the maps on display at a national conference, OSU is throwing the window wide open.

○

Exhibit 3.2. Map of the Ohio State University Neuroscience Program Student Research Foci

Neuroscience is an interdisciplinary field, with the common goal of studying and understanding the brain. Researchers can study different "model systems," arranged by size from the atomic and molecular level through the organismal and population level. Likewise research can be categorized by the primary research technique. In the depiction below, these two different ways of categorizing a research project are arranged on the two axes of the graph. The field of neuroscience includes research projects at the intersections of most, but not all, techniques and model systems. The OSU students "mapped" twenty-one student research projects being conducted in 2005. The size of the circle indicates the duration of the project (large circles have been underway longer).

   This diagram reveals that students are clustered into a relatively small number of locations—the department's specialty areas—rather than being equally distributed across the discipline of neuroscience. A similar graphic could show the distribution of faculty research foci, and the comparison of the two could reveal mismatches and gaps that need filling. Likewise, other scatter plots could depict the evolution of one senior researcher's body of work, the research underway at another institution, recent nationally funded research projects, and so forth.

G. Butcher, interview with the authors, May 9, 2007

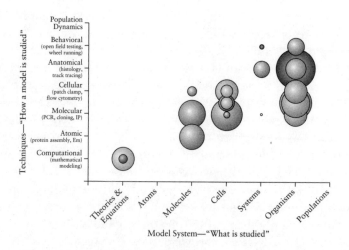

Higher education has traditionally been ambivalent about comparative data (consider the love-hate relationship that campuses have with *U.S. News & World Report* rankings), and the possibility of No Child Left Behind–like assessment mandates coming to higher education is alarming. But going public with metrics and data has the potential to open up important lines of discussion and planning. Sharing data across campuses opens the window for departmental reflections leading to formative assessment of programs. As a result of exactly this kind of interaction, the Howard University chemistry department learned that its curriculum was far more rigid and heavy on coursework than other departments. Making the curriculum more flexible was one of three major pillars that informed a comprehensive program revision; the new plan has promise for enhanced professional development, and for speeding up students' transition into research (see the Howard University department of chemistry's Web page, Flexible Student-Specific Curriculum, at http://gallery. carnegiefoundation.org/cid.).

Better Designs for Better Learning

This chapter began with a look at the qualifying exam as a case of the mixed messages doctoral programs often convey about what it means to know the discipline deeply, and about the goals of the PhD. It seems appropriate, then, to end the chapter by looking at how that experience can be remade and improved through a process of clarifying purpose, data gathering, and deliberation—in this case by using a professional development portfolio. But, first, a little more needs to be said about this pivotal moment in a doctoral student's education.

The experience of the CID departments argues for the benefits of deliberating about purposes and practices, and qualifying exams are, in fact, a particularly strategic site for focusing those deliberations. For the student, the exam (by whatever name) is the bridge or transition between the coursework and dissertation-research stages, or, to put it differently, between knowledge-absorption and knowledge-creation. For faculty, the exam is a perch from which to scrutinize the student and the program. At the time of the qualifying exam one can look both forward and backward, asking "Did you learn what we tried to teach you?" and "Are you ready for what comes next?" At its best, the exam allows careful judgments about whether students have a sufficiently broad understanding of the field of which they will be a steward, and if they are prepared to drill deeply and become specialists.

The Professional Portfolio

Like most history departments in this country, the doctoral program at the University of Kansas had a long tradition of asking students to demonstrate their mastery of the field in a comprehensive exam before moving into work on the dissertation. Many successful scholars have survived and even thrived on their exam experience, and this tradition has therefore seemed to serve the field well. Over the past several years, however, faculty in the Kansas program began to question its continuing usefulness.

For one thing, the field itself has changed. "At one time the so-called 'comprehensive' examination indeed comprised the entire key historiographical canon," a department document reports. "But the enormous growth in the varieties of history and concomitantly in the secondary literature has made genuinely comprehensive knowledge impossible" (Levin, n.d.). The traditional "data-dump exam," as it came to be called, in which students are asked to write under a strict time constraint with no books or other documents to consult, "has nothing in common with how historians do their work," says Eve Levin, the KU history department's Director of Graduate Studies (E. Levin, interview with the authors, August 2, 2006). There were other issues as well: lack of consistency in the structure, administration, and standards applied to the exams, and a sense that the quality of the work, even from the best students, was often disappointing.

Moreover, the department had data pointing to the exam's negative effect on student progress. As Levin explains, this was a clear "slowdown point" for students. The PhD program was officially set at five to six years, and preparation for the comprehensive exam was expected to take no more than a year, but many students were spending much longer and falling badly behind. Indeed, department data showed that the period between completing coursework and the completion of exams was sometimes two and a half years. "The data were slippery," Levin concedes, "but the overall pattern was clear."

What to do? Predictably, faculty were concerned about doing away with a tradition that was widely recognized and respected by their peers in other settings. And certainly the program needed a way to certify students' command of the subject matter and methods of their field, and to ascertain readiness for the dissertation phase of doctoral work. Was there a better way?

The solution that eventually emerged was the professional portfolio, a collection of artifacts designed to help students document their own histories as emerging scholars. Through it (as the student handbook says), "students demonstrate their command of their fields and their preparation to undertake dissertation research. It should be designed with this purpose in mind."

Students begin constructing the portfolio in their first semester of doctoral work. A detailed timeline indicates what elements to create and collect at various points along the next several years. The portfolio allows for individual emphases and interests, but some elements are required: a curriculum vita, all research seminar papers, any published historical works, and a 15–20 page professional essay explaining why the student selected his major fields, how those fields might be integrated and related to one another, and what he understands to be the leading research issues. The portfolio also includes a dissertation prospectus, materials about teaching, and other items important to the student and his sense of his own trajectory and goals. In the semester following completion of course work, students present the professional portfolio to their committee for discussion in the oral exam that follows.

The portfolio is still relatively new, but already there are signs that the approach is bringing tangible benefits to students and to the program. Students choosing the portfolio option (it is required for new students, but advanced students can choose whether to shift to the new approach) are moving through the program more quickly. New students also report that the portfolio model was a consideration in their choice of programs. In general, student "buzz" about the option is positive.

And for good reason. The portfolio assignment reflects several important principles of effective doctoral education as it is conceived in this volume. First, it assumes that self-assessment is and should be ongoing and embedded in each student's professional life, rather than episodic. Second, it shifts some of the responsibility for assessment from the faculty to the student, and does that early on. It allows students to assume increasing responsibility for their own formation, to learn important skills of reflection and critical self-assessment, and to develop habits of documentation that will serve them well as they enter professional life (Levin notes that the portfolio deliberately bears some resemblance to the promotion and tenure dossier). Third, the portfolio provides a structure—a scaffold, if you will—for developing skills and habits of mind that will stand graduates in good stead in their future workplaces. For these reasons and others, portfolios are now attracting attention as an alternative to traditional assessment tools in doctoral education (Cyr and Muth, 2006, p. 215).

It is important to say that the portfolio is only one of a number of changes designed to reinvigorate the Kansas history program, including two detailed Progress and Professionalization Grids describing the progression of steps and tasks that students should be undertaking throughout the program. (For the grids and other artifacts from the department's recent reforms, see the University of Kansas department of history's Web page, History Department, at http://gallery .carnegiefoundation.org/cid.) The biggest change of all, program participants report, is that "the department has developed a new self-confidence about who we are and what we are doing." That confidence would seem to be affirmed by the interest of other history PhD programs in the use of the portfolio. According to Levin, Duke and Ohio State have both been exploring the idea, and, at a recent American Historical Association meeting, a session featuring KU's work drew a large and enthusiastic crowd. In its final report to the CID, the department notes, "We now see ourselves as becoming a benchmark for the nation—pioneers in the realm of graduate education." From our point of view as CID organizers, work on the portfolio is also testimony to the power of data and deliberation to catalyze creative change.

A Culture of Inquiry and Evidence

Becoming a steward of the discipline should be a goal for every doctoral student and therefore for every faculty member working with doctoral students. But it is incumbent upon faculty not simply to consider whether their advisees are developing as stewards, but whether their program in its entirety encourages all students to become stewards. Programs that embody the ethic of stewardship take collective responsibility for the quality of what they do. Such programs work toward shared visions of purpose, and they create occasions and mechanisms (mirrors, lenses, and windows) for understanding what works, why, and how the program might be improved in the future. Rather than be content with anecdotes and impressions ("My advisee understands the purpose of the qualifying exam," or "I've never heard students asking for more feedback on their teaching"), the program promotes a culture of inquiry and evidence in which faculty members bring their habits, skills, and values as scholars to their work as educators.

Every department must, of course, pick its own starting point for investigation and analysis. Transitions are good targets, because so much is at stake. Some departments in the CID elected to focus on the first year for this reason. Others began with career preparation, effectively starting with the transition out of graduate school. In due course a number of programs chose to think carefully about and experiment with the candidacy examination, but this was not easy, and it was rarely the first thing on the agenda. The point is that nearly any starting point leads eventually to consideration of purpose, and this, in turn, guides changes in the doctoral experience from start to finish. Difficult dialogues about purpose are a foundational first step because they ripple out in so many directions.

As Carnegie Foundation president Lee S. Shulman argues, there are "inherent obligations and opportunities associated with becoming a professional scholar/educator, and especially with the responsibilities to one's discipline symbolized by the PhD." Chief among these is the responsibility to "treat our courses and classrooms as laboratories or field sites in the best sense of the term, and contribute through our scholarship to the improvement and understanding of learning and teaching in our field" (Shulman, 2000, pp. 157–158). In the next chapter, we'll look at three principles that both emerge from this process and can guide it.

ENDNOTES

1. This quotation appears in Shulman's unpublished "President's Report" to the board of The Carnegie Foundation for the Advancement of Teaching (Shulman, 2002, p. 3).

2. The Council of Graduate Schools describes the examination as follows: "Virtually all universities require an examination for admission to candidacy after the student has completed appropriate courses and seminars. This examination also has different labels depending, for the most part, on the tradition of the institutions (it is often called a general, comprehensive, or qualifying examination). Regardless of its title, its purpose is to determine the student's readiness to undertake independent research." The CGS policy statement continues, "In many institutions students are essentially on probation for the first two years of graduate study. They are 'admitted to candidacy' for the doctoral degree by the end of the second year or the beginning of the third after a number of qualifying procedures have been satisfactorily completed. . . . The qualifying procedures may include one or more of the following: formal coursework, proficiency examinations in language and/or other research tools, comprehensive (or general) written and oral examination, and one or more research papers showing evidence of the ability to do original work" (Council of Graduate Schools, 2005, pp. 24–25).

3. The student survey asked, "Has the educational purpose of each of the following requirements or expectations been clearly conveyed to you? Qualifying exam or process (the requirement for Advancement to Candidacy)?" The choices were yes, no, or N/A if not an expected part of the student's program. In total, 74 percent of students surveyed chose Yes, with little variation among the disciplines: chemistry, 74 percent; education,

66 percent; English, 72 percent; history, 73 percent; mathematics, 88 percent; and neuroscience, 83 percent. The quotations come from open-ended items that followed.

4. Respondents were asked to use a 5-point scale ranging from 1 = extremely individually determined to 5 = shared by all faculty. For this table responses of 1 or 2 were combined to represent "individually determined," and responses of 4 or 5 were combined to represent "shared understanding."

5. Graff has made these mixed messages the subject of a now-classic work in the field. His volume *Beyond the Culture Wars: How Teaching the Conflicts Can Revitalize American Education* (Graff, 1992) has deeply influenced thinking not only in departments of English but in higher education more generally. In a nutshell, he argues for a curriculum that foregrounds political and theoretical debates, making them the focus of discussion rather than a set of hidden assumptions that students are left to figure out for themselves. His newer contribution, *Clueless in Academe: How Schooling Obscures the Life of the Mind* (Graff, 2003), follows on this theme, suggesting ways that teachers can make the "moves" of academic argument and discourse more transparent and available to students.

6. Nebraska's commitment to recruiting and graduating women in mathematics has brought huge gains. In a period of ten to fifteen years, the department went from a decade in which the PhD program graduated virtually no women to a situation in which women constitute 40–50 percent of the entering doctoral class and 40 percent of graduates. The program won the Presidential Award for Excellence in Science, Engineering and Mathematics Mentoring in 1998, given by the White House. Under the leadership of then-chair James Lewis, the $10,000 prize was then used to leverage further, local funds to create a conference for undergraduate women in math. That event has now grown into a national conference held since 1999, the Nebraska Conference for Undergraduate Women in Mathematics, funded by the NSF and National Security Agency, that attracts some 200 undergraduate women.

7. A fuller account of the University of Pittsburgh English department's commitment to innovative self-assessment and inquiry into student learning appears in a chapter on the CID in an edited volume on assessment of doctoral education (Golde, Jones, Bueschel, and Walker, 2006). Data are also to be found in the University of Pittsburgh Department of English's Web pages, The Comprehensive Exam, the Profession and the Doctorate and Matching Regulations to Intellectual Orientation, at http://gallery .carnegie foundation.org/cid.

8. The most comprehensive assessment of doctoral programs in the United
   States is the periodic review conducted by the National Research Council
   (NRC). The resulting ranking of departments by discipline has been used
   extensively by faculty members and administrators across the country. Not
   all fields are included; education is one notable exclusion in the 2006–2007
   assessment.

   In the 1982 and 1993 assessments, the quantitative measures included
   faculty research productivity and awards garnered. Equally important
   were reputational ratings of the scholarly quality of program faculty and
   of program effectiveness, as determined by a survey of graduate faculty.
   Although these rankings measure some important characteristics of the
   faculty, who are critically important contributors to doctoral education,
   reputational rankings certainly do not comprehensively assess the quality
   of the educational program. As the NRC book itself points out, "The reputational rating of a program is related to the level of involvement of faculty
   in research and scholarly activities. . . . Reputational ratings do not tell us
   how well the program is structured, whether it offers a nurturing environment for students, or if the job placement experiences of its graduates are
   satisfactory. . . . Reputational standing does not take into account other
   elements in the 'quality of faculty performance,' such as contributions to
   teaching of graduate and undergraduate students or contributions to the
   welfare of the department, the institution, or the larger academic community" (Goldberger, Maher, and Flattau, 1995, pp. 22–23).

   For the 2006–2007 NRC assessment, efforts were made to collect more
   data that speak directly to scholarly quality and educational practices.
   Measures of the latter include institution-wide policies and practices (such
   as health insurance), the educational environment (including time to degree
   and completion rates, diversity of the faculty and student population), and
   program-level policies and practices (including orientation, requirements
   for candidacy, teaching requirements, office space, travel support for
   professional meetings). In addition, a pilot student questionnaire was sent
   to advanced doctoral students in five fields: English, economics, physics,
   neuroscience/neurobiology, and chemical engineering.

4

FROM EXPERIENCE TO EXPERTISE

PRINCIPLES OF POWERFUL FORMATION

---

*Assistant Professor: Full-time, tenure-line position for a scholar
of promise with a proven record of research success, a history of
peer reviewed publications, and a demonstrated facility for
teaching. The University is deeply committed to fostering cross-
disciplinary collaborations and promoting community
engagement. The applicant will be expected to teach two
introductory courses, two upper-level undergraduate courses, the
undergraduate research practicum, and a graduate seminar of her
or his design employing pedagogies that tap the potential of new
technologies. Candidates should submit a curriculum vita,
representative publications, a statement of teaching philosophy,
teaching evaluations, three letters of reference, and provide
evidence that their work expands the frontiers of knowledge.
Stewards of the discipline are most welcome to apply.[1]*

WHERE THE GOLD STANDARD FOR NEWLY MINTED PhD's twenty-five years
ago was likely to be the promise of significant research productivity, today's
job postings (like the composite we have assembled as our epigraph here)
are likely to call for "a proven record of success," a "history of publication," and "demonstrated facility" in the teaching arena. In some fields,
expectations include a track record of securing external funding, or

experience providing leadership for complex long-term projects. At the same time, there are calls for doctoral programs to do a better job of fostering creativity, the ability to work in groups, independent thinking, and "the courage to follow insight" (Bargar and Duncan, 1982, p. 13). Some observers worry that doctoral programs turn out students who know a great deal about far too little, calling for a kind of "general education" and breadth that better match the requirements of life and work in an increasingly interconnected world (Stimpson, 2002). In short, doctoral students today must be ready for a fast-changing, highly fluid, competitive, and demanding professional world, be it in academe, industry, or government. Already high expectations are escalating every year.

Traditionally, higher education has addressed escalating expectations from the job market by adding new elements—a special workshop on grant writing, a course on writing for publication, or a seminar series covering "professional development" topics. But a central conclusion of the CID is that simply adding experiences to an already full plate is unlikely to lead to the kinds of expertise needed today and in the future. Adding requirements (formal or informal) risks either that many students will ignore them or that time to degree will keep growing; the additive approach also leaves inherited expectations unexamined and unaltered. Tinkering with program elements will not be sufficient to meet the challenge of providing an increasingly diverse pool of students with the highest quality preparation. Serious structural and cultural changes are required for meaningful formation in a world that will surely demand more of society's most educated citizens.

Formation, as readers will recall from Chapter One, is the process through which the intellectual and social practices of a discipline are gradually internalized by novice practitioners. Becoming a mathematician (or historian or neuroscientist) requires knowing the subject matter of the field at a very deep level; content knowledge is essential. It also requires learning to "think like a mathematician" (or historian or neuroscientist). That is, subject matter mastery is necessary but is not in itself sufficient to the formation of scholars. Learning to present oneself as a member of a discipline, to communicate with colleagues, and to apply ethical standards of conduct is part and parcel of formation. Creativity, responsibility, and leadership are also critical areas for attention in programs that aim for excellence. (The theory and practice of doing this well—what the CID began to call the pedagogy of research—is an area of inquiry that deserves considerable attention by researchers and scholars from many fields.)

In this chapter we propose three principles for student formation: (1) *progressive development* towards increasing independence and responsibility, (2) *integration* across contexts and arenas of scholarly work, and (3) *collaboration* with peers and faculty in each stage of the process. Like stewardship, these broad principles pertain across disciplines and settings and, as we have seen in our work with CID programs, can help frame the kind of reflection and inquiry advocated in the previous chapter.

Our intent in proposing these principles is to create a framework that can pull together the mix of practices that constitute the graduate student experience and move students more efficiently towards expertise. The idea is not to add new elements, but to shape and reshape existing ones to be more educationally formative. The principles reflect ideas about how people learn and the vision of stewardship that informs this volume. Our premise is that doctoral graduates could be better served by educational processes that explicitly address the rapidly evolving roles they assume upon graduation.

Progressive Development

Most doctoral programs begin with a dependent stage, before students are expected to make the transition to the independent stage where they take primary responsibility for conducting original research and creating knowledge.[2] There is much to be said for this model. Students enter graduate programs from very different backgrounds—and in some fields with little experience in the area they have chosen. Many are well served by focused time spent "mastering the knowledge base of their disciplines and specialty areas, learning their discipline's theories and methods, and establishing relationships with peers, faculty, and their adviser" (Lovitts, 2005a, p. 140). This two-stage model has parallels in professional education. Medical school, in part because of the famous Flexner Report sponsored by the Carnegie Foundation, begins with two years of basic science coursework followed by more specialized, clinical work (Flexner, 1910). But more and more medical education programs today are looking for ways to build authentic practice into the program from the beginning, and doctoral education, too, is struggling to find alternatives to the two-stage model. This shift, which we saw embodied in various ways in CID programs, is a trend of great promise, as it builds expertise and allows for a gradual increase in difficulty, responsibility, and opportunities to act as a professional colleague. In this way, the trend is toward the old saw: if you want to become an expert (if you want to get to Carnegie Hall), practice, practice, practice! And our first principle, progressive development, points to the importance of practice—guided, repeated, intentional, self-conscious effort—in forming the skills, habits, and dispositions that fully prepare scholars to contribute to their disciplines.

Forming Researchers: Early and Often

The prevailing assumption is that doctoral programs are highly effective at preparing researchers and scholars, however much they may fall short in preparing students for a full range of professional roles and responsibilities. And yet, by the time the CID concluded, it became clear that this assumption deserves to be critically probed and perhaps challenged. The Carnegie surveys of faculty and graduate students suggest that most students reach acceptably high levels of proficiency as novice researchers by the time they are at the end of their programs (see Table 4.1). Nevertheless, we are troubled by the relatively large group (perhaps as much as a quarter) that may not. Further, when we asked students about areas of development to which their programs should pay more attention, over 20 percent focused on research preparation.[3] A 2001 report revealed tremendous variation among the disciplines as to whether students reported the opportunity to take progressively more responsible roles in research, and about a third did not believe that coursework had laid a foundation for conducting independent research.[4] Perhaps most telling were the conversations at the CID summer convening devoted to the preparation of researchers. Faculty and students alike confessed that their programs did not seem built on a clearly articulated theory of how researchers and scholars are formed. Regardless of discipline, fostering creativity and teaching students how to ask good research questions were perceived as hard challenges as yet undone. Taken together, these facts suggest that it is inappropriate to assume that all students receive excellent preparation as novice researchers, even if they are at the "top" universities.

There is reason to believe that the nature and origin of the problem may be quite different among the disciplines. In the sciences, involvement in research usually begins early, in the adviser's lab, but many students do not have opportunities, either early or late, to practice developing an original research question and independently designing a research project. In the humanities and social sciences the problem is a bit different. The dissertation is typically the first substantial research project, often begun in the third or fourth year, and students may flounder for lack of preparation in how to conduct research: "I did not really get a chance to do a research project that involved primary sources in my field until I started the dissertation," one history student reported on the CID survey. "This is a big problem, because I felt like I was in the archive, by myself, inventing the wheel all over again."

Clearly these problems have multiple origins. But what is clear is that students are not well served when the development of independence, creativity, and initiative is delayed until the second stage. The leap from

Table 4.1. Perceived Research Proficiency of Students at End of Program[5]

Faculty respondents	High level of proficiency (4–5)	Low or middle level of proficiency (2–3)	Unable (1)	Don't know or not applicable
Asking a good research question	76%	16%	0%	9%
Independently analyzing and interpreting data (or text)	76	14	0	10
Proficiently employing research techniques	81	10	0	9

Student respondents (dissertator stage)	High level of proficiency (4–5)	Low or middle level of proficiency (2–3)	Not at all (1)	
I can design AND carry out a line of research or scholarship of my own devising	75	24	1	
I can generate interesting questions that are worth investigating	78	21	1	

Sources: *Carnegie Graduate Student and Graduate Faculty Surveys*

course-taking to independent scholarship strands too many students "at the threshold of their first major creative, independent research project unprepared for the work it entails because their educational experiences leading up to the dissertation have not prepared them for the style of thinking necessary to think about and produce the original product required" (Lovitts, 2005a, p. 147). Further, the presumption of indepen- dence at the later stage makes it hard for students to seek out faculty men- toring and peer support as they undertake their most difficult challenges.

The good news is that some programs have created opportunities to develop students' habits of mind and skills of research from the outset, starting early and continuing often. These opportunities build on lessons from inquiry-based learning at the undergraduate and K–12 levels, and their focus on hands-on research and collaborative group work distin- guishes them from didactic instruction in research methods, valuable though it may be. The trend towards an early introduction to research is catching on in a variety of fields.

In the humanities, the new approach may take advantage of the increasing ease of access to original documents offered by digital reposi- tories. The department of history at Duke University has redesigned four core courses as a result of CID participation. Now, first-year students have hands-on research experience with an emphasis on finding and using a variety of primary sources. One product of this work is a summer research grant proposal; the summer research itself, again working with primary sources, generates the data that students then use to write two polished research papers in their second year. Professor Susan Thorne notes, "We are emphasizing polished written work, one of the motiva- tions behind our shift from exams to a portfolio system of prelim certifi- cation" (S. Thorne, e-mail to the authors, March 22, 2007). The revised program in mathematics education at Michigan State University exempli- fies another progressive approach to hands-on research experiences that build in size and complexity: all of the mathematics education courses offered as core requirements of the new program require research proj- ects. These relatively small projects provide students with opportunities to design, conduct, and report on research from their very first semester in the program. The projects can also form the basis for later practical requirements and pilot studies for dissertations. In addition, the program now incorporates a master's degree stage, which means that doctoral stu- dents complete a master's-level research thesis along the way to their PhD (see the Michigan State University Division of Science and Math Educa- tion's Web page, Systematic Induction into Research, at http://gallery .carnegiefoundation.org/cid).

Useful orientations to research activity are also possible outside of formal courses. For example, the University of Minnesota Graduate Program in Neuroscience's orientation program familiarizes students with research in a retreat-like setting at the university's Biological Field Station at Lake Itasca, introducing the process of research rotations and collaborative team projects in the summer before the beginning of the formal academic year. The program raised the money for state-of-the-art lab equipment that is shared by all faculty and students in this unique setting, allowing students to choose topics independent of faculty grant constraints. (More about this program appears in Chapter Six.)

The department of mathematics at the University of Illinois at Urbana-Champaign started a summer program in order to accelerate the critical transition from coursework to research. Research Experiences for Graduate Students (REGS) was conceived by the Graduate Affairs Committee in 2002–2003 as part of CID discussions. In 2002, twenty-one first- and second-year graduate students worked on research projects in various formats. The norm is one or two graduate students working with one or two faculty members, but the arrangements are highly flexible. Some do group projects and some undertake individual research, often with a faculty member who does not become the adviser (see the University of Illinois at Urbana-Champaign mathematics department's Web page, REGS, at gallery.carnegiefoundation.org/cid). There is no assumption that the project will be related to a thesis project. The primary goal is to increase the "research maturity" of the REGS fellows; the pairing up of advisers and advisees is secondary. Students who dislike the field or adviser in which they do a REGS experience "get to change horses before midstream." "The triumph of REGS is that it increases readiness for research in a way that coursework does not," and, as a result, "the department has funded this program each year since its inception," asserts faculty member John D'Angelo (J. D'Angelo, e-mail to the authors, February 15, 2007).

Our point is that there are many ways to integrate hands-on research experiences into the early years of doctoral study, and to do so in ways that are both authentic and iterative, moving from fairly simple, discrete tasks and projects to the more complex, multifaceted, independent inquiry expected in the dissertation project and beyond. The repetition of these activities, and the provision of feedback on their success, is key to the progressive development of skill, confidence, and independence.

Forming Teachers: Learning from Experience

The benefits of progressively challenging, hands-on experience also apply to preparation for teaching. Certainly some students receive excellent preparation, but too often this is more a matter of individual initiative than of program design and departmental accountability. Just as the CID uncovered concerns about the preparation of researchers, serious anxieties surfaced with regard to teaching (see Table 4.2). About a quarter of student respondents assess their own teaching proficiency in the low or middle ranges, which roughly matches the assessments of those faculty members who feel able to render judgment. But it is also troubling that a quarter of the faculty assert that they are unable to assess their own advisees' teaching proficiency. And when we asked students to which areas of development their programs ought to pay more attention, over a quarter focused on teaching preparation.[6]

These data simply add to a loud chorus that has been sounded at doctoral universities for the last fifteen years. Where teaching experience is available, it may not be required. And where it is required, there is no guarantee (or structure to ensure) that experience actually leads to greater understanding of the complicated dynamics of teaching and learning. In teaching, as in other complex practices, more experience does not automatically lead to more expertise.

Many students get stuck at a particular phase in their development as teachers. For example, they may have limited experience as TAs whose duties may be restricted to grading for a year or two early in the program (as happens in chemistry), or they may have a great deal of responsibility for teaching the same introductory undergraduate course over and over again (as in English and math). Although some programs have a special emphasis on preparing international students to teach—a responsibility often handled at the institutional rather than program level—the language problem is often addressed by isolating these students from teaching responsibilities. There is considerable difference among the disciplines of the CID in the proportion of students at the dissertation stage who report a high level of proficiency in their own ability to "design and teach a course in their field" (see Figure 4.1). It may be that this confidence is related to having had the opportunity to take increasing responsibility as a novice teacher while in graduate school (see Figure 4.2). We were not surprised to see that the fields in which graduate students are financially supported primarily by teaching assistantships are the ones that have structured these opportunities for increased responsibility. The students seem to have reaped tangible benefit in terms of their pedagogical preparation.

Achieving confidence and competence as a teacher, as with developing research expertise, requires a consistent, progressive development of skills and responsibility. This is more readily accomplished when teaching is understood more broadly than simply as work in the classroom.

Table 4.2. Perceived Teaching Proficiency of Students at End of Program[7]

Faculty respondents	High level of proficiency (4–5)	Low or middle level of proficiency (2–3)	Unable (1)	Don't know or not applicable
Preparing a syllabus	53%	18%	2%	27%
Evaluating assignments or examinations	59	14	1	26
Giving lectures	61	15	1	23
Student respondents (dissertator stage)	High level of proficiency (4–5)	Low or middle level of proficiency (2–3)	Not at all (1)	
I can use a variety of instructional strategies when teaching	73	25	2	
I can design AND teach a course in my field	75	23	2	

Sources: *Carnegie Graduate Student and Graduate Faculty Surveys*

Figure 4.1. Percentage of Students at the Dissertation Stage Reporting Reaching a High Level of Proficiency in the Ability to Design and Teach a Course[8]

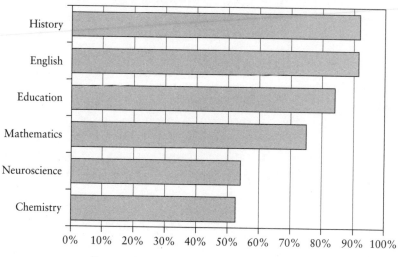

Source: *Carnegie Graduate Student Survey*

Figure 4.2. Percentage of Students at the Dissertation Stage Reporting the Opportunity to Develop Increasing Responsibility as a Teacher[9]

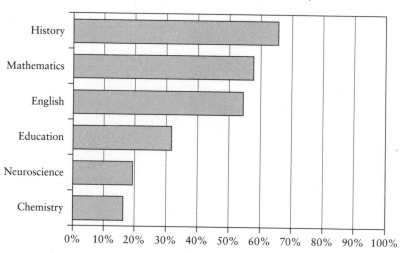

Source: *Carnegie Graduate Student Survey*

An expansive definition includes presentations at seminars, giving posters and papers at conferences, and mentoring peers and undergraduates. And, of course, the variety and number of opportunities depends on the discipline and type of institution. For instance, although students in the lab sciences report limited opportunities to teach outside of required teaching assistantships in the first or second year, these students may have many opportunities to practice presentation skills and informal mentoring relationships in the lab context. It is critically important, however, that these activities be framed as acts of translation or teaching—that is, reminding students that such activities as giving a paper, presenting a poster, or making the "elevator pitch" about their research are fundamentally pedagogical. The simple move of repositioning the task into the category of "teaching" rather than "research" opens new areas for feedback. Rhetorically, administrators often tout the mutually reinforcing nature of inquiry and pedagogy; this is a way to bring that promise to fruition for graduate students.

Of course there are also more straightforward approaches, and the sciences are important settings for programs that explicitly lead students toward expertise in teaching. Consider, for example, the Department of Anatomy and Neurobiology at the Boston University School of Medicine, which is one of the few neuroscience programs that requires their PhD students to serve as TA's in courses in anatomy, neuroscience, and histology offered to medical students. In addition to required TA training and assessment programs (including the use of teaching portfolios), the department's Vesalius Program offers opportunities for progressive growth and strong faculty mentorship in teaching throughout the years of doctoral study. The program begins with "Teaching in the Biomedical Sciences I—Theory," a course in which students learn how to generate course materials (syllabi, outlines, exam questions, course evaluations), determine which teaching methods work best for different learning styles and venues, and begin to hone their presentation skills. Following completion of this first course, Vesalius students participate in the Practicum, a mentored teaching project in which they "put theory into practice, working in collaboration with a selected faculty mentor in one of the following formats: large lecture, small lecture or seminar, or proposing a new course" (Boston University School of Medicine Department of Anatomy and Neurobiology, n.d.). Students who complete the sequence are then promoted to instructors, with continued faculty mentoring, during their years in the program.

The Vesalius Program illustrates the power of discipline-specific programs that integrate content mastery and instructional techniques, as well as the opportunity for mentoring and feedback from experienced teachers in the field. The sequence of activities begins early in the program, builds in and toward complexity, and student learning does not end at the completion of the program. This is an excellent example of a progressive approach to learning to teach, as well as an example of the power of a program that offers its students access to multiple mentors, a topic we will return to in Chapter Five.

Forming Professional Identity

PhD's can expect to exercise considerable influence in their professional lives. They may be called to lead academic research projects, departments, and universities. They may lead by shaping the flow of ideas through their scholarly work, or by championing promising new directions in teaching and research. Some are called to lead in the public sphere of policy research, analysis, and decision making, while others apply their knowledge and skills as leaders in business and nonprofit organizations. While leadership development is built into the formal curriculum of business and management programs, explicit attention to leadership skills is much rarer in doctoral programs. That said, a number of universities have identified such work as a promising new direction (see for example Stanford University Commission on Graduate Education, 2005). Indeed, the traditional triumvirate of academic service—campus, discipline, and community—offers rich opportunities for leadership development for doctoral students, following the same principle of progressive practice that guides teaching and research.

In spite of a mixed reputation among faculty members, service to the university can play an important role in doctoral student formation. As one history faculty member noted on the CID survey, "I believe strongly in bringing graduate students, as they are ready, fully into all of the issues that make up a professional life in the academic profession. Having them participate actively in searches, learning in broad outlines how departments actually function, learning both the highs and the lows of how decisions get made; all of this is vital to a well rounded outcome in terms of success in the future." Serving as a graduate student representative to departmental or school committees also provides a safe setting within the local intellectual community to learn about academic politics and to see (good and bad) models of faculty leadership. Other readily available leadership activities include student-organized journal clubs, seminars, and colloquia—and participation in projects like the CID.

At a slightly higher level of responsibility, students can be introduced to service to and leadership in the discipline. This might mean serving as

a reviewer of conference proposals, journal submissions, or grant applications. Such activities can be sequenced to build toward greater independence and responsibility. For instance, a faculty member might include
simulated reviews as course assignments; a next stage might be to collaborate in, say, co-authoring an actual review of a journal submission; and,
at the "high end," graduate students might take independent responsibility for reviewing conference proposals. Students might also serve as conference session chairs, as respondents, or as members of a conference
planning group. In such settings the audience is larger, including potential
employers, and the reputations of the program as well as the students are
at stake. These are activities that typically take place after a few years of
doctoral study, and the student's advisers play a critical mentoring role.

Perhaps the highest-stakes arena of intellectual engagement can be
found in service to the larger community outside academe, an area in
which doctoral programs can learn from longer-standing undergraduate
service-learning programs. Real-world contexts are complex and conse-
quential, and many doctoral students are therefore eager to use their
emerging skills in such settings. The commitment to developing "citizen-
scholars" has caught on at several campuses, led by the example of the
University of Texas at Austin (see Exhibit 4.1). This progressive learning
approach introduces community engagement early on, in a highly supportive, supervised setting, and moves students gradually toward more
confident roles as leaders, partners, and experts in the world at large.
Positive experiences in these applied settings sustain commitment, and can
help motivate students throughout the program and push for higher levels
of achievement.

There are a number of approaches to building skills in community
engagement: some are focused on policy, and others emphasize research
partnerships. Many universities—most often through their schools of
education—have partnerships in K–12 schools, often in challenging social
contexts. Doctoral students begin as research assistants in these complex
real-world environments, and may over time develop independent
research projects in these communities as well (Berliner, 2006, p. 282).
The program in public history at Arizona State University is a good
example of how productive this approach can be. Established in 1980,
the program has produced a steady stream of successful graduates working in the fields of historic preservation, public policy, management of
cultural properties, museum and library studies, and scholarly publishing.
The program provides a full range of coursework and requires a
320-hour internship. Students are also required to attend short courses

○

Exhibit 4.1. Creating Citizen-Scholars in the Intellectual Entrepreneurship Program at the University of Texas at Austin

Thousands of graduate students at the University of Texas at Austin have become "citizen-scholars" through the Intellectual Entrepreneurship (IE) program. Since 1997, IE has helped graduate students to use their disciplinary expertise to make meaningful and lasting differences in their academic disciplines and communities. They learn to leverage knowledge for social good through cross-disciplinary credit-bearing courses (in consulting, communications, applications of technology, entrepreneurship), internships, a consulting service, and faculty-student-community action seminars. Students are challenged to develop a professional identity as intellectual entrepreneurs who create knowledge and solve problems in diverse realms; along the way many students construct a vision for their professional lives inside and outside of academia (Cherwitz and Sullivan, 2002).

IE programs show promise for increasing the diversity of the graduate student population. After participating in the IE pre-graduate school internship, psychology and communications major Ana Lucia Hurtado was able to connect her coursework and career dreams in an internship, thereby integrating her personal commitments, intellectual interests, and professional ambitions (in her case as a lawyer, mother, and community activist). IE programs for undergraduate and graduate students tap into a need that may be particularly important for minority students—to give back to their communities. In the words of IE program founder and director Richard Cherwitz, "The spirit of intellectual entrepreneurship seems to resonate with and meet a felt need of minority and first-generation students, who acquire through it the resources to bring their own visions to fruition" (Hurtado, 2007, p. 50).

○

offered by visiting professional historians, which, together with the development of the new Public History Alumni Database, introduces students to a wider network of role models and potential mentors.

Expanding this notion into new degree formats, the University of Wisconsin has recently launched a new dual-degree program combining a neuroscience PhD with a master's degree in public policy. By integrating coursework in both programs, graduates will be dual-degree professionals who can "help ensure that scientific perspectives provide an important contribution to the policy process." Program coordinators argue that "with the pace of neuroscience discovery accelerating dramatically, the demand for skills to navigate public debate and decision making will only grow" (Brunette, 2006).

Programs that progressively emphasize public service and leadership as a vital component of intellectual development have chosen a special niche in the academic landscape, one that attracts highly committed students and faculty. Some distinguished scholars are looking beyond local educational, social, or industrial settings and arguing for a year of international study to prepare students for the emerging realities of globalization (Elkana, 2006, p. 84). This is another widespread practice in undergraduate education (the "junior year abroad") that graduate programs could explore to good effect. Currently, humanities students who are studying cultures or archives located in other countries typically travel, but may find their ability to interact with other scholars limited by time, finances, or university structures. Scientists occasionally have the chance to apprentice in a collaborating lab located halfway around the world. Indeed, the NSF, as one funding agency, has offered international travel supplements to grants in many of its directorates for the reciprocal exchanges of investigators and students between the United States and other countries. Encouraging and enhancing such arrangements will surely have multiple advantages.

As these examples suggest, opportunities to learn from service in all arenas have tremendous educational and formative power, and should be available to all students. The good news is that CID survey data suggest that many students across disciplines are engaging in community service activities, as shown in Table 4.3. (Student participation in departmental service activities is shown in Table 6.1.) The bad news is that few programs employ a progressive model for developing leadership over time: from smaller audiences and venues to larger public arenas, from relatively simple issues to complex public policy debates, and from participation to leadership. There is tremendous potential for programs to create a progression of opportunities to form scholars with a balanced professional identity. The integration of these activities with research and teaching is key to making this work fit into the busy lives of students.

Integrative Learning

Making the preparation for various scholarly roles more iterative, more developmental and progressive, requires rethinking the structures that support student development in the areas of scholarship, teaching, and service. The second key principle to keep in mind is that integrating these

Table 4.3. Percentage of Students at Dissertation Stage Reporting Participation in Community Service Activities[10]

	Chemistry	Education	English	History	Mathematics	Neuroscience
Took part in civic or advocacy activities related to my discipline (writing legislation, writing an opinion piece, giving testimony)	5%	21%	16%	18%	2%	7%
Gave a formal talk about my research to an audience outside of my discipline (alumni, civic organizations)	16	35	18	28	12	22
Took part in an educational event aimed at the public (museum display, Brain Awareness Week, a public history project)	14	21	20	34	8	46
Took part in an educational event aimed for K–12 students or undergraduates (majors day, tutoring, literacy programs)	31	46	28	31	35	39
Proportion who participated in at least one of these activities	**42**	**65**	**50**	**59**	**40**	**69**

Source: *Carnegie Graduate Student Survey*

areas of development in the curriculum creates opportunities to learn more in the same amount of time and to learn each of these areas more deeply. The twin advantages of efficiency and effectiveness make integrative learning a key strategy for maximizing student formation.

What do we mean by integrative learning? Integrative learning refers to the capacity to make connections across settings and over time—from one course to another, from one discipline to another, between the classroom and community settings, and among the domains of teaching, research, and academic service (Huber and Hutchings, 2004, 2005). Integrative learning also entails the ability to put theory into practice. A recent study of quality in doctoral dissertations concludes that those whose work is identified as outstanding are "very creative and intellectually adventurous. They love, and are passionate about, what they are doing, and they display intense curiosity and drive. They leap into new territory and transfer ideas from place to place" (Lovitts, 2005b, p. 19). These are critical abilities for scholarly success. The problem is that graduate programs do not take advantage of opportunities that already exist to promote these kinds of connections.

Sites for Integrative Work

There are a number of ways to promote integrative learning within the established structures and elements of doctoral education. The practice of research rotations may, for instance, play more than one role in the formation of scholars. Rotations are a strategy used primarily in the biological sciences for selecting advisers and matching students with the research lab that will become their home. The idea is that the adviser-advisee relationship should be tested (like a short interval of dating) before being made permanent (the marriage). Students are expected to conduct two or three research rotations during their first year of graduate school. Most programs encourage students to sample widely among departmental faculty during the course of their rotations. Typically students work fifteen to twenty hours a week for six to ten weeks in each rotation, conducting a small research project as a vehicle for learning about the work that is done in that lab. A rotation-sized research project should, ideally, allow the student to make a genuine contribution, but be feasible for someone who is new to the lab and often to that subfield and its techniques, as well.

Although the explicit goal of research rotations is fostering a good match between student, research lab, and faculty adviser, there are other ends that can be accomplished at the same time, particularly if one is deliberate about designing them into the experience. Research rotations can promote inter-lab collaborations, with students serving as links; that is, the experience forges relationships with both people and ideas that continue during the student's subsequent work. Research rotations can also be opportunities for students to integrate research and teaching; some programs ask students to prepare a poster or short presentation of their work at the end of the rotation, giving them a chance to translate their accomplishments as a researcher into terms that are meaningful to others.

However, although research rotations sound like a good idea, even in another laboratory science the idea is greeted with skepticism, as CID chemistry departments discovered. As a reporter for chemistry's newspaper of record, *Chemical and Engineering News,* explained, "Although [rotations are] the status quo in biology departments and even many biochemistry departments, the notion is deeply controversial among many chemistry faculty and students. Detractors raise concerns that range from how to pay students to the possibility that rotations are nothing but a fruitless elongation of the doctoral program." That said, the chemistry department at the University of Michigan has mandated rotations, and learned that they do not affect time to degree. Students increasingly endorse rotations, perhaps because of "the appreciation of a broader education that comes with scholarly maturation" (Everts, 2006).

The practice of research rotations is ripe for strengthening as an integrative experience. Individually, rotations should link classroom learning to hands-on research practice. Cumulatively, they expose students to a variety of theoretical and methodological approaches that can serve as a foundation for novel problem-solving approaches as students develop their research interests. All of these goals can be advanced by being clearer about the integrative intention behind rotations. This insight, in turn, calls for a careful examination of the rotation assignments, to ensure that they provide an appropriately broad range of experiences. Even as the process of "narrowing" to a research project is critical to timely completion of the program, it can obscure the value of having a broad exposure to a variety of theories, methods, and subfields in the early years of the program.

In the humanities and social sciences, the integrative purpose accomplished by rotations may be met through the "parade of stars" course in which different faculty members present their research each week, or the series of seminar courses where students "shop" for an adviser and research focus. Once again, methodological and content matters are on display in such settings. However, these experiences can be made much more powerful by making their integrative purpose more explicit. For instance, students might be asked to interview three or four faculty members and their students as part of their exploration of alternative theoretical perspectives.

Another example of how existing elements can serve the cause of integrative learning comes at the time of the comprehensive or qualifying examination. Such exams often ask students to demonstrate an integrated understanding of the content of their field, bringing together what they have learned in an explicitly cumulative demonstration of their understanding. An interesting variation we noted in some neuroscience programs is to ask students to prepare and defend a formal grant proposal in a field distinct from their dissertation. This task is designed to promote breadth and versatility, and, because dissertation projects are almost always funded by grants to faculty, may be the only occasion a student has to practice the skills of grant writing. The ability to put theory into practice—by writing a research proposal, for example—is one of the hallmarks of integrative thinking. The qualifying examination and dissertation proposal defense can serve as critical assessments of this capacity. These elements can be designed as formative assessments, helping students to make connections, as well as summative evaluations, examining the extent to which they have done so.

In Chapter Three we discussed another variation on the comprehensive examination: the professional portfolio developed in the history department at the University of Kansas. The English department at Indiana University is experimenting with portfolios as a way to provide more holistic reviews of doctoral students. Based on their experience and success with teaching portfolios, faculty concluded that annual reviews of integrated portfolios of student work would encourage doctoral candidates to reflect on their progress through the program at regular intervals. This requirement would meet several goals, including creating a practical, non-punitive review; promoting more regular and uniform advising; creating an occasion for sustained reflection on scholarship, writing, and pedagogy; fostering more thoughtful integration of student work in the domains of teaching, research, and service; encouraging greater student responsibility for their own professional formation; and preparing students to meet the expectations for tenure. According to the department, "the portfolio and the annual review meeting are essentially occasions for student self-assessment. Insofar as the student presents and discusses her work to members of the faculty, it is also a chance for the student to perform as an aspiring professional. The role of the faculty in these meetings is primarily advisory: asking questions to clarify a student's goals, offering guidance, etc. To a great degree the faculty are modeling questions we would like to see a student ask herself." Most of all, the portfolio and its review are an opportunity for the student herself to "pull the pieces together" (Indiana University Department of English CID Committee, 2004).

Looking beyond CID departments, a quite different model for fostering connections is I-RITE—Integrating Research Into the Teaching Environment, a program developed at Stanford University to assist young scholars to persuasively communicate the significance of their research to the larger public, including undergraduate students, funders, policymakers, and laypersons. Making the "elevator pitch" requires connecting specialized research to public concerns. As the program's Web site notes, the ability to think in the integrative, broad-based way such tasks require comes with high stakes: "Individual researchers who are unable to clearly express their ideas in ways comprehensible to non-specialists experience problems during job-talks, when writing proposals or communicating with the media, and in other professional and personal situations." The program asks graduate students beginning their dissertation work to write a brief description of their research that would be accessible to undergraduates in an introductory course in the field. A network of peer reviewers then provides feedback for revision. Since it was established in 1999, the program has involved graduate students, post-doctoral fellows, and faculty on more than 400 campuses around the world. It has evolved, as well, to include an I-SPEAK component, and a partnership with the National Communication Association aimed at learning how experts develop the skills to communicate complex information to a general audience (Stanford Research Communication, 2007).

The Integrative Dissertation

Debate regarding the usefulness of the dissertation has been simmering for decades. Standards by which dissertations are judged are unclear to students, and faculty members complain privately that poorly written, poorly conceptualized, and poorly executed dissertations are often passed to appease a colleague or to simply get a student out the door (Lovitts, 2007). Recognizing that many dissertations fail to be translated into useful, public scholarship, one scholar quipped that most dissertations, "like John Brown, lie mouldering in their library graves" (Tronsgard, 1963, p. 493). And whether one attributes poorly written dissertations to a lack of writing skills or to sloppy thinking, the litany of criticisms is likely to echo this summary: "As an academic exercise, the dissertation became primarily the instrument by which students demonstrated to their professors that they had a thorough grasp of research in the field. It became overburdened with exhaustive reviews of the scholarly literature . . . bogged down in a superfluity of discursive footnotes, and even the language changed to the defensive, obfuscatory, stilted prose now referred to as dissertationese" (Olson and Drew, 1998, p. 59).

Nevertheless, the dissertation remains firmly ensconced as the capstone experience of doctoral education. An important formative experience, it has many obvious integrative aspects. Regardless of disciplinary norms around content or form, the dissertation requires students to put theory into action, consider multiple lines of evidence, and display a comprehensive understanding of previous scholarship in the field; it is strongly linked to the development of research skills and content area mastery. The question is, Is it possible to make this signal capstone experience an even more powerful site for integrating the multiple domains of stewardship?

In the University of Michigan chemistry program, the answer is yes. The program offers doctoral students significant experiences in the scholarship of teaching and learning through Chemical Sciences at the Interface of Education (CSIE), an interdisciplinary fellowship program for students interested in pursuing academic careers. Students are supported in completing course and project work above and beyond that of their colleagues, with the idea of integrating an emergent area—namely the teaching and learning of chemistry—into their preparation in chemistry research. In addition to seminars and workshops on aspects of faculty careers such as proposal writing, authorship, and the peer review process, the centerpiece of their activities is to design, implement, assess, and document an instructional project. These projects are done in collaboration with the chemistry faculty, and generally constitute a reform or innovation that the faculty member was interested in pursuing but did not have the time or energy to complete without assistance (University of Michigan Department of Chemistry, 2001).

It is important to note that the impact of this model is not on graduate students alone. Instructional development teams are generally intergenerational (as are research groups), involving undergraduate and postdoctoral collaborators. Michigan's undergraduate students who enroll in the new or revised courses directly benefit from these activities as well. What is perhaps most notable, however, is how this work is starting to be connected with the element of doctoral education most clearly identified with research expertise: the dissertation.

At the CID convening at the Carnegie Foundation during the summer of 2005, a member of the University of Michigan chemistry department

team presented the table of contents of a 2003 doctoral dissertation by
Ryan Sweeder, subsequently hired as a faculty member at Michigan State
University. The title of the dissertation was a surprising combination of
topics, an odd academic couple: "New Reactions of Germylene with
Ketones and Assessment of Studio General Chemistry." As Lee Shulman
observed, "The notion that a student in chemistry at the University of
Michigan would submit a dissertation that combines lab science with
educational science and have it accepted by this department is quite simply astonishing" (Shulman, 2005, p. 1). Sweeder's dissertation is, in short,
an "existence proof" of the possibility of making the dissertation a more
integrative genre, capacious and flexible enough to bring together work in
the chemistry laboratory with work in the laboratory that is the chemistry
classroom.

As these examples suggest, integration is both a bold ambition and an
achievable goal. Helping students connect their experiences at multiple
levels, through iterative progressive experiences, can help form scholars
with the expertise to travel nimbly and creatively through the changing
landscape of knowledge—both today and in the future.

Collaborative Learning

Scholarly versatility and deep expertise can be developed together using
the insights of progressive and integrative learning. But this can only take
a scholar so far. The CID essayists spoke almost universally of the need to
prepare doctoral students for collaborative work, something they saw as
essential in the twenty-first century. The emphasis on specialization and
individual effort (originality and independence) in doctoral training,
and on rewards for individual success in academic careers, has supported
a culture of competitive individualism in the academy that impedes
the development of students and of knowledge. Today's harder, bigger,
more complex problems call for multiple perspectives and collaboration.
The goal of learning to collaborate is too important to be left to chance.

Occasions for Collaborative Work in Doctoral Education

While independent work is essential to the doctoral experience, many
fields have developed occasions and strategies that bring students (and
others) together for important forms of learning from and with one
another. In CID convenings, we found that the examples below are com-
monplace in some fields but unknown in others, making them grist for
useful exchange across disciplines. Each of these elements can also be

used more purposefully to develop longer-term habits and capacities for collaboration.

JOURNAL CLUBS. Most commonly found in the sciences, journal clubs are reading groups that convene regularly to discuss papers in recent research journals. These groups are usually multigenerational, including faculty, post-docs, advanced and novice graduate students; all are considered equal participants. Typically, they are organized around specialized themes. For example, the neuroscience program at the University of Wisconsin recently sponsored such journal clubs as: Axon Guidance; Brain and Behavior; Neural Cell Death and Survival; Cerebral Ischemic Damage; and Transmitters, Circuits, and Plasticity. Sessions are organized around a single article, selected because of its currency and relevance to the interests of participants.

Journal clubs generally meet weekly for about an hour. Each week a different person presents the selected paper to the group, although the expectation is that everyone has read the paper in advance. There is a standard format for presenting the papers: summarize the paper, locate it in the larger landscape of the field, describe the research approach in sufficient detail that the audience can understand it without becoming lost in the details, explain why the paper is important, critique the paper. (Do the data and analysis withstand scrutiny? Are there contradictions or competing hypotheses? and so forth.) The discussion focuses on the big picture: the paper's strengths and weaknesses, how it extends the field, potential applications of the work, and what questions need to be answered in light of current findings.

Journal clubs illustrate the power of collaboration for keeping abreast of advances in the field—an imperative for all scholars, after all. In addition, they provide an intellectual community for learning the norms of scholarly exchange. In most science programs students are expected to participate in several journal clubs throughout their graduate careers. The norms and structures of these experiences teach participants to compare perspectives, debate differences, respectfully disagree, and build on the thinking of others—skills and habits that are critical to successful collaborations both inside and outside academe.

DISSERTATION WRITING GROUPS. Writing groups are another powerful tool for collaborative learning and peer mentoring. Students in the humanities and social sciences often rely on dissertation writing groups to combat the isolation that is common in the later stages of their doctoral work. In general, groups meet weekly, and one or two group members present written work for detailed feedback at each meeting. While journal clubs are explicitly multigenerational, writing groups are usually formed by those at roughly the same stage of their graduate student careers.

At their best, dissertation writing groups provide a safe place to try out new ideas, take intellectual risks, and share work that is in its infancy. The reciprocal obligations of membership—you give me feedback this week and I'll read your chapter next week—teach habits of constructive criticism that improve the work and even raise the collective intelligence of the group. Such groups can also usefully incorporate faculty members or even outside speakers. One well-known example is the University of Chicago's year-long Graduate Research Workshops for faculty and graduate students. For more than twenty years, these workshops have been an integral part of the university's intellectual life in the humanities and social sciences. More than sixty workshops, some of which have continued for more than a decade, provide regular occasions for students and faculty to share work in progress with one another (University of Chicago, n.d.).

Though getting candid feedback can be stressful, and peers can be harsh critics, the benefits of participation outweigh the costs. A writing group can also be a source of emotional support in a setting that often feels impersonal and anonymous; group members become colleagues with whom one can vent, bolster, encourage, sympathize. In short, the writing group becomes a community in which members collaborate to complete their respective projects, along the way inculcating skills of getting and giving feedback.

Of course writing groups maintain the focus on individual work and are generally restricted to peers in the same field. But in some settings, interdisciplinary groups are starting to take hold. Some universities are experimenting with formats that connect graduate students across a wide range of fields in writing and discussion groups with the primary goal of fostering innovative and creative thinking, but also in anticipation of collaborative projects. One example beyond the CID circle is found at the Graduate School of Arts and Sciences at New York University. NYU launched the Graduate Forum to "encourage interdisciplinary inquiry into intellectual and moral problems, to question the foundations of the disciplines, and to experiment in translating basic research into a language accessible to a variety of audiences without oversimplification." The members of the Forum are the dean and ten master's and doctoral students drawn from all quarters of the university. Membership is for two academic years, and is predicated on "the capacity for innovative thinking, the ability to contribute to interdisciplinary inquiry, and an interest in the new technologies of education" (New York University, 2004). At monthly dinners Forum members take turns making formal presentations of their work; cross-disciplinary discussion follows.

If the goal is to expand the frontiers of knowledge and understanding, it is worth asking how these multidisciplinary efforts might be a stepping stone to collaborative work that is more significant than sole authorship can produce. Indeed, in some fields, compilations of journal articles with multiple authors are already accepted as dissertation projects, and one can imagine research teams submitting jointly authored dissertations.

Even in humanities fields where such moves are far from common, the trend towards greater collaboration is challenging the notion of the dissertation as solitary, individual work. Stanford University English professor Andrea Lunsford sees this future:

> While students should always have the choice of taking a narrow and highly defined topic (gambling in eighteenth century writing, early modern women's prefaces to translations, a reading of two 1930s women poets), they should also have an opportunity to engage the kind of project that calls for more than one researcher (one that, for example, requires complete fluency in several languages, one that requires expertise in digital media, one that combines two or more disciplines). Allowing for collaborative dissertations will present a great challenge to our imaginations and our organizational abilities. . . . But they are not impossible to conceive [Lunsford, 2006, p. 366].

Principles and Imperatives

Our work in the CID has persuaded us that the framework of three principles presented in this chapter can propel important improvements in doctoral education, not by adding new elements that could exacerbate the time-to-degree problem and further stress overloaded students and faculty, but by making more of the program elements that already exist. Reshaping the "regular" work of the PhD to make it more progressive, more integrative, and more collaborative is a route to greater effectiveness and efficiency on the part of doctoral programs—and to more powerful formation on the part of students. This view of improvement brings with it two imperatives.

The first pertains to faculty: Over the last several decades, research in the "brain sciences" has brought forward a host of ideas about how learners move from novice to expert. Experts not only know more; their knowledge is more structured. They have highly developed "schemas" that allow them to bring their knowledge to bear on new problems with remarkable speed and accuracy. These "schemas" are developed through iterative practice combined with purposeful reflection and self-monitoring (Bransford, Brown, and Cocking, 2000). Faculty members have a responsibility to become familiar with emerging principles and insights that can guide student's transition from experience to expertise. Moreover, they are responsible for bringing to their work with students the same habits of inquiry and evidence-gathering they bring to their research, asking hard questions about whether (and which) students are meeting program goals and how those goals might be more successfully pursued. This commitment to self-examination, deliberation, and improvement may well be the central contribution of the CID, and the principles of progressive, integrative, and collaborative learning set forth in this chapter provide one set of lenses for enacting that commitment.

The second imperative refers to students: One of the key findings from several decades of work on how novice learners move toward advanced forms of understanding and action is that expert learners—those who continue to grow and develop throughout their careers—have a keen sense of how they learn. "If students are to continue improving their performance after the end of formal education, they have to be prepared to shape their own learning processes, that is, diagnose their needs for improvement, seek out their own activities, and plan, monitor, and evaluate this entire process" (van Gog, Ericsson, Rikers, and Paas, 2005, p. 78). And so, while faculty have a responsibility to shape program elements in ways that create rich experiences of formation, students too must be responsible, active, intentional agents in their own learning. In this spirit, the three principles presented in this chapter—though they are not, certainly, the only possible points to draw from the research on learning and expertise—may be helpful compasses for making the most of the road to the PhD.

A third imperative emerges here as well: Real improvement must be a joint venture in which faculty and students are genuine partners. Education is a complex, deeply personal process in which the quality of interaction between teacher and learner matters at least as much as the formal design and requirements of the program. Thus, in the next chapter, we turn to the very human business of apprenticeship, a long-standing tradition in doctoral education that can, we argue, be powerfully reshaped by the principles of formation.

ENDNOTES

1. The epigraph is a composite based on job postings from a variety of disciplines and contexts. Of course the final line is a reflection of the CID project.

2. Most researchers divide graduate studies into three stages: conventionally the first year, pre-candidacy, and the dissertation stage (Bowen and Rudenstine, 1992; Council of Graduate Schools, 1990; Lovitts, 2001; Tinto, 1993). We used a similar categorization for the students responding to the CID survey. The expectations and duration of the second and third stages vary considerably among the disciplines. Barbara Lovitts (2005a, p. 140), a noted researcher on graduate education, says, "In some disciplines, the dependent stage focuses exclusively on course taking; in other disciplines, the sciences in particular, the dependent stage involves a combination of course taking and closely supervised or managed research."

3. The graduate student survey asked respondents to select from a list of twenty-one choices three areas of development to which the program should pay more attention. Of students at the dissertation stage, who have had the most complete experience with their program, "the ability to design AND carry out a line of research or scholarship of my own devising," was selected by 31 percent of chemistry students, 30 percent of those in education, 7 percent from English, 10 percent of history students, 21 percent of mathematicians, and 26 percent of neuroscience students. This item was selected more than any other by students in chemistry and education.

4. The *At Cross Purposes* report of a survey of over 4,000 doctoral students in eleven disciplines at twenty-seven universities found that many students did not believe that the opportunity to "take progressively more responsible roles in research" was available to them. Overall, a quarter of the humanities students said this opportunity was available, and half of the students in the social, biological, and physical sciences agreed with the statement (Golde and Dore, 2001, Table W-3 and special analysis). 30 to 40 percent of student respondents disagreed with the statement that "course work laid a good foundation for doing independent research" (Golde and Dore, 2001, Table W-16 and special analysis).

5. The faculty survey asked, "Considering a typical student you advised (as primary advisor or dissertation committee member), how proficient were they at these aspects of research by the time they received the doctorate?" Respondents were asked to use a 5-point scale ranging from 1 = unable to 5 = excellent, with the additional choice of "Don't Know or not applicable." For this table responses of 4 or 5 were combined to represent a high

level of proficiency, and responses of 2 or 3 were combined to represent a low or middle level of proficiency.

The student survey asked, "To what extent have your experiences in your doctoral program contributed to your knowledge, skills and habits of mind in the following areas?" Respondents were asked to use a 5-point scale ranging from 1 = not at all to 5 = to a great extent. For this table responses of 4 or 5 were combined to represent a high level of proficiency, and responses of 2 or 3 were combined to represent a low or middle level of proficiency.

6. The graduate student survey asked respondents to select from a list of twenty-one choices three areas of development to which the program should pay more attention. Of students at the dissertation stage, who have had the most complete experience with their program, "the ability to design AND teach a course in my field," was selected by 28 percent of chemistry students, 25 percent of those in education, 22 percent in English, 29 percent of history students, 23 percent of mathematicians, and 42 percent of neuroscience students. This item was selected more than any other by neuroscience students.

7. The faculty survey asked, "Considering a typical student you advised (as primary advisor or dissertation committee member), how proficient were they at these aspects of teaching by the time they received the doctorate?" Respondents were asked to use a 5-point scale ranging from 1 = unable to 5 = excellent, with the additional choice of "Don't know or not applicable." For this table responses of 4 or 5 were combined to represent a high level of proficiency, and responses of 2 or 3 were combined to represent a low or middle level of proficiency.

The student survey asked, "To what extent have your experiences in your doctoral program contributed to your knowledge, skills and habits of mind in the following areas?" Respondents were asked to use a 5-point scale ranging from 1 = not at all to 5 = to a great extent. For this table responses of 4 or 5 were combined to represent a high level of proficiency, and responses of 2 or 3 were combined to represent a low or middle level of proficiency.

8. The student survey asked, "To what extent have your experiences in your doctoral program contributed to your knowledge, skills and habits of mind in the following areas: I can design AND teach a course in my field." Respondents were asked to use a 5-point scale ranging from 1 = not at all to 5 = to a great extent. For this figure, responses of 4 or 5 were combined to represent a high level of proficiency. Data for all students at the dissertation stage were reported in Table 4.2.

9. The student survey asked, "While pursuing doctoral studies, which of these teaching activities have you performed? I had successive teaching opportunities in which I took increased responsibility (e.g., from grader to section leader to independent instructor; or from lab assistant to head lab manager to developing labs)." The figure shows the proportion of students at the dissertation stage who responded affirmatively.

10. The student survey asked, "While pursuing doctoral studies, which of the following community service activities related to your discipline have you engaged in? (Check all that apply.)" The table shows the proportion of students at the dissertation stage in each discipline who responded affirmatively.

5

APPRENTICESHIP RECONSIDERED

*Imagine a graduate program defined as a set of loose,
informal apprenticeships and mentorships between students
and faculty members: chaos and nightmare, enough to put
several echelons of associate deans out of business. Graduate
education as a free space of association, collaboration, and
inquiry? Administratively unacceptable, surely. Such a model
could work only by trusting that faculty members, given the
freedom to rethink their roles as educators, could and would
devise relevant forms of training.*

—Peter Brooks[1]

ONE OF THE STURDIEST AND MOST DISTINCTIVE FEATURES of doctoral
education is that so much of the important teaching and learning takes
place in a one-to-one apprenticeship between student and faculty member. Intellectual biographies and retirement *festschrifts* offer moving tes-
timonials to outstanding advisers and mentors, and the relationship is
important enough that most PhD's list their dissertation chair's name on
their CV, thereby claiming a link in the chain of intellectual lineages.[2]
Indeed, it can fairly be said that apprenticeship is the signature pedagogy
of doctoral education.[3]

The tradition of close work between a faculty "master" and student
"apprentice" has its roots in medieval guild culture, which took hold in
the early university as well. This central relationship is not the only
approach to graduate teaching and learning, but "elbow learning" in
seminars and labs has certainly been the prevailing pedagogy of graduate
education throughout its evolution in American universities.[4] Historian
William Cronon testifies to its enduring power: "This master-apprentice

relationship remains utterly central to doctoral education at its best. . . . When it works, it produces intensely personal relationships that can last a lifetime. Those of us lucky enough to have had generous and inspiring graduate mentors know how essential they were to our success. We owe a debt to them that can never be repaid, save by working as hard as we can to pass along the same kind of gifts to our own students" (Cronon, 2006, pp. 346–347).

As Cronon's comment recognizes, "when it works" the relationship can be very good. Certainly it beats many of the Darwinian alternatives: the sink-or-swim theory, the talented-students-will-self-discover theory, or the high-pressure-crucible theory. Unfortunately, when the relationship is bad, it can be horrid. At its worst, it has contributed to murder and suicide, but more common problems are student attrition and the demise of passion and love for the field. Indeed, the downsides of the apprentice-ship model are several.

For one, apprenticeship tends to be a reproductive model of mentor-ing, which "subtly reinforces social as well as intellectual conformity" (Damrosch, 2006, p. 39). From chemists in the CID we heard repeatedly that the prevalent system in which students affiliate early with one faculty member and his ongoing line of laboratory research means that students may graduate unable to formulate their own line of inquiry. More insidi-ously, apprenticeship often means complete dependence on one faculty adviser, who, through ignorance, convention, or malice, neglects, abuses, or exploits the student. Stories abound—some splashed on the pages of the *Chronicle of Higher Education*—of advisers who expect students to run personal errands, of calls to the lab on Thanksgiving to see which students are working, of appropriation of intellectual property, or worse. The traditions of solo sponsorship are often coupled with traditions of faculty autonomy that leave students feeling they have no recourse when they are mistreated or, more commonly, when a relationship sours. The culture of privacy extends so far that faculty members and departmental leaders are reluctant to intervene in dysfunctional situations. On the other hand, students who have had beneficial advising relationships often refer to themselves as "lucky," highlighting the almost random and haphazard access to high-quality advising and mentoring. Surely, effective teaching and advising of doctoral students should not be a matter of luck!

Classic apprenticeship, done well, is a powerful experience, but in a forward-looking examination of doctoral education one must ask: Is this the best way to support the formation of scholars in the twenty-first cen-tury? Our answer is that it is not. The master-apprentice system—even at its best—falls short of what is required to develop stewards of the discipline.

The solution, it seems to us, is not to abandon the apprenticeship model but to reclaim and urge it in directions more purposefully aligned with the vision of learning that is needed from doctoral programs today, combined with known ways to foster that learning. Simply put—and we are aware that language matters here[5]—we propose a shift of prepositions: from a system in which students are apprenticed *to* a faculty mentor, to one in which they apprentice *with* several mentors. This chapter therefore explores what such a shift might entail, drawing on insights from the CID, and then turns to more conceptual underpinnings for reconsidering apprenticeship and its role in doctoral education.

Apprenticeship *With* Defining Features

Typically, images of doctoral apprenticeship are closely connected with advising and mentoring—a faculty member and a student talking in the faculty member's office. But apprenticeship should, in our view, be understood more broadly as a theory of learning and a set of practices that are widely relevant. Seen this way, apprenticeship can and should inform and strengthen all aspects of the doctoral program, whether during advanced classes, in the course of working in the lab, while teaching undergraduates, during seminars, while having conferences in an office, or in hallway conversations. Standing in stark contrast to Darwinian approaches to doctoral education that generally provide students little guidance and, at the other extreme, to formulaic programs in which students progress in lockstep fashion, apprenticeship pedagogies demand purposeful participation by both students and faculty. Apprenticeship as we see it has five defining features important to highlight here.

Intentionality

Apprenticeship pedagogy entails deliberately making visible and explicit those aspects of scholarly and professional expertise that are typically taken for granted and thus unarticulated—and this is no easy task. It requires that faculty not only be expert but understand their expertise well enough to conceptualize the whole, break the whole apart into constituent components, and help students integrate them back into the whole (Grossman and others, 2005). In teaching the elements of being an expert researcher and scholar, mentors must construct occasions and assignments that allow students to practice key tasks and move in step-by-step fashion toward more accomplished, independent practice. In this way, effective mentors provide structured support for students' learning. "Scaffolding," to use the language of education, "is the support the master gives apprentices in carrying out a task. This can range from doing almost the entire task for them to giving occasional hints as to what to do next" (Collins, Brown, and Holum, 1991, p. 2).

Consider, for example, the process of asking a good question—essential to the work of scholars in every discipline and field. Inquiry is prompted by curiosity. It starts with posing questions to advance the frontiers of knowledge and provide new ways of understanding. Effective researchers are able to discern the important or pressing questions of the moment, to form a vision of what constitutes a "meaningful" question, to judge which problem areas are interesting and ripe for investigation, and to identify manageable questions to pursue. Ideally, as students develop, they move from accepting questions that others pose to critically evaluating questions, to posing and defending questions of their own, and ultimately to asking questions that cohere into a research program that extends over time. Unfortunately, as one mathematician told us on our survey of faculty, "this is one of the hardest things to learn. Most students never learn it." CID essayists point to the need to focus more clearly on helping students identify problems and formulate significant research questions. As an historian of science, Yehuda Elkana hits hard on this point: "In doctoral education, too often the chance to learn this process is absent altogether; the mentor assigns the problem or a problem is engaged quite uncritically. Instead, problem choice should be a major focus of the entire doctoral program—a primary responsibility for the candidate to exercise. The student should choose, defend, critique, and examine from various points of view a problem of her own choosing" (Elkana, 2006, p. 76).

Thus, one of the activities of the CID was to analyze the process of question-asking and begin to think about how it can be more intentionally built into the multiple contexts in which faculty mentors interact with students. On the CID faculty survey we asked "What experiences and activities are most effective for learning to ask good research questions?"[6] and then used the answers to construct the case study of Ken, a fictional graduate student whose experiences represent a composite of survey responses.

Throughout his graduate program, his assignments and experiences integrate opportunities to identify and then ask research questions. In a first-semester course, Ken is asked to read four articles and identify the research question in each. He brings his list to class and the instructor leads students in a lively discussion. After agreeing on the questions and in some cases trying to write better ones, the class debates their importance, and then tries to craft additional questions that the authors could subsequently explore. Later in the semester, Ken begins to attend a departmental seminar in which advanced graduate students and faculty members discuss their current work. As urged by the director of graduate studies, Ken uses the seminars to practice identifying the key questions in everything he reads and every talk he attends. Some of the speakers, he realizes, set their questions in a large framework and context, and others focus more on the particular. Some questions seem more important than others, and, from the Q&A, it seems others share his assessment.

In his second year, Ken takes a course in which the instructor challenges every student to write a research question, preferably in one to two paragraphs, that derives from the topic of the week. The students pair up and give each other feedback on their questions. Later, for his qualifying exam, Ken must propose and defend a project that is substantially different from his dissertation research. One of the criteria for evaluation is whether the question is interesting, important, and tractable. As Ken moves toward preparing his dissertation prospectus, he begins meeting with the faculty members he is considering for his dissertation committee to discuss his evolving ideas for what to investigate and how to proceed. He is surprised, but pleased, when they take his ideas seriously and offer feedback without condescension. They help him keep his questions manageable. As his prospectus moves from draft to draft, he is invited to join a writing group of other students who are at the same stage. Through these experiences with fellow students and faculty, Ken learns to appreciate colleagues who can find flaws, give a well-considered (if hard to hear) assessment, and suggest improvements.

Even with all this preparation, Ken's dissertation phase has many moments of frustration when the obstacles seem insurmountable. When he seeks help, sometimes the strategic question from a committee member points him to a solution, and other times he is left to puzzle through the challenges on his own. As he prepares for several job interviews during which he will propose future lines of inquiry, Ken recalls that "research" had once seemed a mysterious process. He now realizes that his program has managed to turn that mystery into a series of steps he understands, employs—and, yes, can even teach to his own students in the future.

This idealized account of the doctoral program may not have many counterparts in reality, but it demonstrates a number of experiences that are based on apprenticeship principles. For faculty members this kind of apprenticeship approach means self-consciousness, and intentionally creating opportunities for practice and development over time. For the student it means taking responsibility for practicing what they are learning in order to improve. It also means developing habits of self-reflection about what they are learning and comparing their efforts with the work of experts. As mentoring support is reduced, the student takes increased responsibility for independent work (Collins, Brown, and Holum, 1991, p. 10). Readers will recognize that this is a version of the iterative, progressive learning described in Chapter Four.

Multiple Relationships

The traditional apprenticeship model is typically conceived as a pairing of two individuals, but the multifaceted, integrative learning expected of today's PhD's requires growth on a number of dimensions. It is rarely the case that one relationship can meet all those needs. Today's students are thus best served by having several intellectual mentors. Incoming students, for instance, have evolving research interests that may not align perfectly with those of a single faculty member. And even if students' interests closely parallel those of a single professor who becomes their adviser, novice learners benefit from seeing the field through different theoretical or methodological perspectives represented by different members of the department. Multiple mentors can also increase the number of possible connections and collaborators available to each student. As several departments in the CID discovered, students want and would benefit from connections outside the department as well.

It is certainly the case that some students already identify several mentors, and there are clearly disciplinary differences, with multiple mentors considerably more common (in fact, often the norm) in the humanities than in the sciences, as illustrated by Figure 5.1. If the idea that every student should have multiple mentors is taken seriously, it seems that those in science fields can learn from their colleagues in the humanities.

In English, for instance, and other humanities, students are likely not only to have research mentors but to have one or more mentors in the area of teaching. Indeed, English departments often have a faculty or staff person (sometimes more than one) dedicated to mentoring graduate students who are teaching introductory writing courses. This strategy is useful for improving the quality of undergraduate instruction but also recognizes that graduate students are developing their professional identity, which encompasses a number of roles, including teaching.

Mentoring relationships can develop in a variety of settings, sometimes serendipitously, sometimes (even better) by design. For instance, a course assignment may become grist for more extensive interaction (such as a conference presentation or master's thesis) between the faculty member and student—particularly in those humanities or social science fields in

Figure 5.1. Number of Faculty Advisers or
Mentors Students Identify[7]

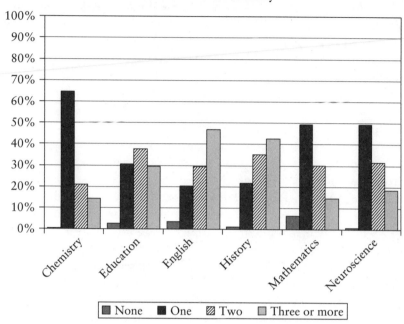

Source: *Carnegie Graduate Student Survey*

which students take classes for the first two or three years of graduate study. In other cases, multiple mentors can be systematically "designed in." The University of North Carolina School of Education has instituted a series of "inquiry groups" that bring together faculty and students interested in a particular topic and research problem. These groups provide early research opportunities in a field where traditionally the dissertation has been the only opportunity a student has had to conduct an investigation. Such groups also ensure that students interact with more than one research mentor in the course of their work (see the University of North Carolina at Chapel Hill School of Education's Web page, Inquiry Groups, at gallery.carnegiefoundation.org/cid). And in the lab sciences, as described in Chapter Four, research rotations can serve the added purpose of connecting students with multiple research mentors.

Of course, effective apprenticeship *with* cannot depend completely on the faculty. Multigenerational approaches are required. Not only does this mean new thinking about faculty roles, but student roles and responsibilities must change as well. The mathematics department at the University of Southern California is experimenting with "mentoring triplets," which bring together a faculty member, a new graduate student, and an experienced graduate student with the goal of successful orientation of the new student into graduate school life (see the University of Southern California mathematics department's Web page, Promoting Effective Advising and Mentoring at gallery.carnegiefoundation.org/cid). Science labs naturally provide what could be called "cascading mentoring," in which advanced students teach those more junior. Post-docs mentor senior graduate students, senior graduate students mentor junior graduate students, and junior graduate students mentor undergraduates.

In the same spirit, the neuroscience program at Boston University has created what they call a "full circle" model of mentoring that includes graduate students, faculty, post-docs, and alumni. As explained by Professor Todd Hoagland, "New graduate students are assigned two mentors when they arrive in our department, one student and one faculty member. The student is usually a senior grad student who volunteers for the position, and they are matched according to similar research/teaching interests or lab identification. The new student generally feels comfortable asking the senior student anything and everything . . . they are a bit more guarded with the faculty mentor, at first. Faculty mentors are assigned and then can change over time as the student's interests evolve" (T. Hoagland, e-mail to the authors, August 15, 2006). Whereas post-doctoral fellows are often relegated to the periphery of departmental life, they play a pivotal role in the BU model. Hoagland says, "Our post-docs have begun to mentor graduate students on the ins and outs of the post-doctoral experience and how to land a great opportunity. The post-docs also teach in some of our courses and are at times paired up with graduate students in the teaching laboratory."

This circle is being closed as the department has started to communicate more closely with alumni, who are valuable role models for graduate students, post-docs, and junior faculty. They can offer advice on career trajectories for graduate students, and sometimes help place students and post-docs in jobs and post-doctoral fellowships. The department now has an alumni coordinator who tracks departmental graduates and keeps records on where they are and how to get in touch with them. Some have gone off to industry, business, law, and various nonacademic pursuits, but most have stayed in academia. The program keeps in touch with this network of alumni through a quarterly departmental newsletter. "Alumni and faculty are lifelong colleagues, so the circle wraps around completely," Hoagland concludes.

Collective Responsibility

Unfortunately, we know that many students do not have access to the apprenticeship experiences necessary to fully develop their potential. The unintended consequence of pairing students with a single adviser (a situation that is mitigated but not wholly solved by multiple advisers) is that some students fall through the cracks and do not participate in meaningful mentoring relationships at all. Like teaching more generally, apprenticeship teaching is often practiced as a private activity—and privacy is certainly an ingredient in establishing the kind of trust and candor that are needed for meaningful learning. But the value of privacy must be balanced against the collective responsibility of the larger community of the graduate program to ensure that apprenticeship experiences are available to all students in a full range of settings. Holding one another accountable for students' development does not mean being intrusive. What it does mean is having more of the kinds of conversations that already occur in some settings: "Mike is working with you as a TA, isn't he? How well did his recent lecture go?" "Can you talk with Leslie about her upcoming conference presentation? I think you could be helpful to her." Making students' development everybody's business means integrating the process of guidance and feedback into daily life. In short, our reenvisioned form of apprenticeship demands a culture of shared responsibility for students' learning, in which all parties have shared and transparent expectations, holding one another accountable, and providing formal and informal safety nets.

A shared vision of the program's purposes and central goals for student learning is a first condition for collective responsibility. (Readers will recall we discussed the value of creating a shared vision of departmental goals in Chapter Three.) Such a vision allows the department to set expectations and frameworks for mentor-student relationships: a timeline and process for formally and informally identifying mentors, for instance, and guidelines for the scope of conversation and documentation for annual reviews.

Discussing and agreeing on norms and standards may seem overly bureaucratic to some—and there are many who argue that mentoring is a matter of "chemistry," not something that can or should be systematically built into the organizational culture. But a shared understanding of what is expected goes a long way toward reducing the potential for misunderstanding, abuse, or simply slipping through the cracks. For example, one departmental expectation can be that faculty members and students meet regularly to set (and revisit and revise) mutual expectations for their relationship.

Of course, students as well as faculty must be accountable. Without question, one of the assumptions of apprenticeship is that students are responsible for, and thus must be more intentional about, their own learning. They must define their own goals, near-term and for their careers, and then seek out experiences that will move them toward those goals. This is easier when the faculty and department set clear expectations for timely student progress and for the characteristics of high quality work (Lovitts, 2005b, 2007). By the same token students can, and should, hold one another accountable for their progress as learners, and even push one another toward higher levels of performance.

For the benefit of both students and faculty, the program must have formal mechanisms for ensuring accountability and resolving conflicts. The University of Wisconsin neuroscience program has created a dense web of safety nets to ensure that students are making timely progress and receiving the necessary mentorship and support. These include the First Year Committee (it plays the role of adviser before an adviser has been chosen); the adviser; the dissertation committee; and the departmental steering committee (charged with ensuring the well-being of students and adjudicating any disputes between adviser and dissertation committee). Ultimately, the chair of the neuroscience program has final responsibility and oversight.

Simpler approaches are also possible. The students in the neuroscience program at Boston University select one faculty member as the departmental ombudsperson. Students can approach this person in confidence and seek advocacy and advice in resolving problems. At the very least, the faculty director of graduate studies (DGS) should serve as the department's first line of defense. It is the responsibility of the DGS to monitor student progress and offer informal counsel to students and faculty members. The DGS can help ensure that every student has at least one actively engaged faculty mentor. The rest of the dissertation committee, or other committees in the department, can also play these roles. Human relationships are complicated, and mentoring is no exception; tensions and conflicts are inevitable. But mechanisms for conflict resolution (see Exhibit 5.1) and processes for strengthening apprenticeship relationships are important ingredients in meeting the department's collective responsibility to student formation.

Recognition

In our survey of CID faculty members, we asked "Is there someone whose advising you try to emulate?" Most frequently respondents identified their own primary adviser as a model (38 percent), but the most striking

◯

Exhibit 5.1. Conflict Resolution Workshops at Michigan State University

The Graduate School at Michigan State University created a program for graduate students and faculty to develop skills in conflict resolution using an interest-based approach. The workshops use video vignettes that depict moments of conflict between graduate students and faculty. By discussing these commonly occurring scenarios, participants are able to explore the substance of the issues and craft creative solutions for the situation. This provides them the tools to successfully set mutually understood expectations in their own advising relationships. The goal is to prevent problems through proactive expectation-setting before misunderstandings escalate into conflicts.

The program does not assume that all issues in graduate education are negotiable or that the power differential between faculty and graduate students must be reduced; faculty are clearly still responsible for setting and maintaining standards. The program also does not assume that all conflict is to be avoided. On the contrary, conflict over ideas is part of the intellectual core of graduate education.

This program was originally supported by the Fund for the Improvement of Postsecondary Education and the William and Flora Hewlett Foundation and has spread to many other campuses. The program is a strategy for reducing attrition, which can result from serious conflicts, especially in the later years of graduate study. For information see the program's Web site at http://www.msu.edu/~gradschl/conflict.htm.

◯

finding was that "no one" was the second most common response (33 percent). (We did not ask how many had an "anti-role model" although several volunteered that fact.[8]) On the one hand, we were rather shocked by this finding, but on the other, it was no surprise. Few graduate programs have structures or processes in place through which faculty or doctoral students (who will likely be mentors themselves at some point in some setting) can learn the skills and values entailed in apprenticeship pedagogy. An important step toward realizing the vision of apprenticeship presented here is to recognize that being a good mentor is not an innate talent, or a function solely of "chemistry." It also involves techniques that can be learned, recognized, and rewarded.

A first step toward this recognition is to create occasions for faculty members to learn about and discuss one another's apprenticeship philosophies and strategies. Opportunities to discuss challenging moments might be particularly useful. Because mentoring is a relationship, it cannot be reduced to formulaic "moves," but it can be improved by documenting and sharing practice. In fact, some British universities are offering professional development workshops on graduate student advising (Eley and Jennings, 2005). In this country, attention to training and preparation has been advanced by investment from the Howard Hughes Medical Institute, which recently supported the development of an extensive curriculum on student mentoring, called *Entering Mentoring* (see Exhibit 5.2).

A further step is to make effective mentoring, advising, modeling, and other forms of apprenticeship pedagogy a focus for recognition and reward. When faculty members invest in their relationships with students they reap direct benefits from their students' scholarship, as well as enormous amounts of reflected glory. But apprenticeship pedagogy rarely comes with public accolades or rewards. Shifting the culture around these roles will be easier if, as the National Academy of Sciences has urged, they are more firmly embedded "in institutional systems of rewards and promotions" (Committee on Science Engineering and Public Policy, 1997, p. 66). And some campuses have taken steps in this direction. Since 1987 Arizona State University has given an Outstanding Doctoral Mentor award that comes with a $5,000 cash prize and, as an added bonus, recipients' essays on their advising philosophy are posted on the university's Web site. Selection criteria include "a demonstrated record of graduate teaching excellence, a successful record of chairing doctoral committees with timely degree completion rates, an ability to attract doctoral students to ASU through active recruitment and academic/scholarly reputation and a demonstrated commitment to diversity in the mentoring process" (Arizona State University, n.d.). Similarly, the Duke University Graduate School presents the Dean's Award for Excellence in Mentoring, and in 2006 the University of Pittsburgh followed suit with the Provost's Award for Excellence in Mentoring.

Recognition need not come from the top. Students can take the lead. The Graduate Student Senate at Washington University in St. Louis and the Graduate Student Council at Harvard University make annual awards to outstanding faculty mentors and laud the recipients on the Web. Nor must such awards always be given at the university level. The students of the Graduate Women Educator Network in the Indiana School of Education annually recognize outstanding mentors who serve graduate students. After several years, the award is beginning to change the culture in the school; student organizers report that conversations

○

Exhibit 5.2. Resources for Mentoring Graduate Students

Entering Mentoring. A Seminar to Train a New Generation of Scientists, by Jo Handelsman, Christine Pfund, Sarah Miller Lauffer, and Christine Maidl Pribbenow. University of Wisconsin Press, 2005. http://scientificteaching.wisc.edu.

> Syllabus and materials for an eight-week course on teaching graduate students to mentor younger students. It has also been valuable as a seminar for faculty members.

How to Mentor Graduate Students: A Faculty Guide, and *How to Obtain the Mentoring You Need: A Graduate Student Guide,* by The Graduate School, University of Washington, 2005. http://www.grad.washington.edu/mentoring/GradFacultyMentor.pdf & http://www.grad.washington.edu/mentoring/GradStudentMentor.pdf

> A pair of guidebooks to help graduate students and faculty members understand good mentoring and learn to work together. Includes practical advice that can be tailored to many campus settings.

Effective Postgraduate Supervision. Improving the Student/Supervisor Relationship, by Adrian R. Eley and Roy Jennings. Open University Press, 2005.

> A set of case study scenarios with focused questions and suggestions for resolution. Many are based on real-life examples and relate to research.

Adviser, Teacher, Role Model, Friend: On Being a Mentor to Students in Science and Engineering, by the Committee on Science Engineering and Public Policy. National Academy of Sciences, 1997.

> Short handbook on mentoring and advising for faculty members.

A Graduate Student Guide: Making the Most of Mentoring, by Carol Mullen. Rowman & Littlefield, 2006.

> Book for graduate students on getting the most out of graduate school by taking an active and assertive approach to career planning and seeking mentorship.

Working Effectively with Graduate Assistants, by Jody Nyquist and Donald Wulff. Sage, 1995.

> Taking a developmental approach, this book gives practical advice for meeting the variety of challenges inherent in supervising graduate teaching and research assistants.

○

about mentoring and recognizing mentoring have increased. In addition, the annual faculty review process recognizes the award as evidence of a significant teaching contribution (see the Indiana University School of Education's Web page, Mentoring Award, at gallery.carnegiefoundation .org/cid).

Respect, Trust, Reciprocity

Ultimately, apprenticeship depends on relationships, and like any relationship, apprenticeship relationships are more likely to flourish when they are based on and cultivate the qualities of respect, trust, and reciprocity. These qualities are important not simply because they make the relationship more pleasant; they are necessary conditions for learning. To put it differently, they are three legs of a stool that will not otherwise stand. And, as we will discuss in Chapter Six, they are attributes of healthy intellectual communities.

Starting from a stance of mutual respect is a hallmark of effective apprenticeship. In an academic setting, respect for ideas is especially important. The mentor's ideas and feedback must be incorporated into the student's work in a way that recognizes the teacher's greater experience but that also respects the student's growing intellectual independence. The student's ideas must be given room to grow and develop. Personal respect (which does not presuppose affection or friendship) is also important and can build on respect for ideas.

Respect builds trust, the second leg of the stool, and trust is essential for new ideas to flourish. And of course successful interactions increase trust, so over time a positive cycle takes hold. On the CID faculty survey, an historian noted, "I try to develop trust as a basis for building a personal and working relationship with the student. I believe that trust encourages students to work hard and creatively, primarily because they know that they can depend on me to give them the guidance and support that they need." Together, trust and respect are the best ways to combat student uncertainty and fear. For instance, many are reluctant to confess career goals (such as teaching in a community college) that might be perceived as unserious or that may not boost the faculty member's standing in the field.

Reciprocity within the relationship is the third leg of the stool. It is generally obvious what students gain from a mentoring relationship with a faculty member—training, advice, sponsorship, funding, support, encouragement, and feedback. Faculty members gain something, too—new ideas, infusions of energy and excitement, the satisfaction of developing the next generation, and intellectual legacy. Approaching the relationship from a stance of reciprocity reduces the chance of power differentials becoming so great that they are unhealthy. A faculty member in the humanities, for instance, looks at the sciences and sees, "even the most senior and junior members count on one another, and . . . joint publication and grant applications acknowledge and formalize the structure of mutual dependency" (Davidson, 1999, p. B4). Celebrating interdependence seems the right thing to do.

How to do this? In working with CID faculty and students, we were struck by several strategies that foster these humane qualities:

KNOW ONE'S SELF AND EACH OTHER WELL. Apprenticeship relationships are truly personalized education. All students bring to graduate school a unique combination of knowledge, skills, prior experiences, goals, beliefs, personal identity, education, and family background. This combination of ingredients, in turn, "affects their abilities to remember, reason, solve problems, and acquire new knowledge" (Bransford and others, 2000, p. 10). In addition, because of their diverse backgrounds, students have different needs, motivations, and ways of responding to challenge. Conditions that some find inspiring leave others feeling daunted and even alienated; challenges that motivate some to greater achievements are dispiriting to others. Apprenticeship pedagogy demands that the faculty member understand each of her students and individualize instruction. Likewise, the student can be expected to learn about and understand the preferred working styles of the faculty mentors he works with. The time this takes pays off with greater learning.

But knowing each other is only half of the equation. Good working relationships are easier when each party knows herself well enough to understand and express her own needs. Self-knowledge is largely the product of iterative reflection and openness to input and feedback. The tangible benefit is ever increasing fluidity in dealing with a wide variety of other people. These attitudes inspire a cycle of positive change.

COMMUNICATE CLEARLY. Apprenticeship relationships are improved with clear communication, especially about expectations. What are the assumptions about the roles of students and faculty? What is the scope of the relationship: research, teaching, career development, values, professional identity, work-life balance? What are the rules of engagement? What modes of communication are preferred, with what frequency, and with what expectations for response? Many misunderstandings can be avoided with clear and frank communication from the start.

Making expectations explicit, and putting them in writing, is a huge step forward. In this spirit, the University of Illinois department of history developed department-wide guidelines for advising. Once the student has identified a main adviser, that person becomes the primary source for the student, specifically for intellectual matters, such as "advice about minor fields and specific courses, response to written work and communications with reasonable promptness and attention, and guidance in selecting an appropriate dissertation topic and input on the dissertation proposal." Equally important, the guidelines spell out the student's responsibilities in the advising relationship, such as "giving the adviser fair warning about deadlines for letters of recommendation or other requests, regular communication with the adviser to inform her/him of progress in the program, and communication with the adviser regarding personal problems that may impede or hinder progress." The full document includes sections on timing for acquiring an adviser and the process for changing advisers (see the University of Illinois at Urbana-Champaign history department's Web page, Adviser-Advisee Guidelines, at gallery.carnegiefoundation.org/cid). Defining shared expectations becomes even more important as programs move to multiple mentors.

But it is not necessary to wait for department-wide consensus about such matters. Individual faculty members can make their expectations clear. In this spirit, many faculty members give statements of their advising philosophy and expectations to their students or put them on the Web so potential advisees can see them. (See Exhibit 5.3, for an example.) In healthy intellectual communities, these matters are openly discussed among faculty and students so that good practices can be emulated.

PROVIDE REGULAR FEEDBACK. A good apprenticeship relationship is marked by regular and candid communication. Apprenticeship pedagogy demands feedback to improve practice and develop the ability to

---

Exhibit 5.3. An Advising Agreement

Robert Gross, James L. and Shirley A. Draper Professor of Early American History at the University of Connecticut, gives this statement to his doctoral students outlining the obligations of both parties in the adviser-advisee relationship. It was published in the *Chronicle of Higher Education* (Gross, 2002).

Let me make explicit what I expect in a dissertation and how I see my roles as your adviser. A doctoral dissertation in American studies must stake out a historical, cultural, or literary problem, explicate its significance in relation to the existing scholarship, make clear how the inquiry engages broad questions about American society or culture, and then lay out a clear research design, by which the intellectual problem will be addressed. The investigation must identify a body of pertinent primary sources, published and unpublished, and describe clearly the methods, approaches, and theoretical presuppositions it brings to bear upon the subject. In describing and analyzing the sources, the dissertation must draw upon and relate its conclusions to all the relevant scholarship, including books, journal articles, and other dissertations. The conclusion should generalize from the specific findings of the study to the larger issues the study engages.

As to my roles, I see myself as your principal editor, whose job it is to note errors of spelling and grammar, identify infelicities of expression (awkwardness, clichés, unclear formulations), and set forth problems in the larger presentation, especially in the structure of chapters or the work as a whole. Secondly, I read your work as a critical scholar, assessing the logic of your argument, the pertinence and the persuasiveness of your evidence, and the acuity of your analysis. Third, I will offer suggestions of pertinent books, articles, sources, and propose various approaches, methods, lines of interpretation. Finally, despite the critical stance all these roles involve, I am also your chief cheerleader, who will do everything possible to enable you to produce a first-rate dissertation and secure a top academic job. Whatever faults your work may show along the way, they will not dispel my support and enthusiasm for your career.

What do I expect in return? First, that you send me a text that is always spell-checked, grammatical, documented with footnotes in appropriate style, and as clear as you can make it. Second, that you respond to my comments and, if you choose to ignore or reject them, tell me why in an accompanying letter. I get frustrated and cranky when I invest lots of time in reading and reflecting on student work and my suggestions seem to get lost in space. Third, it is useful for you to recognize that both of us operate under time pressures, with all sorts of obligations and deadlines to juggle, and that you alert me when I should expect to receive draft chapters and leave me roughly a month to read and comment on your work. Ordinarily, I return manuscripts within two weeks' time, and a month is my outer limit. Beyond that, you have a right to complain.

○

self-monitor and self-evaluate. For starters, there should be clear and frequent opportunities to check in about how the student's ideas are developing. Sometimes—this seems to happen more commonly in the fields where scholars work alone—a mutual disengagement pact can form, and weeks and months can pass without the student and adviser having a conversation. "Some students hide when they get stuck, and I might go several months before insisting that they check in," a CID survey respondent from history said. A possible antidote to such delay is illustrated by a CID faculty survey respondent from chemistry, who explained, "I have graduate students provide me with a weekly update and plan for the next week during their entire graduate career in my group." This schedule may be too relentless for some, but it suggests what is possible on the "high end."

In addition to assessing the progress of students' work, mentors have a responsibility to evaluate their overall formation, as well. What ought the student accomplish—in research, teaching, leadership—by the end of the first year, the second year, and so forth? The University of Kansas history department, for example, developed a Progress Grid that offers guidance about degree requirements, and a second Professionalization Grid that provides a schedule of recommended professional and leadership activities including: acquire a professional outfit (year one), deliver a guest lecture (year two), take a position on a department or university committee (year three), present a paper at a professional conference (year four), and mentor more junior graduate students and dream about future research projects (year five). The Grid provides a wonderful map of formation at its fullest and is easily adapted to any discipline or department (see the University of Kansas history department's Web page, Curricular Changes, at gallery.carnegiefoundation.org/cid).

Ideally, time is set aside, at least once a year, for faculty to work together to formally evaluate each student's progress. This is one way faculty can take collective responsibility for ensuring that all of the students in the department are making timely progress. Typically the faculty will discuss each student, what the student has achieved during the year (progress through formal requirements like courses and exams, research accomplishments, courses taught, as well as broader professional formation), and set goals for the next year. Evidence of student development in many arenas can be examined in conjunction with a student self-assessment. Regular reviews are also a way to intervene with students who are stuck or not meeting expectations, and thus ensure that the department is meeting its educational responsibilities. When integrated into the doctoral program, robust regular reviews (recall the portfolios described in Chapters Three and Four) can become part of the culture, signaling the department's commitment to students' formation along multiple dimensions, as well as the understanding that students and faculty share responsibility for it.

Every apprenticeship relationship grows and changes, and so the expectations for and terms of working relationships themselves ought to be revisited regularly. How frequently do faculty and students communicate and about what? In what ways should the relationship change? What is not working well? What friction points have emerged and how can they be ameliorated? Recalibrating expectations is important, as needs can change over time. "As time progresses and I learn more about the student, I try to tailor my advising to better fit their needs," a neuroscience faculty member told us. Ideally, of course, faculty members use this as an opportunity to solicit a candid assessment about how they themselves can improve. For all these reasons, periodic conversation about the relationship itself is essential.

TAKE TIME. Relationships require an investment of time. It is frankly troubling to hear of faculty members who take on dozens of student advisees; departments that condone or even encourage such a system are clearly on a dangerous slope. We are equally concerned about students who, often for very good reasons, attend graduate school on a part-time basis and may be effectively unable to participate in meaningful apprenticeship relationships or in the other activities that help integrate students into the intellectual community of the department.

How much time is enough? Obviously there are no hard and fast rules; we are simply arguing against too little interaction. Every mentor must determine the frequency and duration of meetings. "I really am very flexible in my advising and the time spent, depending on the particular needs of the student at a given time. I may spend a whole afternoon one week, and only five minutes the next. The goal, however, is always to get the student the necessary information, and answer all questions to the extent possible." The mathematics faculty member who said this on our faculty survey spoke for many who tailor their advising to student needs. Many also share the perspective of this faculty member from an English department, who candidly pointed out, "Students who are proactive get more of my time."

Currently the assumption is that mentors and students spend the most, and the most intensive, time together in the student's final year. Accepting for the moment that this assumption is true, strong disciplinary differences prevail. Figure 5.2 shows how often faculty members report spending

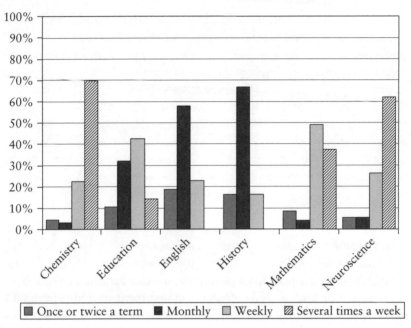

Figure 5.2. Frequency of Meetings with Doctoral Advisees
Within a Year of Completing the Dissertation
Reported by Faculty[9]

Source: *Carnegie Graduate Faculty Survey*

time with their advisees who are nearing graduation. In some fields there
is a great deal of variation, and in others—notably history and English—
"monthly" is the prevailing response. It is not surprising that in the lab
sciences, where faculty and students effectively share office space, meetings may occur several times a week. Respecting different intellectual traditions, we would nevertheless argue that the humanities might take a
page from the sciences in this regard.

Furthermore, effective apprenticeship learning may mean spending
time differently. It is in the early stages of their work, after all, that students are struggling to understand the complexities of scholarly practice,
making their first forays into authentic research, getting their pedagogical
feet wet, and trying out a new professional identity. It is at this stage that
high levels of supervision and guidance are most needed. Such an investment not only strengthens student formation at the crucial first stage of
work; it may well have the ancillary benefit of reducing attrition, much
of which can be attributed to failure to integrate into the academic community of the department (Golde, 2005; Lovitts, 2001).

Whether at the beginning or end, time can be invested more or less wisely. To illustrate, two scholars in composition studies describe the process of "joint texting" in which a faculty member literally sits with the student and together they edit the student's text on the computer in real-time. The instructor talks through the revision process (making her thinking explicit and visible to the student), and then invites the student to do the same. The student can see how the work changes, and, for instance, how authorial voice is asserted (Kamler and Thomson, 2006, pp. 53–57). Rather than spending hours making the same corrections over and over in the margins of a manuscript, a faculty member using this approach spends one hour with the student. Revision comes to be understood not as a process of implementing changes requested by the professor but as a way of thinking about the use of language. Not only is the payoff a higher quality text but also greater independence on the part.

Conceptual Underpinnings

The vision of apprenticeship *with* presented here is not something invented by the CID, certainly. Many of the most encouraging concrete practices—and the principles behind them—can be gleaned from careful observation and analysis of what the best mentors and teachers do, but our understanding of how and why these practices work has been enriched by findings over the last several decades about how people learn (summarized in Bransford and others, 2000). To date, this work has had much wider circulation in K–12 and undergraduate education than in graduate studies. New findings from the learning sciences have anchored a number of Carnegie Foundation programs on preparation for the professions. As the study of preparation for the law remarks, "A great contribution of modern cognitive psychology has been to place apprenticeship, so understood, once again at the heart of education" (Sullivan and others, 2007, p. 26).

While much of the research on apprenticeship and expert learning has focused on the workplace, John Seely Brown and his colleagues use the term "cognitive apprenticeship" to describe the pedagogy of apprenticeship as applied to intellectually complex practices in a schooling context. The education of novices is best focused not on acquiring information, they tell us, but rather on learning the concepts and procedures that enable the expert to use knowledge to solve problems. It is "cognitive" because it focuses on intellectual skills and practices, because it makes thought visible through formal representations (talking, writing, mathematical equations, and the like), and because it expects teachers and learners to think explicitly about what they're doing (Brown,

Collins, and Duguid, 1989; Collins, Brown, and Holum, 1991). It is "apprenticeship" because students move through increasingly complex assignments, getting feedback that leads to improvement. "By giving learners the opportunity to practice approximation to expert performance, and giving the students feedback to help improve their own performance, educators are fostering an apprentice-like experience of the mind, cognitive apprenticeship" (Sullivan, 2005, p. 207).

In fact, Brown and his colleagues observe that doctoral education can be a model for other levels of schooling.

> [A]dvanced graduate students in the humanities, the social sciences, and the physical sciences acquire their extremely refined research skills through the apprenticeships they serve with senior researchers. It is then that they, like all apprentices, must recognize and resolve the ill-defined problems that issue out of authentic activity, in contrast to the well-defined exercises that are typically given to them in textbooks and on exams throughout their earlier schooling. It is at this stage, in short, that students no longer behave as students, but as practitioners, and develop their conceptual understanding through social interaction and collaboration in the culture of the domain, not of the school [Brown and others, 1989, pp. 39–40].

Considering the parallels between doctoral education and professional education (educating doctors, lawyers, nurses, clergy, engineers, and the like) reminds us that students are apprenticing for the work they will be doing in the future. This returns our attention to questions of purpose and the need for clear links between the elements of graduate education and the possible futures for which those elements are meant to prepare new scholars. Not only are students acquiring a strong knowledge base they are building skills, and developing the professional judgment to apply their knowledge and skills responsibly and routinely. In short, these students are developing professional expertise. This is true not only for doctors and lawyers, but also for chemists, historians, and (as our final story below illustrates) neuroscientists.

And a Final Story

To illustrate some of the principles of effective apprenticeship pedagogy, and to point to what can happen when the features highlighted here come together (and how they map onto the principles of progressive development, integration, and collaboration sounded in the previous chapter), we offer a brief case study of a student we had the good fortune to come to know during the CID. As we write this account, Maureen Estevez is about to defend her dissertation at Boston University.[10]

The story begins with Estevez's time as an undergraduate. "I started college as a liberal arts major. I was terrified of math, chemistry, and physics and avoided them like the plague. I got straight A's in these courses in high school, but for some reason I thought they would be beyond my capability in college. But I had a fascination with the human body and decided I would take all courses I needed in order to get into the cadaver dissection laboratory course. To make a long story short, I very gradually, one toe at a time, stepped into more and more science, math and even engineering courses. It turned out that I loved these courses, and I excelled in them. But I still didn't really know where I was going with them."

Estevez began her graduate work in engineering, at the recommendation of one of her undergraduate professors. As it turns out, she was "miserable," partly because she was taking inappropriate courses but also, she confesses, because "I liked using engineering concepts to help me solve biological problems, but I wasn't flourishing in a purely (and very hard-core) engineering program. I was realizing I didn't really want to be an engineer." This realization prompted a careful appraisal of her driving passions and life goals. "I had gone to that school without a clear vision for what I wanted to do, but a PhD program is so difficult, so consuming, so challenging that a student must have a clear vision of their goal, so that they have something for which to persevere."

Interestingly, it was a desire to teach ("it's all I could really think about wanting to do") that led Estevez to her current program at Boston University. The equal emphasis on research and teaching fit her perfectly. And by the time she arrived she was well aware of the importance of a good fit with an adviser who would understand and coach her effectively. "Initially I was very concerned about finding a lab in which to work. I knew that I wanted to work with a Principal Investigator who would be able to mentor me well, someone who would be able to invest time and energy into shaping me into a neuroscientist and a researcher. I surely was neither when I entered graduate school. But the message I seemed to get from other graduate students was 'Good luck finding that . . . that doesn't exist anymore. Most professors are bogged down with a million things (writing grants, writing papers, teaching, administering, traveling) and are not really able to spend any time with you in the lab. Maybe you'll see them once a month.'"

She kept looking and found a mentor whom she clearly trusts and respects. "Dr. Cornwall (who prefers to be called by his first name, Carter) is in his early sixties and has been working in his field for over thirty years. He's a cross between da Vinci and MacGyver. Give this guy a microscope, a paper clip and some duct tape and he'll kludge together some crazy device to record action potentials from neurons, then go home and read French poetry while building furniture in his basement. I'd say 90 percent of who I am now as a researcher is because of my mentor."

Rather than letting Estevez flounder or micromanaging her, Dr. Cornwall began by teaching her the relevant techniques, and then giving her the freedom to develop her own experiments. "Carter apparently saw potential in me even though I had no experience in his field and was quite intimidated by the racks of electronic equipment in the lab. But, I remember him telling me, 'Everything you see here, I can teach you. It looks incredibly difficult, but each part is simple in and of itself, and you can learn it all.' This was one of the turning points for me. Up until that point in school, whenever I had seen something that looked difficult or intimidating, I immediately turned away. I was overwhelmed by the fear of looking stupid."

Cornwall describes his philosophy in similar terms. His definition of research is "the programmed breaking of things to find out how they work." He tells all of his graduate students, "Your job is to make mistakes on a regular basis." He concurs that Estevez did not know how to fail. The strategy he uses to help students learn to take risks is to tell them that "failure lies in *not* breaking something or making a mistake every day."

A second strand of his advising strategy is to have enormous confidence in his students and not to have plans for them in advance. He encourages them to find a piece of his grants that interests them, do some experiments, and see what sparks their passion. "If you have confidence in students," he confided, "it is enabling like nothing else." Estevez agrees, and says, "Somehow Carter's confidence in me triggered the thought that I really could learn anything in time, and it was okay that I didn't know anything to start. I've since discovered that many grad students (particularly women) have similar fears . . . fears of being discovered as an imposter in the field, that they don't belong there and they've been pulling one over on everyone all this time."

Cornwall spends a lot of time with his students, breaking the research process into "serial steps," which is relatively easy because his lab is small. Estevez elaborates, "Carter spent many hours with me my first year in the lab. He was teaching me a technically very difficult technique to record current from single photoreceptor cells. Essentially, the technique involved about 50 steps, each of which depended upon the success of the previous step, and each had about a fifty-fifty chance of succeeding (until you get good). The final goal was to isolate a single intact photoreceptor cell from the retina of a salamander or toad, to draw that cell into a perfectly-fitting recording microelectrode and then keep the cell alive long enough to manipulate and harass it in all sorts of ways in order to piece apart the molecular machinery of this tiny little beautiful neuron. But on top of this feat, the experiments are all done in complete darkness with a night goggle-type microscope apparatus."

In the best traditions of apprenticeship, Cornwall had to determine when failure was the best source of learning. "My adviser was very attuned to moments when he needed to step in and teach, and moments when he just needed to let me struggle. It was like trying to fly to the moon, and I spent my first year and a half in the lab failing at it over and over again, day after day and week after week. I had never failed so much in my whole life. I explain all this because one of the most important experiences that has facilitated my development as a scientist and a scholar was learning to fail."

Not only did Cornwall communicate his confidence in her scientific potential in their one-on-one communication, he conveyed his respect by treating her like a colleague at the first scientific meeting she attended. "He let me tag along and introduced me to every person he knew." This seemingly trivial act bewildered her at the time. "He treated me like a colleague even if it was undeserved," she said. "I hadn't created any data. I was *so* fresh."

But in keeping with the vision of multiple mentors, Cornwall is not the only person in the picture. Estevez's learning is facilitated by the department and the larger communities in which she interacts.

The BU neuroscience program emphasizes teaching through its Vesalius Program described in Chapter Four. In order to finish the program, participating students complete two practicum projects with a teaching mentor, such as designing a syllabus, giving a lecture in a medical school class, or completing a research project on teaching. Estevez chose to determine the effectiveness of using 3-D clay brain models, instead of conventional 2-D drawings, to teach neurofunction to medical students. She sought out a faculty member who is very knowledgeable about research on learning to help her design and implement her study. Their conversations ranged widely about the art and science of teaching and she soon felt "that he was on my team." Although he was not knowledgeable about her area of neuroscience, he became part of her dissertation committee. He ultimately played a crucial advocacy role when the rest of the committee wanted her to conduct another year's worth of experiments.

In her account she emphasizes how difficult it is for her peers to find multiple faculty members with whom they can develop trusting and supportive relationships; most know only their own adviser and perhaps one other faculty member in a collaborating lab. Without mechanisms for faculty and students to get to know one another (seminar courses are rare in medical schools), mentoring relationships cannot develop.

Estevez's second practicum in the Vesalius Program involved teaching one unit of a medical school physiology course. She describes the load as "pretty heavy," although students in the humanities would find teaching part of one course every year unimaginably light. Once again, she is experiencing colleagueship with new mentors. "The actual training and practice in teaching is great, but most importantly it provides a shift in the way we students interact with faculty . . . from being their students to being their colleagues. I'm sitting with them in a conference room discussing how we'll design the final exam, how students are doing and so on." Working on the CID provided a similar opportunity for apprenticeship learning with multiple mentors. "I started feeling more like a professor, a colleague to my professors, rather than a measly grad student. I could visualize myself continuing in the academic profession because I was seeing it modeled right then and there."

Estevez concludes her account by reflecting on how her experiences have progressively built on one another, and on her emerging identity as a scientist who is part of the scholarly community and who can integrate research, teaching, and service. "After a year or so of failing in the lab, my research finally took off and I've been finding lots of interesting things. I am also publishing papers, going to meetings, presenting posters, and even got to give a talk on my research at a big national meeting. I've formed some good collaborations with other scientists through Carter, and those collaborations have opened doors for additional publications (and also potential post-doc positions). I was even invited to give a seminar talk on my research through one of our collaborations. These talks are usually only given by professors or post-docs, so it was a real honor for me to be able to do this as a graduate student. I remember getting down from the podium after the talk, hearing the applause, and all of a sudden realizing, 'I am a real scientist. When did that happen?'"

Making Apprenticeship Work

In this chapter we have argued that the term *apprenticeship* has taken a lot of knocks, many for good reasons. But apprenticeship learning has a long history for a wide variety of professions and occupations around the world; without a doubt it is a model worth saving, and continues to be the signature pedagogy of doctoral education. The apprenticeship relationships illustrated by Maureen Estevez, Carter Cornwall, and the entire BU neuroscience program are quintessential examples of apprenticeship as a powerful route to the formation of scholars. The kind of apprenticeship we argue for—apprenticed *with* rather than apprenticed *to*—is critical for the twenty-first century because it puts ideas and learning at the center of relationships. There are many who have argued that American doctoral education is limited by structures and practices that are faculty-centered rather than student-centered. We reject both of those in favor of a learning-, idea-, and knowledge-centered perspective on doctoral education.

Apprenticeship relationships can be conducted in a way that promotes tremendous learning while also making effective use of faculty members' time. This will not, of course, be entirely smooth or easy. Many have no direct experience with "elbow learning," giving them little on which to build. Too many of today's professors are successful despite the mentoring they did (or did not) receive, rather than because of it. A twin challenge is that most of us do not know how others perceive us, and it is challenging to solicit candid input. Faculty members must be willing to ask for help, which requires some humility and vulnerability, but has the payoff of becoming a better mentor. Our vision of twenty-first-century apprenticeship is admittedly ambitious, and interim steps to improvement are possible. Faculty and students alike can begin by examining what they do now and assessing whether it works. There are plenty of examples of alternative ways to meet similar goals, and if asked ("Can other ways be more effective and efficient?"), most people are very willing to share ideas.

Apprenticeship challenges faculty members' prevailing mindsets and habits of work. Every faculty member cannot serve every student, even when there are shared interests; sometimes the match is not productive. It is important to recognize when it is best to step back and let others play a more central role. Our ideas about mentoring require letting go of the notion of sole "ownership" of a student and recognizing that students are better served with multiple mentors, albeit with one or two taking primary responsibility for the team. It may seem on first blush that things are going well, but periodic checkups are always in order. Does every student have access to mentors? Do faculty understand the new demands on emerging scholars in a rapidly changing world?

Bringing our vision to fruition will be difficult because the values and structures of academe often work against it. In many science departments, the system of federal research funding ties students to one faculty member, and the pressure to quickly produce results works against investing time in each student's individual development, regardless of whether there might be a long-term payoff. Without these grant-based production imperatives, the humanities and such fields as mathematics are more inclined to committee-based mentoring, and yet the practice of meeting with students on a weekly basis has not yet taken hold. Perhaps this is in part because, as one CID-leader lamented, "in the lab sciences every student is *worth* a paper a year, and in math every student *costs* me a paper a year." Letting go of deeply ingrained assumptions and actions based on a calculus of short-term self-interest requires imagination and courage. But we are firmly convinced that the payoff in terms of knowledge advancement and student development is worth the risk.

Apprenticeship also challenges prevailing mindsets and habits of work for students. Too many students approach doctoral education as if it were a continuation of the prior sixteen to eighteen years of schooling, with the student as the relatively passive recipient of the knowledge ladled out by faculty members, and success measured by correctly completing well-defined assignments in a fixed timeframe. Instead, doctoral students must be active managers of their own careers, purposefully charting a course and asking for what they need, while remaining open to new ideas, input, and opportunities heretofore unimagined. Although many students enter graduate school relatively unaware of what is demanded of them, ignorance is no excuse. Students must also actively combat the fear that reasonably arises from financial and intellectual dependence. Admitting feelings of ignorance and fear to colleagues and acting collectively is an essential strategy.

It is never too late to change. Students and faculty can take individual action, and individual actions add up to collective cultural change. A learning-centered view of doctoral education means that every academic department should be a lively intellectual community, celebrating the advancement of learning and knowledge. And intellectual communities are the topic of the next chapter.

ENDNOTES

1. Brooks's quotation is from "Graduate Learning as Apprenticeship," an opinion piece that appeared in the *Chronicle of Higher Education* (Brooks,

1996). Brooks is currently Sterling Professor of French and Comparative Literature at Yale University and, at the time he wrote this, was Tripp Professor of Humanities and chair of the Department of Comparative Literature at Yale.

2. The mathematics genealogy project documents intellectual lineages in mathematics (see http://www.genealogy.ams.org/). Hyman Bass, former president of the American Mathematical Society and author of a CID essay, has twenty-five students and ninety descendents. His lineage can be traced back thirteen steps through Johann Carl Friedrich Gauss to Otto Mencke who received his PhD in 1665 from the University of Leipzig.

3. "Signature pedagogy" is a term coined by Lee S. Shulman, to describe "characteristic forms of teaching and learning . . . that organize the fundamental ways in which future practitioners are educated for their new professions" (Shulman, 2005, p. 52). Examples of signature pedagogies include the case dialogue method of teaching in law schools and bedside teaching on daily clinical rounds in medical education. Signature pedagogies are windows into the cultures of their fields because they incorporate into the operational acts of teaching and learning assumptions about how to teach knowledge and skills (such as how to think like a lawyer) and implicit assumptions about professional values (pp. 54–55).

4. The term "elbow learning" is how the first president of Clark University, Dr. G. Stanley Hall, a noted psychologist, described students and faculty working side by side in research labs. Hall was revered among his students for his seminars, as well as for creating a vibrant intellectual atmosphere in Clark's early years (Ryan, 1939).

5. We carefully deliberated about our terminology. "Adviser" indicates a formal role, and most doctoral students have an adviser. But advising, particularly in the early years, is ancillary to learning; it is often done sporadically and focuses on checking off requirements. In the later stages, advising narrows its focus to dissertation research and writing. Dissertation advisers (also termed "chairs" or "directors") play key roles in the formulation of the dissertation project, its execution, writing, and defense. But the term "adviser" presupposes unidirectionality; it does not have room for reciprocity, nor does it foreground student learning to the extent we desire.

   The word "teacher" might be the obvious choice when learning is the central goal of the relationship. But, somehow, in the university context, teaching is associated with classroom settings, and in doctoral studies, classrooms are only one of many important teaching and learning venues.

   In general, and in this volume, our preference has been for the term "mentor." In common usage it cuts a wider swath than does adviser or teacher. Mentors play an advocacy role, and the term *mentorship* conveys sponsorship and support that extends beyond the years of graduate school. We were also drawn to the term *mentor* because popular usage assumes that anyone can, and perhaps should, have multiple mentors. The term reminds us of the active role students take in identifying and cultivating mentors (this is often advocated as a compensatory strategy for those who may find themselves marginalized in an organization by virtue of their minority status). Furthermore, mentorship is aligned with the idea of stewardship. It connotes the development of a person's complete professional identity, not limited to particular skills or tasks. The term implies affection and care, but, like stewardship, it is associated with aspiration. It is not about being nice or friendly, but rather about setting the conditions that elicit high-quality work. In this book we do not precisely distinguish between mentors and advisers, but note that when such a distinction is drawn, as Nettles and Millet do in their detailed survey of thousands of doctoral students, 25 percent report that they do not have a mentor (Nettles and Millet, 2006, p. 99).

   We opted for the term "student," as accurate and relatively unladen with baggage. "Apprentice" carries many negative connotations of subservience and great power differential; the student simply has no voice. "Protégé" and the neologism "mentee" do not sufficiently emphasize learning.

6. The faculty survey asked an open-ended question, "Students become proficient at aspects of research by participating in many activities and experiences, such as reading articles, working on a research team, presenting research findings at meetings. For your students, what experiences and activities are most effective for learning to ask a good research question?" In total, 455 faculty members responded to this question, and we coded the responses into ten broad categories that emerged from our reading of the responses. Any single response could be coded into any or all of the categories, although none was coded into more than six, and 90 percent of respondents identified one, two, or three strategies. Taken together, their answers illustrate the principles of apprenticeship pedagogy at work.

   The ten categories were as follows: (1) Reading—read research papers or literature; (2) Talking—discuss with adviser and other members of research community; (3) Courses—work done in seminars and courses; (4) Listening—learning by listening to others talk about their work; (5) Presenting—presenting work to an audience; (6) Writing—translating and explaining; (7) Doing it—designing and performing research; (8) Guided—research and apprenticeship, especially one-on-one work with adviser; (9) Other; (10) Don't do it/don't know.

7. The student survey asked, "How many faculty members do you consider to be your advisers or mentors?" The choices were: None; one; two; three;

four or more. The figure shows the distribution of answers within each discipline for all student respondents for the survey, regardless of stage in the program. For this figure responses of "three" and "four or more" were combined.

8. The faculty survey asked, "Is there someone whose advising you try to emulate? (Check all that apply.)" Three quarters of the respondents picked only one of the options, and fewer than 2 percent picked none of the options. The proportion picking each choice were: doctoral adviser, 37 percent; no one, 33 percent; colleague at this or another university, 25 percent; another faculty member from grad program or post-doc, 22 percent; someone else, 7 percent; and undergraduate faculty, 5 percent. Of the forty-nine individuals who listed someone else, seventeen of them specifically mentioned their post-doctoral adviser. Six also specifically mentioned negative role models with comments like, "reverse emulate" and "within the limits of professionalism, I try to do for my graduate students what I felt my own adviser failed to do for me."

9. The faculty survey asked, "How frequently do you typically meet outside of class with students for whom you are the primary adviser? For students within a year of completing dissertation." The options were: once or twice a term; once a month; once a week; two to three times a week; daily; not applicable. Responses of "not applicable" were dropped from the analysis. Responses of "two to three times a week" and "daily" were combined to represent "several times a week." Notably, 34 percent of neuroscience faculty and 20 percent of chemistry faculty selected the category "daily," a selection made by very few of the faculty in other disciplines.

10. Maureen Estevez attended three convenings at the Carnegie Foundation, and credits her participation in the CID with giving her a number of formative opportunities and experiences. This excerpt is drawn from a longer account she provided to us. We also interviewed Carter Cornwall.

6

CREATING AND SUSTAINING INTELLECTUAL COMMUNITY

A community is more than a spring and fall picnic and a few select brown bag sessions. There is no real vision for what communities we have, need or can develop.

—CID student survey respondent, education

Intellectual community is the most important facet of any doctoral community. Students need a supportive community among themselves and collegial relations with faculty. The opportunity to present one's work to such a community, to respond to work in progress by a faculty member, and to interact informally all function to raise students' sense of their own potential and help them learn to function as junior colleagues.

—CID faculty survey respondent, history

ANNA IS A BRAND-NEW DOCTORAL STUDENT, and she has been looking forward to returning to academia after being away for a few years. She has thought a lot about her research and teaching interests and is thrilled when she sees a flyer announcing a departmental seminar by a well-known scholar in her field. She knows she is unlikely to have an opportunity to question him in person again, so she prepares some ideas to try out for the discussion after the talk.

Anna is pleased to see lots of people at the seminar, including many of the senior faculty. This is exactly the kind of experience she has been hoping for—a setting in which all the members of the departmental community come together to discuss the big ideas in the field. A reception is planned for after the talk, so Anna looks forward to meeting more of her colleagues in an informal setting.

The talk is everything Anna hoped for, and, as the presentation concludes, she knows exactly what question she wants to ask, albeit a little nervously. Marshalling her courage, she is one of the first with a hand in the air. But again and again she is passed over, and she soon realizes that all of the people asking questions are senior faculty.

It also begins to dawn on Anna that the questions she's hearing are not really questions; they are more like speeches, not really intended to invite engagement with the speaker and unrelated to other "questions." Anna turns to the veteran grad student next to her with a quizzical look. "What's going on?"

"It's always like this," he whispers. "The faculty use these events to one-up each other and rehash old arguments." She'll get to know the pattern soon enough, he suggests, pointing out that most grad students don't bother attending anymore because they end up just talking to each other, not to the faculty or the guest.

He's right, Anna thinks. The crowd includes only a scattering of graduate students. And though she hasn't completely given up on meeting the speaker at the reception afterwards, Anna realizes that her earlier enthusiasm is fast evaporating. With the beginnings of a hollow feeling in her chest, she wonders if she has been misleading herself about being a part of this community.

------------ o ------------

Doctoral students bring different motivations to their work, but for most of them passion for the field tops the list. Like Anna, they want and expect to be surrounded by others who share their passion; they long to be part of an intellectual community. And they are right to want this. Intellectual community is not simply a feel-good atmosphere, not just "a spring and fall picnic." Nor is it an end in itself. Intellectual community serves multiple purposes, from improving knowledge production to reducing isolation and attrition. In the words of a recent report from the American Historical Association: "[A]t root [departments] all have the same purpose: sustaining an intellectual community that advances the learning of all members. A graduate program is more than courses and examinations and hours in the archives. There needs to be an open engagement with ideas; public conversations about research, pedagogy, and professional issues; and discussions that place history in a larger culture" (Bender and others, 2004, p. 98). Intellectual community is a condition, indeed the foundation, for the core work of doctoral education: building knowledge.

In the work of the CID, we have come to appreciate just how true that proposition is. We fully expected to focus with our campus partners on new ways to think about, say, the dissertation, and the qualifying exam. We expected to focus on new directions for the disciplines and their implications for the future of doctoral education. We expected debate around the practices of advising and mentoring. What we did not fully anticipate was the importance that intellectual community would come to have in the project's work, and the extent to which students would contribute to, shape, and enrich that community. Again and again, CID faculty and students seized on the concept of intellectual community as central to the character and quality of doctoral training; nearly every other aspect of the program depends on and contributes to the development of such community.

Intellectual community affects how people wrestle with ideas (is there honest exchange or hostile subversion?); how teaching is valued (do people recognize which faculty and graduate students are good teachers?); how students learn to engage with senior colleagues (do faculty patronize students or are they open to the potential of junior colleagues?); how failure is treated (are risks supported or avoided?); how people work together (is collaboration actively promoted by the structures of the department?); how independence and creativity are encouraged (do students have multiple, planned opportunities to tackle new questions and projects?); how the department and its members stay connected to the field (is there energy and excitement in work that is pushing new frontiers?). All of these facets—and many others—affect not only the intellectual life of a department, but the formation of scholars and the contributions they will be prepared to make as stewards in the multiple settings in which they work and live.

Because intellectual community is intangible, it rarely gets the attention that goes to more concrete elements of doctoral education, such as the curriculum or qualifying exam. Yet its implications are significant. Students who do not become engaged with the departmental community are more likely to drop out (Lovitts, 2001; Tinto, 1993). And a recent study from Harvard highlights an important finding: new faculty are more likely to value collegiality over salary, a significant shift from prior generations (Collaborative on Academic Careers in Higher Education, 2006).

If departments are to be competitive in attracting and retaining talented faculty and students, they must concern themselves with issues of intellectual community.

In this penultimate chapter, we focus on intellectual community as a synthesizing concept that pulls together our major themes: the formation of scholars, integration of research and teaching, and stewardship. Intellectual community is also essential to the new vision of apprenticeship set forward in the previous chapter. Our aim is to assert the importance of intellectual community, identify its central characteristics, describe strategies for fostering it, and explore its role in the various stages of scholarly formation.

The Importance of Intellectual Community

Paradoxically, given its importance, intellectual community is difficult to pinpoint. In fact, it is often most noticeable by its absence, as in Anna's story. However, it is also a subject that has prompted a good deal of attention outside academe. Today's literature on business and organizational theory abounds with advice about how to create a culture that promotes productivity, creativity, and the growth of knowledge. In *The Social Life of Information,* their well-known study of the information-technology industry, John Seely Brown and Paul Duguid (2000) point to the power of the social setting in a knowledge economy. In one example, they describe how Xerox customer service representatives routinely gathered with their colleagues over meals or breaks. It was in these settings—informal and social—that they solved problems, shared ideas, and provided support. Their range of experiences and wisdom meant that this unplanned, informal community of practitioners was far more valuable to the reps—and ultimately to the company—than their formal training and documentation.

Brown and Duguid see these kinds of communities—in which information has its "social life"—as essential to settings in which knowledge is the key currency of exchange. "Become a member of a community," they say, "engage in its practices, and you can acquire and make use of its knowledge and information. Remain an outsider, and these will remain indigestible" (2000, p. 126). Similarly, Barton Kunstler, writing about "hothouse" conditions that promote productivity and creativity, highlights the value of collective wisdom and practice: "Many of our greatest achievements occur precisely because a group of individuals acting in concert *elevated* the ethical, intellectual, creative, and social character of each group member" (2004, p. 3, Kunstler's italics).

The importance of culture and community has also become clear in academic settings, particularly in undergraduate education. Perhaps the most robust area of work has focused on "learning communities," various arrangements for linking courses and organizing intellectual work around unifying, cross-cutting themes. These arrangements have provided new opportunities for faculty to share ideas and work collaboratively, and for undergraduates to engage with each other and their instructors in new and deeper ways. In short, "[i]f the right social conditions, institutional structures, personal relationships, and opportunities for personal expression can be created, stimulated, and nurtured, then we can make our campuses more invigorating places to work and learn" (Tepper, 2001, p. 7).

When it comes to graduate education settings, the picture may not be so rosy. Indeed, some would claim that doctoral programs are settings in which independent intellect trumps intellectual community—and that the purpose of the PhD is to identify and cultivate individual genius. But our view is quite otherwise. Certainly there are examples of individual geniuses who seem to generate breathtaking new ideas alone. For these individuals—be they students or faculty—the approach has been simply to leave them alone. But those who flourish in true isolation are few and far between, and their experience is not likely to be a useful template for designing programs that must serve the large majority.[1]

And, in fact, individual achievements may not be as individual as they seem. As Kunstler continues, "The hothouse effect . . . asserts that such singular 'creatives' are more likely to emerge from within a group of skilled practitioners than from isolation" (2004, p. 3). The kind of reciprocal mentoring described in the previous chapter is a relationship in which ideas flow both ways; the collaborative settings described in Chapter Four, too, invite the lively exchange of ideas and feedback (think of the dissertation writing group, for instance) which characterizes intellectual community. The point is that for both novice and experienced scholars intellectual energy and passion are triggered by engagement with the field and its pressing questions— be that in the department or beyond (imagine a rolling conversation of the kind that characterizes the very best scholarly conferences and seminars). In this sense, intellectual community has a kind of chicken-and-egg quality: ideas are both magnets for and products of communities.

Characteristics of Intellectual Community

Throughout this volume we point to the need for multiple models, shaped by discipline, institutional setting, student interests, and faculty profiles. The same is true of intellectual community, which comes in many forms and flavors. And of course a program or department may have multiple communities and subcommunities. However, our work and the work of researchers in many fields suggest that there are certain qualities of communities that make them more vibrant, enriching, stimulating, welcoming, and more suited to the formation of scholars and to the knowledge-building agenda of graduate education.

Shared Purpose

Our CID partners emphasized one thing as most important for intellectual communities: shared purpose. Indeed, as a much earlier study points out, one of the ways "in which the academic department can be characterized as a community is in the degree to which the goals and purposes of the department seem to be clearly understood and, more important, fairly widely shared" (Hartnett, 1976, p. 73). That is, purpose is more than a shared agenda for how to operate; it is a community-wide commitment to help students develop into the best scholars possible so that they, in turn, may contribute to the growth and creation of knowledge.

It is no accident, in this regard, that intellectual community is one of the central commitments and achievements of the University of Nebraska mathematics department described in Chapter Three. Pressing themselves about their own purposes and goals, program faculty gave voice to the many "taken-for-granteds" in the department. The document they collaboratively produced reflects a powerful sense of shared responsibility and stewardship, the hallmarks of intellectual community. And no doubt the conversations leading to the document helped to forge intellectual community as well.

Diverse and Multigenerational

An intellectual community able to stimulate new ideas and development is one with an appreciation for the generative potential of multiple perspectives. Far from requiring agreement on everything, true intellectual exchange must include a wide range of opinions that can challenge and inform thinking. Not only, to use a phrase from Chapter One, is scholarship segregated likely to be scholarship impoverished; scholars who are segregated, who are not actively engaged in a community of diverse viewpoints and healthy debate, may find their work intellectually malnourished.

Departments that deliberately seek out a wide representation of backgrounds in their students and faculty are more likely to encourage diverse perspectives and ideas. Often, doctoral programs approach the topic of diversity as a concern for numbers of people who can be counted in different ways—and attention to access is a crucial agenda. But an equally important motivation for diversity is to ensure a wide range of viewpoints that enrich intellectual exchange. Every member of a community benefits from new and different ideas, and both individuals and the collective enterprise of knowledge building benefit from greater diversity.

In addition, a vibrant intellectual community is multigenerational—one in which students are integrated as junior colleagues. Students are in a distinctive position to contribute to intellectual work precisely because they bring fresh eyes. Research teams that include newer scholars who have yet to suffer that "hardening of the categories" that sometimes characterizes the work of more seasoned scholars benefit from creative ideas and angles on the topic. Indeed, one of the most significant findings of the CID is just how great a contribution students can make to the intellectual life of the department.

Flexible and Forgiving

The most productive intellectual community is one that provides opportunities for experimentation and risk taking. Learning, after all, means making mistakes and testing inchoate ideas. And failure, as Maureen Estevez learns from her mentor (in the story that ends the previous chapter), lies in "*not* breaking something or making a mistake." Mistakes, that is, can be a source of strength, not a waste of time or resources. Unfortunately, departments are often structured (and funded) in a way that leaves little time and few resources for projects that might not pan out, and in an academic culture that increasingly values "productivity," the need for reflection and thought is profoundly undervalued. Creating a space—literally and metaphorically—to try out new ideas, to "take a flyer," to play, and to step back and reflect on what has been learned is essential to intellectual community.

Respectful and Generous

Chapter Five points to the importance of apprenticeship relationships in fostering student learning. Likewise, an intellectual community depends in large measure on positive relationships. It is not necessary for each member of a department to enjoy every other person; everyone need not be best friends. But clearly intellectual community is strengthened by close ties, and the general atmosphere ought to be civil, respectful, generous. As an earlier study on doctoral education discovered, students want a "sense of community or togetherness," which the researchers described as "a social network of relationships as well as a professional, discipline-oriented, community of scholars" and a "spirit of cooperation, openness, and trust as opposed to an environment in which suspicion, jealousy, and a pervasive sense of paranoia seems to capture the essence of departmental activities" (Hartnett, 1976, p. 71). Without creating a climate of political correctness, treating one another respectfully—regardless of difference of opinions—is a necessary and valued aspect of a community. Indeed, without an atmosphere of respect, it is not possible to engage in genuine intellectual interaction. As one CID participant explained it, there must be "camaraderie built on engagement, if not agreement."

Members of a vibrant intellectual community are generous with their time, ideas, and feedback. Generosity derives from the assumption that all members of the community ought to be helped to succeed, and, indeed, that other community members bear a measure of responsibility for helping foster that success. Success and achievement are not a zero-sum game; one person's success does not come at the expense of another's. With this understanding in place, community members share opportunities ("Have you seen this grant application?"), intellectual resources ("Here are three articles you might find helpful"), and connections ("Let me introduce you to Professor Kim because you will find each other's work interesting"). Generosity seems to flourish when senior members of the community are confident in their own expertise, and assume the responsibility of stewards to mentor the next generation of scholars.

Each of these elements of intellectual community—shared purpose, diversity, flexibility, and generosity—advances knowledge, ideas, and the formation of scholars. Indeed, the overarching characteristic of intellectual community in doctoral education (or elsewhere) is that it is knowledge-centered, and the process of knowledge building, as we know from cognitive science, is a "fundamentally social" enterprise (Wenger, 1996, p. 3). This perspective implies a need to deliberately build and sustain intellectual community in the various settings available to doctoral education.

Activities That Foster Intellectual Communities

Intellectual community is not simply a matter of ambiance, and it does not happen by accident or by magic. Work is required. Faculty and students (who need not always wait for faculty) must look for and seize opportunities, putting in place whatever activities, strategies, and structures are most conducive to community in their setting. Occasionally this may mean developing new activities, but it may well be that reshaping existing elements and features of the program will bring significant benefits. In any event, the need is not only for ongoing nurturing and attention to the quality of intellectual community; it is for concrete actions that promote such community. What follows, then, are actions and activities that have been especially helpful in the diverse settings of the CID.

ENGAGING STUDENTS FULLY IN THE LIFE OF THE DEPARTMENT. Just as students must have increasingly independent opportunities to teach and do research (as described in Chapter Four), they can also become increasingly involved in other departmental activities as they develop as stewards. A department with a healthy intellectual community is marked by the level to which students are engaged in all of the activities of the department: serving on committees, hosting outside scholars, planning events, mentoring more junior students, and shaping policy. These activities are, in turn, routes into the larger discourse and, as Michael Oakeshott (1962, p. 198) once called it, an "unrehearsed intellectual adventure" that defines the department, and the field, as a community. Students (especially those at the beginning of their program) need explicit invitations and routines for such engagement. For instance, in response to the type of problem described in Anna's story at the beginning of this chapter, the history department at the University of Pittsburgh has instituted a rule for one of its seminar series: the first three questions must come from students. This small gesture speaks volumes about the department's commitment to true intellectual community.

COLLABORATIVE WORK ON CURRICULUM. Like the work that goes into a mission statement or set of departmental goals, curriculum design and course development can bring people together around questions of purpose. In particular, departments that work together to create core courses find that they quickly move from discussions of specific content to larger debates about what a member of their field should know. The faculty in the School of Education at the University of Colorado, for instance, engaged in lengthy discussions about what their students should know and be able to do. Although the process was often contentious, there is now a clear understanding—by both faculty and students—of what coursework and thus what content and skills are expected of all students in the school. This understanding informs an ongoing revision of other aspects of the doctoral program, including comprehensive exams and expectations for the dissertation (see the University of Colorado School of Education's Web page, Reforming Education Research Preparation, at gallery.carnegiefoundation.org/cid). In the University of Michigan chemistry department, doctoral students have opportunities to work with faculty on the design of the undergraduate curriculum, again a chance both to debate ideas and build professional community.

SHARING RESEARCH ACROSS BOUNDARIES. Every department has program areas, and these are often lively intellectual communities in themselves. But sometimes the impulse to focus inwardly means forgetting the opportunity for making connections across intellectual arenas. Thus, one strategy for creating intellectual community is to create research seminars that bridge specialties; such connections are especially important as disciplinary boundaries blur. Connections with others in different subareas or fields can lead to new collaborations. Inviting students to organize these events brings further advantages for both knowledge building and professional training.

OPENING CLASSROOM DOORS. Sharing research ideas—formally or informally—is important. So is knowing what happens in colleagues' classrooms. For graduate students, seeing how and what others teach is an opportunity not only to expand their pedagogical repertoire but also to observe different modes of explanation, different metaphors, and other models for transforming key ideas in the field. For faculty, observing colleagues and students not only communicates interest in their work, but provides a chance to reflect on one's own teaching. Departments in which classroom doors are open (metaphorically and otherwise) are settings for building a particular kind of intellectual community that some are calling a "teaching commons" (Huber and Hutchings, 2005).

ALLOWING RISK AND FAILURE. Important breakthroughs are more likely in settings that allow for risk taking and failure. But it is rare for a department to include these opportunities as an explicit part of the program. Typically, risk taking, if it is invited at all, is encouraged or modeled in individual classes, labs, or advising relationships. Maureen Estevez's story from Chapter Five highlights an example; she describes how her adviser knew when to step in and when to let her struggle, saying, "Your job is to make mistakes on a regular basis." But how can this permission to fail be systematically tapped as a source of learning? One answer was proposed by a CID historian: a seminar series in which speakers describe projects that didn't work, and how they proceeded from those failures, making visible a process that is otherwise invisible, mysterious, and even scary.

SETTING ASIDE TIME FOR REFLECTION. Many of our CID partners, especially in the neuroscience programs, use departmental retreats as a time to step away from day-to-day demands—for a few hours or a few days. Agendas vary from a focused attempt to solve a specific problem to a wide-ranging program that includes formal and informal opportunities to think, discuss, argue, and create. Several of the departments used the CID and its guiding questions of purpose and outcomes as an occasion to hold retreats for their faculty and students. We're well aware that retreats are not everyone's cup of tea, but in an academic culture increasingly captured by "productivity," setting aside time to think, and to build the community in which careful thought is possible, sends a powerful signal.

CREATING PHYSICAL SPACES FOR INTELLECTUAL COMMUNITY. Much of the research on organizational culture points to the value of informal interaction; Brown and Duguid call this "incidental learning" (2000, p. 72). And although such learning is, by definition, not something that can be planned, the chances that it will happen rise when there are places for informal exchange: coffee machines, kitchens, lounges, bulletin boards, and electronic spaces where department members can connect with others and stay apprised of program activities. In this spirit, the department of English at Texas A&M provides refreshments for students each week at a regular time and invites them to get together in a new lounge to talk about whatever issues are important to them.

SOCIAL EVENTS. Although intellectual community requires more than potlucks and softball games, social activities clearly strengthen a community that already has strong intellectual ties. These personal and informal connections not only create goodwill but build foundations for deeper intellectual engagement. In this spirit, many mathematics departments have a tradition of afternoon teas—regular, informal times when students and faculty gather to discuss and share ideas and problems. There is no agenda and everyone is welcome to participate. These occasions allow students to get to know faculty in a relaxed setting.

o

These activities, strategies, and structures are of course only a few of the ways to create and sustain intellectual community. The important point behind them all is that members of a department or program must think deliberately and act purposefully to put in place the elements that will build the kind of culture in which vibrant intellectual life is available to all its members.

Intellectual Community and the Formation of Scholars

Clearly there are many ways to promote intellectual community. But the point is not simply to create occasions but to ensure that these actually foster the intellectual and professional development of graduate students as stewards. "It is easy enough to increase the number of venues and opportunities for intellectual exchange," one CID team pointed out, "but how do we increase the intensity of the engagement with texts and ideas? It is easy enough to get people in a room to talk about their work to others, but how can we more deliberately foster intellectual identities and scholarly personae? Is doing more of the same going to produce a leap in quality?" (See the Washington University in St. Louis English department's Web page, Creating Intellectual Communities, at gallery.carnegiefoundation.org/cid.) These questions put the focus where it should be: on intellectual community as a means, not an end. Simply proliferating activities won't necessarily lead to greater intellectual engagement and development. Rather, these strategies must be linked to and evaluated in light of the outcomes they are intended to produce. With this in mind, and building on the notion of progressive development in Chapter Four, the final section of this chapter explores how intellectual community can advance scholarly formation at three points in the ongoing development of doctoral students.

Becoming Part of a Community

In response to the invitation to "tell us anything you would like us to know about your sense of belonging to a community," many of our graduate student survey respondents wrote eloquently about their experiences, both positive and negative. A student from an English department had this to say: "The sense of community at my institution was actually one of the deciding factors that led me to choose my program over similar programs at other institutions. Especially within my subfield, I find that my colleagues are ready and willing to help each other learn, to confer with each other about each other's current research, and to share our experiences and resources (especially when it comes to teaching). There isn't the sense of cutthroat competition I found at other institutions I visited when I was a prospective student. Overall, I'd say that the collegiality among graduate students enhances the learning environment my institution provides."

These words speak to the importance of intellectual community in the earliest stage of doctoral work—indeed, as an influence on the choice of program. Even if a robust intellectual community exists, there are always new members who need to be brought into the intellectual life of the department. With this challenge in mind, some programs have paid special attention to how students enter and become part of the community.

Of course students bring diverse backgrounds to their graduate work. "Socialization is not a static process in which the newcomers only receive the imprint of the organization," notes a well-known scholar of graduate education. "It is a dynamic process in which the individual newcomer brings experiences, values, and ideas into the organization" (Austin, 2002, p. 97). The challenge lies in finding ways to respect that background while ensuring that students meet the goals and outcomes of the program.

Several education and neuroscience programs focused their CID work on the first year, in part as a way to accommodate the wide diversity of experiences students bring to these programs. The University of Michigan School of Education has restructured its first-year experience to help ensure a smooth transition. The diversity of students' background, age, race, and academic preparation—a strength in an intellectual sense—makes this a challenge. "Our major tools for building community have been instituting a core curriculum for first-year students using a cohort approach." In addition to giving students a consistent and coherent experience of taking classes together and sharing new experiences, this approach is intended to "enrich students' common experiences prior to their engaging in deep specialization" (see the University of Michigan School of Education's Web page, Creating Intellectual Communities, at gallery.carnegiefoundation.org/cid). By addressing the academic and the social aspects of the first year, the education program hopes to reinforce students' connections to the community.

The University of Minnesota neuroscience program faced a similar challenge. When the program started in 1986, faculty members realized that they needed a way to bring together and train students from widely varying backgrounds. To address this need, students new to the program are required to participate in an intensive summer experience before they enter. The Itasca Neurobiology Course is five weeks long, with a new module each week. Faculty members rotate in each week for the new module, teaching in teams of two or three, often with post-docs or senior graduate students. The site is 200 miles from campus, so students and faculty work and live together, forging new collegial relationships during courses as well as recreational activities. "Nowhere else in the country can you walk along the shores of a pristine lake, take in a startling view of a pileated woodpecker and smell the fragrance of the Minnesota ladyslipper, and then sit down at an experimental station in which you evaluate generation of memory traces in a hippocampal slice or explore the synaptic organization of the leech ganglion," program organizers report. "At Itasca, strong bonds are formed between students and faculty both in and out of the lab. Indeed, sometimes the best discussions occur over the breakfast table or during canoe excursions on the lake." Reflecting on her experience, one student noted: "One of the most important aspects of the Itasca program is that it enabled me to cultivate relationships with current and future researchers. By being removed from the distractions of everyday life, it encouraged me to focus not only on neuroscience, but on how to collaborate with others in the scientific community" (see the University of Minnesota Graduate Program in Neuroscience's Web page, Itasca Neurobiology Course, at gallery.carnegiefoundation.org/cid).

Indeed, the program embodies many of the characteristics of powerful intellectual community described earlier in this chapter: a clear sense of purpose, opportunities for risk taking, dedicated physical space, social components, a multigenerational mix of people, and an atmosphere of respect and generosity. Evaluation of the program suggests that they are meeting their goals; for instance, "peer bonding carries over into the formation of study groups that correlate with success in the core curriculum."

Several CID programs have developed structured mentoring programs for entering students. As described earlier, the department of mathematics at USC is exploring the use of "mentoring triplets." New students are assigned both a faculty and senior graduate student mentor, ensuring two different points of access to the departmental community. Ideally, the resulting relationships will continue beyond the first year, as the entering student becomes a veteran and mentor for another beginning student.

Moving from Novice to Full Participant

Once students are acquainted with the departmental community, it is important to shift roles from passive recipient to more active contributor— or, as psychologist Jerome Bruner puts it, between "learning about" and "learning to be" (Brown and Duguid, 2000, p. 128). As observed in a survey of graduate students several decades ago, doctoral students "want to become part of the intellectual community rather than to remain

Table 6.1. Percentage of Students at Dissertation Stage Reporting Participation in Departmental Service Activities[2]

Played a formal role in faculty hiring (such as served on search committee)	16%
Played a formal role in graduate student admissions (such as on committee, hosted student)	31
Served on a departmental committee with faculty	36
Mentored undergraduate students	43
Part of an intellectual network that goes beyond my immediate classmates and includes colleagues senior or junior to myself	50
Mentored other graduate students	56
Gave or received feedback on ideas or work in progress to or from a fellow student	82

Source: *Carnegie Graduate Student Survey*

on its fringes and have a mere bowing acquaintance with scholars" (Heiss, 1967, p. 43). And this transition is a crucial one for all doctoral students as they take on and practice the skills and habits of mind they hope to develop within the intellectual communities they are part of.

So how does the transition occur? With this question in mind, we asked students on the CID survey about their engagement in departmental activities (see Table 6.1). Predictably, responses indicate that informal activities are most common, such as giving and receiving feedback from fellow students and mentoring other students. The good news is that students seem to have found ways to learn from one another. But there are missed opportunities as well. As these data suggest, departments could take better advantage of existing structures to involve students in more formal aspects of the community, like departmental committees on hiring and admission. These experiences can provide real practice with the full range of roles students will encounter as they move into professional settings, and can help move students to full participation in the community.

The data also suggest that whereas students are comfortable in student communities, many have not yet found ways to engage with faculty, formally or informally. One simple route to this end is to ask students about their experiences. Several CID departments had successful "town hall meetings"—open discussions that allowed students to share their experiences and offer feedback on the program. Both faculty and students report learning a great deal that they didn't expect from these meetings. This kind of interaction across roles and generations ensures that a community not only casts a wide net for good ideas but fosters students' development as full participants.

Finally, several CID programs have placed special emphasis on developing the professional and intellectual identities of students. Consider, for example, the Interdisciplinary Program in Neuroscience (IPN) at Georgetown University. With an eye toward reducing the sense of hierarchy that separates faculty and students, the program employs coursework, journal clubs, experiential learning, and "neurolunch," a forum for students to present research to a group of faculty and students, thereby bringing students into the larger disciplinary community of colleagues. Program leaders draw a direct connection between professional success and engagement in the disciplinary community: "The scientific process is not the sole determinant of a neuroscientist's success. They must also . . . meet and share ideas with other researchers, promote the goals of the field and their personal aims to the government and private foundations to procure funding, educate the youth about opportunities for future careers in neuroscience, and raise awareness in the community about the public health issues that neuroscience research addresses" (see the Georgetown University Interdisciplinary Program in Neuroscience's Web page, Supporting Intellectual Community, at gallery .carnegiefoundation.org/cid). Each of the activities highlighted in Exhibit 6.1 helps to form students' professional identities while they are

---

○

Exhibit 6.1. Developing Professional Identity in the Interdisciplinary Program in Neuroscience at Georgetown University

Many of the expectations for an IPN doctoral candidate go beyond coursework and the dissertation. Each of the following activities (some of which are required) serves a clearly identified role in developing the student's professional identity.

- Participate (as a first-year student) in a mock NIH-style study section in which fellow students' mini-grant applications are reviewed according to a protocol that simulates a typical NIH grant review committee to understand the grant writing process and learn to give and take critique.

- Seek co-mentorship for thesis research to diversify sources of guidance and expertise and create interdisciplinary collaborations.

- Give an annual research seminar to the Georgetown community to promote communication between scientists, gain positive and negative feedback, and develop practical presentation skills.

- Write and apply for an extramural pre-doctoral fellowship to attain skills in defending research aims, developing a sound research plan, and responding to critiques.

- Attend and contribute to seminars and journal clubs with outside speakers to expand knowledge and expertise, promote collaboration, and develop networking skills.

- Wrestle with ethical dilemmas in the responsible conduct of science in the "Skills and Ethics to Survive and Thrive in Science" course to develop sound professional judgment. Thesis-level students participate as panelists, and revisit issues from a new vantage point.

- Present research abstracts at professional meetings to share research goals with fellow scientists, the public, and to develop networking and collaboration skills.

- Contribute to a discussion at "Tea-Time," a monthly informal student-faculty gathering in which a controversial topic, often with broader social implications, is on the table for discussion for purposes of becoming an ethical scientist and developing confidence in the student's own knowledge and values.

- Collaborate with the thesis mentor in giving a joint teaching presentation in the "Neuroscience Survey Course," in which first-year graduate students learn about the research topics being investigated in various labs to learn how to communicate complex science to relative novices.

- Teach (and potentially serve as course director) in a student-organized and student-directed "Disorders and Diseases of the Brain" course for undergraduates to develop teaching skills.

- Spend a summer conducting research in a laboratory at another institution (U.S. or abroad) to gain exposure to new techniques, environments, cultures, and research approaches, and to expand the student's network of professional contacts.

- Serve as representatives on program administration committees (admissions, curriculum, student advisory, executive) to gain understanding of program administration and develop leadership skills.

- Publish results in peer-reviewed scholarly journals to communicate ideas and work with the field at large.

Source: *K. Gale, e-mail to the authors, February 9, 2007*

○

still in a supportive learning environment. By taking on this kind of work before graduating, students are able to develop themselves as junior colleagues by playing an active role in the program's intellectual community.

From Department to Disciplinary and Professional Community

Although the department is the students' primary intellectual home, their work also takes shape in the larger context of the discipline or professional field. Thus, as students progress through doctoral programs, their experiences must continually broaden to encompass the larger intellectual community of their field, even as their particular interests may narrow and deepen.

One of the ways that students develop into scholars is through intellectual engagement with others beyond their immediate communities, and we were curious to know to what extent they see themselves participating in this kind of behavior. In the CID student survey, we asked respondents to review a list of common activities that connect students to the larger disciplinary community, and tell us in which activities they had participated. Figure 6.1 shows both the proportion of students who engage in what we consider minimally acceptable participation and the proportion who are more fully engaged in active disciplinary conversations. Well over half the students at the dissertation stage in all of the fields attend conferences and read journals, but far fewer see themselves as participants in broader networks. There is clearly room for more engagement. These kinds of connections and networks are essential to scholarly success, and programs committed to the development of stewards may look for ways to broaden access to such opportunities—and not only in the final stages of work.

Beyond these kinds of scholar-to-scholar connections, formation is advanced by occasions in which students can immerse themselves in other intellectual communities and institutional cultures. Students who have such opportunities are well positioned to make the transition to new professional settings. After all, a student who graduates from one department becomes a colleague in another, and it serves the interests of everyone—graduating students, hiring committees, and industry—if students have had an actual experience of life in one of the diverse organizational settings in which they are likely to work. Some disciplinary societies have focused on helping students make this transition, but the most extensive initiative was the Preparing Future Faculty (PFF) program, originally co-sponsored by the Council of Graduate Schools (CGS) and the Association of American Colleges and Universities (AAC&U).

Figure 6.1. Percentage of Students at Dissertation Stage Reporting Participation in Disciplinary Community Engagement Activities[3]

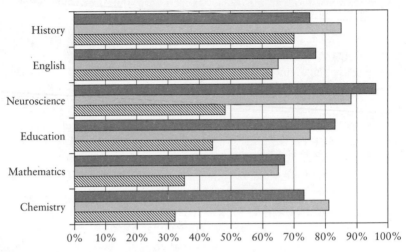

Source: *Carnegie Graduate Student Survey*

PFF is a national movement to transform the way aspiring faculty members are prepared for their careers. As described on its Web site, "PFF programs provide . . . students with opportunities to observe and experience faculty responsibilities at a variety of academic institutions with varying missions, diverse student bodies, and different expectations for faculty" (Preparing Future Faculty National Office, n.d.). The three main features of the project are: opportunities to experience the full range of responsibilities in settings other than students' home institutions; multiple mentors who give feedback on research, teaching, and service; and clustered institutions, including, for example, a doctoral institution, a liberal arts college, a community college, and a comprehensive university. The overall goal is to help students experience in authentic ways the full range of professional and scholarly behaviors expected of them in future positions before they have actually graduated.

Although the original emphasis of PFF was on preparation for academic positions, many universities expanded their activities to include preparation for work in business, government, and non-profit settings as well (often called Preparing Future Professionals). As with the CID, one of the significant contributions of such programs is to encourage faculty and students to think explicitly about connections between doctoral studies and future professional life. Students who participate in these activities have multiple opportunities to experience different types of institutions and communities, intellectual and otherwise, all of which contribute to their development as stewards of the discipline.

Ideally, by the end of their programs, with experiences like these under their belts, and with attention to intellectual community across the trajectory of their development, doctoral students will have made scholarly contributions to their field and developed qualities that make them generous, sought-after colleagues. They will be well positioned to meet the high expectations set forth in the job description that begins Chapter Four. Even more, they will be able to contribute to and create the larger intellectual and civic culture that is at the heart of our vision of stewardship. Donald Hall, a professor of English who has written widely about professional development, describes this vision beautifully in his essay "Collegiality and Graduate School Training." "Collegiality means responsible citizenship within our institutions, embracing the same qualities one would hope for in responsible citizens of our nation and globe: thoughtfulness, attentiveness to the needs of others, a willingness to listen carefully and engage in meaningful communication across and in spite of differences, an ability to work collaboratively to solve problems and set priorities, and, finally, a commitment to ethical treatment of others, and especially those in disempowered positions" (D. Hall, 2006).

Larger than the sum of its activities and structures, intellectual community is both a reflection and a product of the rich exchange of ideas and perspectives that characterizes scholarly life at its best. It is knowledge centered but also relationship based, and its importance lies in creating environments in which all qualified students can succeed in the fullest possible sense, as responsible stewards of their disciplines, academic citizens, and contributors to the larger society.

ENDNOTES

1. An example of how program structure affects students' opportunities for genuine intellectual community is the timing of funding. Fellowship money is often front-loaded and serves as an enticement for students to enter the

program. But this policy often has the effect of shielding graduate students from some of the very activities (for instance, working as teaching or research assistants) that serve to integrate them into the intellectual community of the department. The goal is to give them time to focus on their own scholarship, but an unintended consequence may be that they remain isolated from their peers and other scholars. Consequently, fellowship money might be better allocated in the later years, after students have established the intellectual connections that will allow them to succeed. Alternately, purposeful steps can be taken to include students in formative educational activities.

2. The student survey asked, "While pursuing doctoral studies, which of the following activities related to participating in your departmental community have you engaged in? (Check all that apply.)" Seven of the ten items on the list are shown in the table; it shows the proportion of students at the dissertation stage in each discipline who responded affirmatively.

3. The student survey asked, "While pursuing doctoral studies, which of the following activities related to participating in the broader disciplinary community have you engaged in? (Check all that apply.)" Three of the eight items are shown in the figure; it shows the proportion of students at the dissertation stage in each discipline who responded affirmatively.

7

A CALL TO ACTION

<hr>

There's no shortage of ideas about what *we need to change.*
We have to decide whether or not we want *to change.*

—Tony F. Chan[1]

WILLIAM JAMES FAMOUSLY LAMPOONED "the PhD octopus" a century
ago for its twisted grip on both individuals and institutions (James,
1903). Throughout the intervening years, "ideas about *what* we need to
change" have been widely trumpeted, and the cephalopod has morphed
in important ways. But the evolution must continue. Indeed, in view of
the fundamental transformations taking place in knowledge production
more generally, and within higher education in particular, doctoral education is due for a sea change.

The good news, as evidenced by the stories and examples in this volume, is that the talent to ride the next wave of reform is abundant. As
Kenneth Prewitt observes (and as we quoted in the epigraph to Chapter
Two), "The genius of American graduate education is that no one is in
charge" (Prewitt, 2006, p. 23). No single charismatic leader, no one initiative or project, no solitary organization or group, and no one silver-
bullet remedy can effect the kinds of changes required to take doctoral
education productively into the future. What is needed, rather, is purposeful action on many fronts by a full range of actors—each of whom
brings distinctive strengths (and limitations) as an agent of change. It is
by combining forces that those who care about doctoral education can
now move the enterprise forward, and this final chapter aims to speak
directly to readers who are ready to push ahead.

The Argument

This volume is predicated on a belief that doctoral education provides a uniquely productive seedbed for the next generation of intellectual leaders, and that its continuing health is therefore a matter of extraordinarily high stakes. Our central themes—formation, the integration of teaching and research, intellectual community, and stewardship—reflect the many rich deliberations and lessons from the Carnegie Initiative on the Doctorate, and can, we believe, guide the efforts of those who share our sense that change is not a choice but an imperative.

Our vision of the change that is needed often takes the form of "existence proofs," with special attention to the power of local deliberations among faculty and students. In this spirit, our stories are about those who have examined the purposes of their doctoral programs, evaluated their current program elements, and acted to align their goals and practices more closely. Often the stories are incomplete, and their themes are not all happy ones; some innovations are a success, others are not, and in many cases the jury is still out. Our message to readers is less about particular innovations, successful or not, than about a commitment to the ongoing process of improvement: deliberating about purpose, asking questions about effectiveness, gathering evidence to shape improvements over time, and taking action. Traditionally, graduate education has had few habits and tools for such work, but there are now more and more doctoral settings in which the skills and commitments of scholarship are being turned toward the work of education itself. This emerging culture of evidence promises real advances as doctoral education moves into the coming century.

But evidence is not enough. To change directions in a meaningful way, one needs a compass, and this volume is built around a number of guiding principles; first among them is the concept of scholarly formation along broad, integrative lines. In a context where research so easily trumps teaching, we envision developing each novice scholar into a powerful teacher and researcher simultaneously through repeated practice that moves the student along both trajectories. Other aspects of formation are essential as well, including service, leadership, and ethical practice. And there must be attention to connections among these areas, to the value of combining broad integrative experiences with deep and focused ones, and to the power of collaborative approaches.

With these principles in view, it becomes clear that the traditional apprenticeship model must be enlarged and modified to create a new signature pedagogy for the formation of stewards. Drawing from developments that are evident in some settings and disciplines but not in others, we call for more purposeful, coordinated, multigenerational forms of mentoring and advising, with greater collective responsibility for the student experience. These changes, in turn, can help foster a sense of intellectual community that is at least as important as the curriculum in forming scholars for the various settings in which they will do their work. Indeed, the new apprenticeships can flourish only within vibrant multigenerational learning communities, and when accompanied with well-planned, intentional approaches to doctoral education that are generally missing now. As Carnegie president Lee S. Shulman put it at one of the CID convenings: "The new apprenticeship within a functioning intellectual and moral community: that's the deal."

The challenges to this vision of the possible are daunting—and mostly well known. As so many observers of U.S. doctoral education have opined, there are powerful forces built into the system of faculty rewards and institutional funding that work against the integrative model of scholarly formation and stewardship presented here. Moreover, much of what is needed runs counter to a kind of studied casualness that typically characterizes doctoral education. In this sense, the changes most needed entail not simply a new practice here and there, but deeper cultural transformations.

And of course those transformations must be shaped in light of varied circumstances. There is no single formula or model that will be appropriate in the many different disciplinary and institutional settings in which doctoral education takes place, or that will be applicable to the diversity of students those settings serve. Certainly there is no "one size fits all" curriculum. Indeed, we see this volume as a celebration of the diversity of curricular structures and program elements that support student formation in very different contexts. What works in chemistry may not work in history (though disciplines can clearly learn from one another), and Indiana University presents quite different challenges and opportunities for doctoral education than those at Florida International University. In this spirit, the argument of this volume is that the most important, lasting transformations of doctoral education must be shaped and led by those—faculty, students, and others—who live it every day.

Answering the Call

If readers have found our argument on target, and yet are not inspired to take up the reins of leadership for change, we have missed the mark. To be sure, change requires collective, cooperative action, and one encouraging attribute of the vision set forth in this volume is that the same cast of characters moves from one role to another. The graduate students of the morning are the faculty and alumni of the afternoon. And the great majority of administrators, funders, and accreditors were once graduate students and faculty. So the perspectives, habits of mind, and opportunities to take leadership in service of improving doctoral education are abundant and connected over time. There is strength in the intersection of multiple lenses for understanding the problems and opportunities facing doctoral education.

But a collective is first a group of willing individuals galvanized to action through their own unique leadership opportunities. What, then, can each do? Clearly, the vision laid out in this volume carries with it starring roles for doctoral students and faculty. There are important roles as well for the supporting cast of campus administrators, professional societies, funders, and accreditors. We have recommendations for each of these groups.

Students

Like many social institutions, education (at whatever level) tends to be a kind of closed system; the pieces interlock in ways that make them hard to dislodge. One of the special strengths that graduate students can bring to the process of change, and to their own educational experiences (which are, after all, processes of change), is that they are not yet fully inside the system. Sometimes this sense of being outside may be a source of anxiety and frustration, but it is also a position of strength. Students bring fresh lenses, different perspectives and passions, and an ability to ask unexpected questions about what others may take for granted. As we have noted throughout this volume, doctoral students have been powerful forces for change in the CID.

In this spirit, we urge students to become involved in—and to help lead—a process of self-study and deliberation about the doctoral program they are part of: how it works, how well, and how it must change to meet new challenges. Be part of that process. Join others in the work. You have much to offer by becoming involved.

Moreover, we urge students to find occasions and intellectual communities in which they can engage, repeatedly, the questions that should be fundamental for any scholar: Why do you want to study this field? What is it about the field that ignites your passion? What do you expect from graduate school? What do you need and want to learn? How can you create such opportunities for yourself and others?

Doctoral students who take this kind of intentional approach to their own learning will, in turn, reap benefits from the leadership experience and the satisfaction of being part of something larger. Deliberation with others about the educational process and how it can and should work will make you a better learner—now, as you complete your doctoral program, and in the future as you move into your chosen professional setting as a scholar. Of course it is true that faculty members, individually and collectively, are responsible for creating a culture and a set of experiences in which students develop the necessary knowledge, skills, and values to become responsible stewards. But ultimately you must take charge of your own learning. Expert learners are purposeful about their own learning, intentional about goals and how to reach them, and good at monitoring their own progress. Seek out powerful learning opportunities; look for ways to nudge existing elements and requirements in directions that make them more progressive, integrative, and collaborative. Actively cultivate multiple mentoring relationships and look for ways to make their benefits reciprocal. Ask to be involved in department committees; to host a visiting speaker, or to organize an seminar. Above all, recall that graduate school is one stage of a longer voyage of formation which the learner herself must steer.

Faculty

The word *faculty* refers both to individuals and the collective, corporate entity. Both have the power to shape the character and quality of the graduate student experience, for better or worse. Faculty are role models, program designers and implementers, mentors, and advisers. As such they are, arguably, more "in charge" (echoing Prewitt) of doctoral education and its future than any other single group. What actions, then, can faculty members, collectively and individually, contribute to its improvement?

First and foremost, we urge faculty to see the doctoral education experience through the eyes of a student. Ask yourself the questions about your doctoral program that you would expect a student to ask. And ask students themselves! As we discovered in the CID, faculty perceptions can be quite at odds with the student experience. These disjunctures are invitations (sometimes urgent ones) to inquiry, deliberation, and creative action. Thus, we encourage you to turn your scholarly lenses on the experience of students in your programs. This might mean careful one-on-one conversations, more systematic surveys and focus groups, or regular town meetings where students are seriously listened to. You may be surprised at what you see and hear.

Further, we urge faculty to have the difficult conversations about purpose without which no amount of information can guide improvement. Come together with colleagues to say clearly and explicitly what you individually and collectively seek for your students: What knowledge, skills, and dispositions should the program foster? What does stewardship look like in your field today—and how will it need to look different in the future? What is the purpose of each element of your program, and how are they meant to build on one another? What do you do to ensure that students develop an integrated professional identity that will carry them forward into the challenges of their scholarly life? How can apprenticeship be reframed to be more in keeping with visions of collective responsibility for student formation?

The answers to these questions should point to new directions. Time is limited, change is risky, and ignoring individual career goals is shortsighted. And yet, in the end, time spent inefficiently—enslaved by the status quo—is even more dangerous. And thus we say to faculty: no program, however successful, is perfect. Painful decisions may sometimes need to be made to jettison program elements that no longer serve their purpose. New elements, not currently imagined, may need to be added. Bold thought and action, driven by individual leadership and collective will, are the order of the day.

This vision requires your commitment to ongoing improvement in a culture of evidence. How is it possible to hit the target if there is no target? And if we have a target but don't keep score, how can we know the program is successful? The point here is not simply to collect information and present it to the administration as evidence to support the status quo or a funding request. The point is to use evidence to identify strengths and weaknesses in the program and to share results widely with the goal of challenging complacency and creating a context for positive change. The data will be open to multiple interpretations and challenges, but for scholars whose fundamental commitments are to hard questions and evidence, they cannot be ignored.

University Administrators

The hard work of changing the ingrained habits, customs, and cultures that surround doctoral student learning takes place at the department level as a collaborative effort between students and faculty, supported by program staff. But department chairs, deans, provosts, and presidents have special opportunities to promote boldness in thought and action. In particular, administrators have a duty to listen to the hard truths offered by programs that find their efforts at innovation stymied by larger forces outside their control—but under the university's purview.

For starters, administrators can seize every opportunity to send signals about the importance of the quality of doctoral education. This means speaking out, showing up, joining the conversation. Be a source of hard questions about purpose and practice. Do everything possible to raise the profile of departmental improvement initiatives and to feed that work by making good ideas from other settings available and visible. Building bridges among doctoral programs, on campus and beyond, is crucial because, as the CID demonstrated so well, programs can learn from one another.

Additionally, look for ways to connect successful innovations in undergraduate programs to promising areas of work at more advanced levels. As pointed out repeatedly in this volume, the former is increasingly a site for new approaches to learning, including the introduction to research, and there is much to be gained by sharing ideas about how to move students through a sequence of research activities that leads to creative, pathbreaking scholarly excellence. And of course joining a national project like the Carnegie Initiative on the Doctorate can be a route to new energy, creativity, and prestige—sometimes also to new funding. Even small amounts of money can catalyze serious efforts.

Remember, too, that funding is only one of the rewards that administrators can provide. Visibility is another. As an administrator, you can support promising directions by highlighting them with trustees and with other leaders on campus. Often you are a doorway to funding opportunities, to visibility, to prestige.

Administrators can contribute to this work by demanding accountability, as well. Bring resources, yes, and also ask for results. Departmental reviews should, for instance, be a time for serious deliberation based on evidence, and administrators can create a market for data, working "the demand side." Be clear about how the impact of improvement efforts and innovations will be assessed. As you hold departments accountable for improving doctoral program quality, ask, too, how you will hold yourself responsible for providing resources to accomplish this.

The drive for excellence relies on both competitive energy and collaborative partnerships; using these strategies to reward and inspire innovation is the genius of great administration.

External Partners

A scholar's intellectual community goes well beyond the workplace to a wider set of colleagues and supporters: organized interest groups, such as professional societies, control the major public meetings and publications where scholarship is presented and judged; grant-making organizations have great influence as well; and accrediting bodies have serious oversight responsibilities. Each of these external partners has a role to play in shaping the future of doctoral education.

DISCIPLINARY SOCIETIES. Disciplinary societies have a special power to speak to both faculty and graduate students. Such groups reflect and shape the collective priorities of the field. Fortunately, many of these groups have been active supporters of efforts to bring issues of graduate education into the light, and to prompt and sponsor change—and their efforts can often be enhanced by joining forces with other organizations, from other fields, that are moving in similar directions. But more can be done.

Those who staff and lead these important organizations have unique opportunities to highlight the need for new thinking about doctoral education—be it through conference sessions and speakers, journals and newsletters, or special projects and convenings. Ask yourself how you can keep fresh thinking about doctoral education on the radar screen. Seek out provocative voices and give their ideas room to inspire and shape the debate. Look for ways to signal the emergence of a more balanced approach to scholarship—one that gives serious treatment to public service and teaching, as well as to research. Messages like these will be especially potent coming from organizations that have often been seen as privileging the scholarship of discovery over other academic work.

FUNDING AGENCIES AND GRANT-MAKING FOUNDATIONS. The combination of inside knowledge and outside perspective that funders typically bring to their efforts can be a powerful engine of change. Foundation program officers, as well as those who serve as external grant reviewers, should ask whether funding decisions are promoting new approaches to doctoral education or making these changes more difficult. How can grant guidelines encourage faculty investigators to plan for meaningful student participation? In the case of funding aimed at traditional research, guidelines might push the links with educational practices: How does new research on this or that topic affect the way doctoral students are brought into the field?

More generally, the need is for serious rapprochement between funders and higher education. As reported in a 2006 Carnegie Foundation study of the relationship between foundations and education, frustrations exist on both sides. Those in the funding business say that higher education is insulated in its interests, inward looking, and unaccountable. Higher education leaders say that funders, in their rush for results, are too quick to abandon important agendas that require long-term investment. In short, those involved as funding seekers as well as givers would do well to build bridges, promote understanding, and find ways to ensure that innovations are undertaken in ways that create "educational capital" that others can build on (Bacchetti and Ehrlich, 2006).

ACCREDITORS. Accrediting agencies derive their power from the universities, disciplines, and faculty that they serve. In a real sense, they provide a form of peer review, making sure that institutions deliver what they promise with an appropriate level of quality. Thus, external accreditors can challenge practices in ways that are often difficult for internal leaders to do.

Over the last decade or so, accreditation has put special emphasis on the need for evidence of student learning, but this emphasis has been felt primarily in the undergraduate arena. Now the message is beginning to move to graduate education, as it should. Thus, to those who run and participate in the accreditation process, we say intensify and follow through on the emerging focus on graduate education. Ask institutions to respond to questions regarding graduate student learning, and demand clarity about goals, practices, and assessments of learning. In these ways, accreditation can make a real difference in moving toward the model of self-reflection and continuous improvement advocated in this volume.

The Need to Pull Together

Of course, any program can be improved, and most observers would agree that it is laudable to focus on improvement. On the other hand, time and resources are limited. In the absence of some acute crisis or sudden windfall, it is unusual for a department to engage in a sustained review aimed at program change.

What is the origin of this low priority? We have pointed to promising developments throughout this volume, and pockets of innovation are apparent at all levels of higher education today. But hard truths must be acknowledged. Faculty enter academe because of a desire to advance knowledge and teach young minds; they are passionate about their fields and committed to their students. But along the way many slide into less noble, more pragmatic, and, yes, selfish motives tied up with questions of prestige, funding, and their own advancement. Taking a leadership role in evaluating and redesigning the doctoral program may seem to be a thankless burden, coming at considerable personal expense.

Given the institutional expectations of faculty and their own earlier development, it is not surprising that self-interested attitudes take hold, and service "opportunities" are viewed with skepticism and resistance. There is no point in shutting one's eyes to these realities. On the contrary, we must ask how these "real world" dynamics connect with a call for fundamental rethinking of the PhD. Our answer is that self-interest can in fact be served by investing one's time and mental energy in the quality of the program.

Every doctoral program is in a competitive situation when it comes to attracting and retaining faculty and graduate students. Programs also compete, both locally and nationally, for funding that is growing ever more difficult to secure. In this atmosphere, relatively small differences in the character and quality of the doctoral program will give departments a significant advantage with regard to funding and recruiting, and thus to scholarly productivity and prestige. Programs that have evidence about their effectiveness will surely have the competitive edge. The benefits are cyclical.

Consider, for example, a further theme in the story of Maureen Estevez told at the end of Chapter Five. While celebrating her own good fortune in finding dedicated mentors, Estevez notes that many of her fellow doctoral students feel that they are valued primarily as "cheap labor." Faculty need to do their own research, to publish, to be productive in ways that their fields reward. "What the mentor fails to realize is the long-term benefit (particularly in publications) of investing in the student's welfare," she says. "Yes, in the short term, investing in developing a quality relationship with the student is a big sacrifice of time and energy without immediate publication results. However, in the long term it pays off . . . and many mentors fail to realize this." Citing the example of her own adviser, Carter Cornwall, Estevez writes that he has "such good relationships with his former students that they have gone on to collaborate with him. They include him on projects and publish papers with him. He has generated probably two or three times the number of publications per year (often in prestigious journals) through collaborations with his former students who are now Principal Investigators in other institutions. Had Carter not sacrificed the energy and time to develop those good relationships, he would probably not have those collaborations now, and would not have near the number of yearly publications" (M. Estevez, e-mail to the authors, March 2, 2007).

And on it goes. Much-published, high-visibility faculty attract outstanding students, and the converse is also true; outstanding graduate students attract better faculty and, over a period of time, outstanding graduates enhance the prestige of the whole department.

As one CID faculty participant observed, his department's involvement in the kind of deliberation and reform championed by the CID "has been and will continue to be a valuable catalyst for self-examination, creative thinking and innovation. . . . That's the only reason why I've stuck with it. I can see that there are a number of positive changes."[2] As this comment makes clear, the goal is not utopia but continuing changes that make a real difference for real people as they pull together for improvement.

Unfinished Business

The CID was conceived as a five-year effort, and the years sped by. As we look back on the planning, convening, site visits, data gathering, analysis, and writing, we are struck by how much transpired during that time, not only for us on the leadership team, of course, but for the eighty-four participating departments, many of which made significant changes. That said, improvement is an ongoing imperative, not something about which one simply declares victory and goes home. Indeed, one of the phrases that took hold in the project was "hard things not yet done." In particular, as we look ahead we see hard but fascinating agendas for future investigation—by faculty in their own classrooms and laboratories, by students as they reflect on their educational experiences, and by those seeking to shape and reshape programs to meet emerging challenges. Five sets of issues merit special mention.

First are the **pedagogies of research.** The capacity to engage in careful, creative, groundbreaking inquiry is arguably the acid test in doctoral education; it is what every faculty member most wants to see and most values in her students. But, ironically, not much is known about how to foster this capacity for excellence in research and scholarship. Though important innovations are increasingly in evidence (the use of multiple research mentors, for instance, and the introduction of authentic research opportunities much earlier in students' development), the process through which learners develop expertise as researchers calls out for more systematic study. Insights from cognitive science about novice and expert learners may well be relevant (see, for instance, Bransford and others, 2000; Dreyfus, Dreyfus, and Athanasiou, 1986; Wineburg, 2001). How do novices learn to ask good questions, and to refine their questions as they work toward a research design and scholarly agenda? How do novices' questions differ from those of experts? How does one teach intellectual risk taking? Could doctoral students' work with undergraduates in the classroom or other settings (that is, as novice teachers) be used to sharpen their skills as novice researchers?

As one of the external reviewers of a draft of this volume pointed out, these are questions that call out for fundamental definitional work: What do we mean when we say a question is "interesting" or "good"? What are its characteristic features, and how can we teach, model, or otherwise encourage our students to develop proficiency in asking them? And how, we would add, do we help students distinguish between bold, creative scholarship and sloppy thinking? What skills do students need in order to distinguish between these two? How do they learn to navigate scholarly careers in settings that are increasingly characterized by two countervailing forces—one that rewards and encourages innovative, breakthrough work, and one that is profoundly conservative, associated with peer review, extramural funding protocols, and tenure and promotion standards that, in practice if not principle, almost always weigh quantity more highly than impact?[3] And, to further complicate matters, how does the disciplinary context shape the process of problem finding, question formulation, and research design? How does a good question in chemistry differ from one in history or anthropology?

Additionally, there are questions about which contexts and strategies most effectively prepare researchers. A number of scholars have begun asking about how to teach creative thinking in doctoral education, and to investigate the relationship between expertise and innovation (for example, Bargar and Duncan, 1982; Loehle, 1990; Lovitts, 2005a; Paulovich, 1993). What lessons can be drawn from professional schools—for example, medical educators making extensive use of simulations—about how to help students become more sophisticated researchers? When should students learn from observation and carefully constructed assignments, and when is it necessary to leap into the thick of things, to try, and to risk failure?

Looming large here are questions about the dissertation, an area that CID departments mostly declined to tackle. How might the capstone experience of the PhD be reshaped to encourage more integrative thinking? With a number of practice-based fields (education, nursing, social work, and others) moving to establish doctoral programs, the time is ripe to break the dissertation mold and find forms better matched to the functions of scholarly life in diverse professional settings.

A second related set of issues focuses on what many educators see as a growing tension between **disciplinary and interdisciplinary scholarship.** Indeed, the relative importance of these two ways of framing intellectual work was a proverbial bone of contention in many discussions within the CID. Why, we were asked, would we build a program to rethink the PhD largely around fields that are traditionally discipline-based (though two of our six fields, neuroscience and education, are certainly not)? While in cooler moments most would acknowledge that the focus on discipline versus interdiscipline is not an either-or, the topic has a way of heating up. Consider, for instance, this comment from E. O. Wilson in his work on "consilience": "Our most productive scientists, installed in million dollar laboratories, have no time to think about the big picture, and see little profit in it. . . . We should not be surprised, therefore, to find physicists who do not know what a gene is, and biologists who guess that string theory has something to do with violins" (Wilson, 1998, p. 56).

Hyperbole or not, such views bring into focus the need for further work about how to balance competing goods. The PhD is meant to go deep, but doctoral education must also get smarter about moving students toward the capacity for broad thinking. The Association of American Universities describes "the need for new combinations of disciplinary knowledge and research methods to solve new and complex problems" (2005, p. 1). Catharine Stimpson, dean of the graduate school at New York University, has called for "general education for doctoral education" (2002). What would that look like? What general knowledge should stewards possess—about their own field and about the larger intellectual landscape in which that field exists? And what is the right balance between breadth and depth, between knowing one thing in all its nuance and complexity, and knowing its broader interdisciplinary context? Must the former be acquired before the latter? How do scholars learn to move back and forth between levels and contexts? How strong a disciplinary foundation does a student need in order to productively contribute to an interdisciplinary question? At what point are scholars too hardened to benefit from cross-disciplinary interactions? What communication skills are necessary to make such contributions, and what is the role of doctoral education's social setting in making possible this kind of rhythm and range?

Which brings us to questions about **the culture of doctoral education.** This volume argues that although the formal curriculum and program elements of doctoral education are critical, its more general ethos and spirit—what we call intellectual community—are at least as powerfully formative. This assertion brings with it a whole host of intriguing questions for further study. For starters, doctoral education would benefit from the kind of fine-grained ethnographic mapping and analysis that have been brought to undergraduate education (think for instance of *My Freshman Year: What a Professor Learned by Becoming a Student*, by Rebekah Nathan [2005]), and to other kinds of knowledge-building settings (for instance Sharon Traweek's study of the culture of high energy physics, *Beamtimes and Lifetimes*, which examines life at the Stanford Linear Accelerator [1988]). What are the daily practices, habits, values, and rituals that define the intellectual community of a graduate program, and how do those play out in the work and lives of students? How do these practices and dynamics differ by field (as documented by Janet Donald's study of approaches to thinking in different disciplines [2002], and Tony Becher and Paul Trowler's work on "academic tribes" [2001])? What lenses might different fields bring to questions about intellectual community: What could an ethicist tell us? An historian of science? A scholar of women's studies? A systems analyst? How does intellectual community develop differently in fields dedicated to practice (education is clearly one example) as opposed to those aimed at more theoretical and conceptual work?

More careful exploration of the cultures of doctoral education would also bring into further focus the dynamics of apprenticeship as envisioned in Chapter Five. We recommend multiple mentors and advisers, for instance, and our argument is for much more shared, collective responsibility for student learning. How do groups learn to assume and exercise collective responsibility? What are the most important points in the student's trajectory—critical transitions, for example—when the department should be particularly mindful of the need to exercise this kind of responsibility? Under what conditions do multiple mentors interfere with productive apprenticeship learning? Where does collective responsibility leave off and bureaucracy begin?

In the CID we talked with numerous doctoral students who told us that participation in departmental deliberations (and CID convenings) was a uniquely empowering experience that affected the way they went about their scholarly pursuits. What are the dynamics of these changes, and how could academe harness them more intentionally? How can students be more active, equal shapers of academic culture, and what are the limits and dangers of this shift?

One topic that emerged very little in the CID's work was the role of technology in creating and sustaining intellectual community, and this is an area that would surely benefit from a look at other settings that employ technology for knowledge building and exchange. One thinks of the technology industry itself, certainly, but also of the large-scale online communities that have been growing up around computer games—an especially interesting phenomenon since it is, increasingly, one with which today's and tomorrow's doctoral students have personal experience. As products of a high-tech culture, students now bring habits of interaction, community building, and knowledge exchange that are radically different from those traditional to academe (Brown, 2006). What does this mean for doctoral program design? What should it mean?

A fourth set of issues centers on the changing **backgrounds and identities of doctoral students.** The trends in this direction have been taking shape for several decades now, as suggested in Chapter Two, and there's no single pattern. Some fields are attracting more women, some fewer; some bring in larger numbers of international students, some fewer. And clearly the imperative to bring more students of color to PhD work is ever more urgent, even as the courts put limits on how this can be done. This is not the place to look in detail at demographic data, but rather to underline the more general point that the doctoral student population of the future will and should be more diverse in all kinds of ways that matter to learning—and not in neat pigeonholed ways. Indeed, as the student profile diversifies, new models of apprenticeship and more varied approaches to intellectual community will need to be devised and studied. What might these look like? What is the right balance between individualized approaches and the need for common core knowledge of the field and a shared experience of formation?

This issue has other dimensions as well. Currently (and this was largely true in the CID), doctoral education in most fields is a full-time venture—and this is the optimum arrangement in our view. But it's also true that many full-time doctoral students are working outside jobs to make ends meet, and part-time study (be it official or de facto) may become increasingly common. Arguably, even the sciences will need to find new, part-time models of doctoral education if there is to be any hope at all of increasing the size of the U.S. labor force in the sciences and engineering. And new ways to bring part-time students into true intellectual community must be invented and tested.

But intellectual community is not the only kind that matters. Thanks in part to support from the Sloan Foundation, many research university campuses have been exploring more family-friendly policies for faculty and (increasingly) graduate students. To take just one example (in the news even as we complete this manuscript), Princeton University has announced "a package of new benefits" aimed at giving graduate students more maneuvering room as they seek to balance parenthood and professional development. Meanwhile, scholars at the University of California are working on an in-depth study of graduate students' attitudes that may provide evidence that will push institutions further in this regard. "The biggest problem," says one such scholar, "is that academia has a structure that is still full-time or no time" (Jaschik, 2007).

Our fifth and last set of questions deals with **assessment.** The term itself raises hackles, we are aware, especially in today's climate of accountability, where assessment may seem more like an instrument of external, bureaucratic oversight than a tool for learning. But making judgments about the quality and character of students' progress has always been central to teaching and learning, and more systematic attention to assessment is clearly an agenda for doctoral programs as it is for other levels of education. It is hard work, and it deserves thoughtful, careful attention.

First, there are questions about the assessment of individual students. Consider, for example, the use of the professional portfolio described in Chapter Three. As experience with portfolios grows, questions about their design and use will be ripe for closer examination (for example, see Cyr and Muth, 2006). What combinations of elements and artifacts provide the most reliable and telling window on students' learning at various points on the doctoral trajectory? What is the impact of the portfolio on students' capacity for self-reflection and direction? Can portfolios stand on their own or might they be better used as the basis for an extended interview with students? How might the portfolios developed by history students look different from those of students in the natural sciences? Of course portfolios are simply a case in point. Doctoral education would benefit from efforts to develop and pilot new tools and instruments for assessing the full spectrum of outcomes captured in the notion of formation—that is, not simply in the development of knowledge and skills, but in the growth of professional identity and values.

Second, there are questions about assessing the educational value of particular program elements. Does the qualifying exam as currently constituted teach what it is intended to teach? Do collaborative dissertations teach students more or less about how to conduct research than solo-authored efforts? These are a subset of a vast array of questions about the pedagogy of research, some of which are mentioned earlier in this chapter.

Third, there are questions about the assessment of program effectiveness. Indeed, the CID was largely focused in this direction, encouraging departments to ask themselves hard questions about their purposes and impact. Such work is at the very heart of stewardship. Many of the CID departments developed surveys to explore students' experiences more systematically, and one can certainly imagine future work to refine these instruments and perhaps to share them across settings. But much more can be done, and doctoral programs might look to undergraduate education for examples. Consider the recent study at the University of Washington, where two scholars followed 304 entering freshmen and transfer students as they moved through the college experience from fall 1999 to spring 2003, looking at their learning in six areas through multiple lenses and data sources, including interviews, focus groups, portfolios, and surveys (Beyer, Gillmore, and Fisher, 2007). While there have been national studies of doctoral students (for example, Nyquist and others, 1999), and of graduates (for example, Nerad, 2000; Nerad and Cerny, 1999) that take this longitudinal view, most doctoral programs have not looked systematically at the trajectories of their students over time.

Of course (we hear readers muttering at this point) time is scarce, and the incentives at work in research universities make the agendas described here a stretch. Some of them—such as large-scale, longitudinal studies of students—clearly require special expertise and additional resources. But much of what we are proposing in these five areas for further study invites and, in fact, demands involvement by regular faculty members, who are, after all, in the best position to ask questions about their students' progress toward scholarly expertise. The idea is not to turn historians or neuroscientists into educational researchers but to attend more closely to what can be learned in one's own local setting using the tools and approaches that make sense in that setting. Doing so is part and parcel of good stewardship.

And those who take up these agendas will be in good company. Over the last decade, growing numbers of faculty, in a full range of fields, have come to see teaching as challenging, intellectual work. These scholars of teaching and learning are turning their habits of inquiry on their own students: identifying questions about what and how their students are learning, and sharing what they find with colleagues who can build on these insights. Such investigations have the potential to transform higher education by making the private work of the classroom (or laboratory or other setting) visible, talked about, studied, built upon, and valued— conditions for ongoing improvement in any complex enterprise (Huber and Hutchings, 2005).

Thus far the scholarship of teaching and learning has focused largely on undergraduate education, but those who work with graduate students can both learn from and contribute to this growing movement.

In particular, work on doctoral education can bring questions about how the field itself is conceived and what it means to know the field deeply more fully into the picture. Such questions are in part empirical, aimed at exploring what works; but, perhaps more importantly, they are normative, raising issues about what could and should be, about values and purposes.

Remembering Why

Over the five years of the Carnegie Initiative on the Doctorate, we talked to hundreds of individuals from scores of programs. We heard about what was right and what was wrong with doctoral education, about progress and obstacles, about money, space, administrators, and time. But most importantly, and through it all, we heard about people, and especially about students. As biologist Crispin Taylor puts it in an essay written for the CID, "If we start with the assumption that doctoral education is not only about the discipline advancing knowledge but also about the people—all of the people—who are engaged in these activities, we would examine the adequacy of doctoral programs . . . from the perspective of the programs' major constituent: the everyman-everywoman doctoral student" (Taylor, 2006, p. 46). Another essayist wrote: "If we do not take care of our students, we do not take care of our disciplines. If we do not take care of our disciplines, we fail as stewards of knowledge generation, which is, after all, why we were once students ourselves" (Prewitt, 2006, p. 32).

This is a book about ideas and about the action those ideas might put into play. But more than anything it is about the people whose passion, persistence, and intelligence take doctoral education forward day by day. In this spirit, we dedicate this volume to students past, present, and future whose scholarly formation is the key to so much that matters so deeply.

ENDNOTES

1. Chan is professor of mathematics and dean of the division of physical sciences at the University of California, Los Angeles. This quotation is from an essay written for the CID, "A Time for Change? The Mathematics Doctorate" (Chan, 2006, p. 121).

2. This was in response to the invitation on the faculty survey to provide any comments about the department's experiences with the Carnegie Initiative on the Doctorate. The full quote from this respondent was: "I'm still somewhat skeptical of the overall outcome of the CID. (Are we going to come

up with meaningful data as to the purpose of the PhD?) However, the CID has been and will continue to be a valuable catalyst for self-examination, creative thinking, and innovation within the program. That's the only reason why I've stuck with it. I can see that there are a number of positive changes. Could they have occurred without the CID? Possibly. But not likely."

3. We have borrowed liberally from language from one of our external reviewers, whose identity, alas, we do not know. We are grateful for their observations, cautions, and encouragement.

APPENDIX A: SUMMARY DESCRIPTION OF THE CARNEGIE INITIATIVE ON THE DOCTORATE

The 1990s saw several blue-ribbon commissions and sponsored research reports that offered recommendations to make doctoral education more effective.[1] In their wake it seemed timely to move from talk to action, and so The Carnegie Foundation for the Advancement of Teaching received funding from The Atlantic Philanthropies for a five-year project, which was called the Carnegie Initiative on the Doctorate, or the CID. The initiative, which was funded from 2001 through 2005, was designed to be an action project first and foremost, and secondarily a research project. Its objective was to support selected academic departments' efforts to improve the effectiveness of their doctoral programs. The project invited participating departments to create local solutions suited to what they themselves identified as their needs and problems.

The initiative began with a return to first principles, posing the question: *What is the purpose of doctoral education?* Recognizing that there are many local answers to this question, the Carnegie team began the project by proposing a more general answer: that the purpose of doctoral education, taken broadly, is to educate and prepare those who can be entrusted with the vigor, quality, and integrity of the field. This person is a scholar first and foremost, in the fullest sense of the term—someone who will creatively generate new knowledge, critically conserve valuable and useful ideas, and responsibly transform those understandings through writing, teaching, and application.

We chose the phrase *steward of the discipline* to describe a person who embodies such qualities. A fuller description of a steward's roles and skills, as well as the principles that guide a steward, the moral compass— can be found in the chapter "Preparing Stewards of the Discipline" in our first book, *Envisioning the Future of Doctoral Education: Preparing Stewards of the Discipline—Carnegie Essays on the Doctorate*, a compilation of commissioned essays (Golde and Walker, 2006, pp. 9–14).

Chemistry, education, English, history, mathematics, and neuroscience are the fields on which the CID concentrated. The CID was limited to only six disciplines in order to get to know each discipline very well, have a discipline-wide impact, and also to make meaningful comparisons among fields. In selecting these six we took several dimensions of variation into account—epistemological assumptions, disciplinary history, and career paths of PhD's. By the same token, doctoral education differs across the six fields of study on many measures—time to degree, time to career, attrition rate, funding patterns, demographic diversity of students, and scope and structure of a dissertation. We deliberately chose fields that grant a sizable number of doctorates. We also chose these six disciplines because they represent both core liberal arts fields and emergent interdisciplinary fields. They span the humanities, the professions, the physical and life sciences, and (through history and education) the social sciences.

Not only did we focus on disciplines, but we assumed that the key educational community is the academic department: the nexus of the discipline and the institution. The department is the key community for doctoral education, determining admissions, curriculum, and criteria for graduation. Every department is unique; its history and members of the department shape its culture, climate, and lived practices. Therefore the department is the best leverage point for affecting doctoral training.

The departments that participated in the CID engaged in a process of reflection, implementation of program changes, and assessment that led to the creation of stronger doctoral programs. Participating departments received no money; rather, the Foundation structured a process of deliberation and improvement. The project was relatively loosely framed; each department made its own decisions about how to structure their local process, which aspects of their doctoral program to focus on, particular practices they ought to implement, and evidence they ought to collect. The CID was largely a process of discovery, both for departments and for Carnegie. This book describes what we have learned about graduate education, and it builds on what the departments learned and shared. The next section of this Appendix describes, in broad terms, departmental work. It is followed by a section in which we describe the roles played by Carnegie staff.

Departmental Work

The lion's share of the work of the CID was done by the faculty and students in the participating programs. The most concentrated interactions between the departments and the CID staff were between January

2003 and December 2005. In all, there were eighty-four participating departments and programs. Originally, fifty were designated Partner Departments and thirty-four were called Allied Departments. After the fall of 2004 we no longer distinguished between categories of departments, and began to refer to all eighty-four as Participating Departments (a full list is in Appendix B). Forty-four universities, predominantly large public institutions, were part of the CID. They saw the CID as an opportunity to improve their standing in a prestige-conscious world. Many had more than one department participating, and we actively encouraged these universities to create synergy between departments and spread the lessons of the CID across campus.

Application and Selection

In the fall of 2002, a formal Invitation for Participation was mailed to departments at all doctoral-granting universities in North America, in four disciplines (chemistry, education, English, and mathematics), followed by a similar invitation in history and neuroscience in the spring of 2003. Departments interested in pursuing participation were invited to initiate a prescreening phone call with a member of the CID team. The ensuing conversations were an initial opportunity to get to know one another: the Foundation could learn about the circumstances of each department and what motivated them to consider participating in the CID, and the department could learn more about the approach the Foundation was taking. On the basis of these conversations, only those that might realistically be selected were sent formal application materials. The resulting proposals were quite short—a letter of no more than three pages that answered five questions:

1. How does the department meet the selection criteria? (See Exhibit A.1.)

2. Why is the department interested? Why is the department particularly suited for the project? Is this an auspicious time in the history of the department? Are there other projects it has already undertaken that provide relevant experience?

3. Who will serve as the leadership team? A project of this scope and nature demands the concerted attention of a team of departmental leaders, as well as the support of most faculty.

4. What mechanisms for engaging in ongoing deliberation are proposed?

5. Which critical issues will be the focus of the work? Although we expect the department to engage in a planning process before developing a detailed plan of action, each department will likely identify issues that are especially timely or high priority.

Once the departments were chosen, a Commitment to Engage was signed by the department chair. This outlined the mutual expectations and responsibilities of the department and the Foundation.

Departmental Deliberations and Changes

Participating departments were asked to identify a leadership team of faculty and students. Leadership teams were expected to deliberate seriously, to suggest and implement appropriate changes in the program, and to assess their efforts. This meant wrestling with hard questions: What are the characteristics of a steward of the discipline in our field? What are the desired skills, knowledge, and habits of mind of a PhD recipient from our program? What elements of the program foster those qualities? Which elements of the program should be retained, and which could be changed? Departments then proposed changes in their programs as design experiments that they were expected to document and assess.

○

Exhibit A.1. CID Selection Criteria

The ideal department will see participation in the CID as a way to focus its efforts or as an impetus to implement previously identified program changes in a timely and disciplined manner. By participating in the program the department gains access to some resources and opportunities, increases its visibility in the discipline and with prospective graduate students, and gains entrée into a community of like-minded departments, faculty, and students.

The characteristics of partner departments:

- Respected quality program
- Track record of placing PhD graduates in tenure-track faculty positions at doctorate-granting institutions
- Institutional support, including departmental and extra-departmental resources
- Critical mass of students and faculty willing to experiment, engage in assessment, and share outcomes

○

To provide a foundation for departmental deliberations, Carnegie commissioned sixteen essays—two or three for each of the six disciplines—on the current challenges and emerging opportunities for doctoral education. The essayists were asked to consider how a doctoral program should be structured to meet the challenges and opportunities they outlined. Written by leading scholars—stewards of their disciplines—the essays focus on ideas, not solely on technical details. The essays, and some commentaries on the collection, were included in *Envisioning the Future of Doctoral Education* (Golde and Walker, 2006).

The essays were not intended as definitive prescriptions but rather to provoke debate, and indeed they did. Some departments organized seminars around the essays. Additionally, many departments selected additional readings and materials to prompt their deliberations. Many engaged in self-assessment, surveying their students, faculty, and alumni; conducting focus groups; examining data on student trajectories (admissions, attrition, time to degree, and career placement); and sponsoring department-wide discussions at town hall meetings and retreats. The data that the departmental leadership teams collected were useful in identifying problem areas and crafting solutions.

Departmental efforts took a variety of forms: changes in program requirements, newly created experiences and opportunities, and changes in customary interactions and practices. Concrete innovations included: adding students to departmental committees, career panels featuring alumni, revised core courses and course requirements, changes in the qualifying exams, institution of annual reviews of students and portfolios of student work. Beyond these tangible program changes, CID departments reported a manifest change in the habits of mind of those who participated. Changes continue in many of the eighty-four departments.

Faculty members and graduate students who participated in the CID now approach their programs with an attitude of inquiry. The graduate students of the morning are the faculty of the afternoon, and so the students who played leadership roles in the CID will, we are confident, be more engaged and politically savvy faculty members by virtue of their involvement with the project. In the long run, changed habits of mind can outlast and make more difference than programmatic changes.

The changes that took place in departments might be characterized as incremental changes rather than radical reforms. Moreover, they were implemented at a measured pace, with respect for departmental decision making traditions, rather than being quick fixes slapped into place. In part because the Carnegie Foundation gave no money to departments (although some programs received modest institutional support for travel, graduate research assistants, or surveys), programmatic changes were a response to locally defined needs. Historically, there have been many reform initiatives in which the (often laudable) activities have been entirely predicated on external funding, but many do not persist or become institutionalized once the seed money disappears (Bacchetti and Ehrlich, 2006). We believe that changes prompted by the CID will stick because these were choices made by the department itself, rather than as a response to an external agent.

Going Public

Making knowledge public so that it can be critiqued and built upon is a fundamental tenet of scientific and scholarly inquiry. Likewise, in the service of disciplinary leadership, all CID departments were expected to share insights and lessons learned, initially within the CID circle and later with the disciplinary community and academic audience at large. Reporting was an exercise that flowed naturally from the work of the participating departments and furthered that work.

In addition to providing occasional updates of their work—on the phone, by e-mail, and in person—departments were asked to create Web pages about their work. We asked them to use an electronic Web authoring tool developed at the Foundation, the KEEP Toolkit (KEEP stands for Knowledge Exchange, Exhibition, and Presentation; see www.cfkeep .org). KEEP allows users to easily create *snapshots,* Web pages that provide a quick picture of work in progress and can include documents, photos, Web links, and video.

Snapshots have several advantages over conventional reports. They are multimedia depictions of work in progress that can be shared within and across departments; the KEEP Toolkit allows Carnegie to frame questions into common templates that help readers easily grasp the description and analysis of the departments' work; and snapshots can be modified and updated easily.

Many of the examples of departmental work described in this book are elaborated, often with source documents, in snapshots that are displayed in an electronic gallery (rather like multimedia pictures at an exhibition). We dubbed our gallery *EL CID,* the Electronic Library of the CID. The EL CID gallery contains snapshots depicting departmental innovations and exemplary elements from many participating departments (see gallery.carnegiefoundation.org/cid).

Departments also share their work widely within their disciplinary communities. Many faculty and students participated in workshops and panels at regional and national meetings. Writing about the work has appeared in a number of settings as well. Two conferences were sponsored by CID departments. In spring 2005 the University of Illinois hosted a meeting for neuroscience programs. In November 2005 the history and English departments at Texas A&M University cosponsored a conference called "Shifting Boundaries: The Humanities Doctorate in the Twenty-First Century."

The Role of the Foundation

For its part, the Carnegie Foundation was responsible for the central administration of the CID.[2] CID staff played three primary roles: facilitators, conveners, and researchers. The work of the Foundation was aided by a project advisory committee, a group of national leaders in graduate education.[3] This committee met annually to provide feedback and advice.

Facilitating and Encouraging

The Foundation's role as sponsors of the initiative was to encourage good work, but not to dictate process or outcomes for participating departments. The CID team established an overarching framework for the project, including milestones for progress and schedules for meeting those milestones. To inspire departmental deliberations, we also supplied materials for each discipline related to doctoral education. Rather than micromanaging the work in departments, CID staff were bridge builders, connecting the work underway among participating departments, and in other related initiatives. We recognized that initiatives like the CID do not exist in isolation. Within the life of the department, the initiative is just one of the many activities—both routine and special projects—that take the time, attention, and resources of faculty and students. Likewise, within the larger university community there are always many initiatives and new opportunities being created by the university itself, or fostered by external agents, such as the Carnegie Foundation. We therefore tried to balance setting realistic expectations with continually encouraging and catalyzing the work in the departments.

One strategy for doing so was to visit departments in order to encourage deliberation. In 2003 and 2004, CID staff visited sixty-five departments, including all partner departments. Twenty-six campuses were visited, nineteen of them twice. A Carnegie site visit was not a traditional "accountability" visit; often site visits from funders elicit a dog-and-pony show, glowing presentations by faculty and students who have been well-briefed on how to describe the department positively and to take care to avoid mentioning problems. When Carnegie staff visited a CID department, it was in a spirit of shared inquiry, and included frank discussions with groups of faculty and students. One goal was to increase the number of department members engaged with the CID. Another was to enlist the support and critical encouragement of key administrators. The site visit agenda was purposefully structured as a model of the process of deliberation.

Although the CID was focused on academic departments, as described earlier, the support of administrators was critical. Academic deans, provosts, and presidents all provided encouragement, acted as critical friends, supplied financial resources, and showcased many of the CID participating departments. Graduate deans were particular friends and allies. From the outset, we involved the graduate deans in the project through regular communication, presentations at the Council of Graduate Schools (CGS) meetings, and private conversations on the phone and during site visits. The CGS was an essential partner in facilitating and supporting CID efforts. The development and spread of CID activities will continue to be greatly tied to the efforts and encouragement of graduate deans.

The Foundation also hosted meetings and panels at disciplinary society meetings. These were opportunities to share updates on work in progress. From the beginning of the project we enjoyed close working relationships with the leadership of the relevant disciplinary societies: the American Chemical Society; the American Educational Research Association; the Modern Language Association and the Association of Departments of English; the American Historical Association; the American Mathematical Society; and the Society for Neuroscience and the Association of Neuroscience Departments and Programs. These societies generously provided time and space for CID participants to meet, as well as various outlets to make the work public.

Convening

The signature activity of many Carnegie Foundation programs is a *convening*. The term is meant to convey not only that these meetings are different from traditional conferences, but that the central feature is coming together. The CID was no exception. Much of the shared learning took place in three-day working meetings—a total of sixteen convenings over three years. (Carnegie provided departments with funding for travel to convenings.) Six discipline-specific convenings were held in summer 2003 or January 2004, and another six were held in the summer of 2004.

The discipline-specific convenings were limited to partner departments, and representatives of each campus attended the meeting for their field. The three summer 2005 convenings were cross-disciplinary and organized by themes: developing effective teachers, developing researchers and scholars, and supporting intellectual community. The cross-disciplinary convenings were open to all participating departments (departments were limited to attending one of them) and forty-four departments were included.

Each campus team of faculty and graduate students was limited to two or three participants, so the groups stayed small. We also invited observers—graduate deans, disciplinary society leaders, and leaders from foundations and agencies—to participate in each of the convenings. Many participants attended more than one convening over the years. Returning participants were great resources and helped newcomers learn the ropes. In all, over 260 people came to a CID convening: about 125 faculty members, 100 students, and thirty-five observers.

Each convening had specific goals, and a significant amount of work occurred beforehand—on the part of the planners and the participants—to ensure that those goals were reached. As in a graduate program, clarity of purpose was essential. But beyond the particular goals of any given convening, each convening was planned to create an environment where people trust each other enough to share ideas openly, give honest feedback, and respond respectfully in disagreements. Knowing that we did not have all the answers, we made every effort to create a setting that allowed others to generate and share ideas. Five principles guided the development of the convenings' goals and agenda.

IDEAS AT THE CENTER. Provocative ideas were always at the heart of a CID convening as a starting point of conversations that might have otherwise turned rapidly to the logistical or political (such as matters of how to implement a particular practice or work with specific colleagues). For example, in the first set of convenings we began with a panel of participants debating the commissioned essays for that field. By starting with, and returning to, ideas, participants' attention stayed focused on larger questions of purpose: Why do we want to change our program? Toward what ends? What are promising strategies? These questions kept discussions from foundering on objections and obstacles.

Just as importantly, the agenda always included opportunities to take risks. Convenings gave people time and space to try out (and often reject) new ideas. One year we asked every department to "Describe one idea that would be interesting to implement. It need not be vetted or endorsed by the rest of the department. In fact, you can come up with all kinds of reasons why it won't work or will never be accepted. But it would be so cool and so interesting if . . ." With this kind of permission, no idea was too crazy, too untenable, or too costly. By encouraging true intellectual imagination, new energy and ideas could be tested, regardless of the final outcome.

A MIXTURE OF PEDAGOGIES. From the first communications with CID convening participants, we were clear that they could expect a mixture of formats, including plenary sessions, campus teamwork time, structured small groups, presentations, and social occasions. We paired departments as "friendly critics," expected to give feedback and advice about emerging plans to another department that under other circumstances might have been regarded as a competitor. Basic pedagogical principles helped structure the agenda: we changed the format every couple of hours; we made sure that participants had ample opportunity to actively engage, rather than just listen. Convening tools included worksheets and posters.

Our advance communications about the convenings also highlighted the focus on creating intellectual community (see Exhibit A.2). Members of the group knew what was expected of them and were given opportunities to raise questions and make suggestions. Each day ended with a "one-minute feedback form," with two prompts: "(1) The ideas I found to be most useful and interesting today were . . ." and "(2) My thoughts and suggestions for tomorrow are . . ." Carnegie staff read all of the sheets each evening, and often adjusted our plans accordingly.

MULTIPLE VOICES. Carnegie convenings are deliberately structured to include many opportunities for participants to engage with one another and with the central themes of the meeting, and thus it was important that everyone be able to participate fully. Each participant was expected to share his ideas with others in presentations and discussions, both formally and informally. In fact, during the parts of the meeting in which campuses made presentations, we deliberately structured the proceedings so that the two campus representatives attended presentations in different rooms. This meant that all students and faculty members were responsible for making a presentation. In addition, team members were only hearing half of the presentations, obliging them to listen carefully and share what they had learned with their teammates. This helped level the playing field between students and faculty members on each campus's team. Indeed, many participants, both faculty and students, noted that

Exhibit A.2. A Community of Scholars

Before each convening all participants were sent this philosophical statement:

The participating departments in the CID provide a group of colleagues who are and will be allies in the process of creating the best forms of doctoral education for the discipline. As emissaries from those departments, you will learn from your peers, forge new relationships, and create visions of what is possible. We see the group as a community of scholars, and we have deliberately included graduate students, the next generation, as members of that community. We have also invited a small number of other leaders of the field to attend the convening to provide intellectual leavening to the discussions.

This convening is more than a workshop. It is a crucible for incubating new ideas, and a chance to consider carefully the implications of those strategies, as well as how to document and share your work with the larger disciplinary community. It is a fundamental tenet of our work at Carnegie that all ideas ought to be held up to critical scrutiny and made public. We apply this in the Scholarship of Teaching and Learning through the Carnegie Academy for the Scholarship of Teaching and Learning (CASTL) program, and the same principles apply to the CID.

○

this was the most powerful aspect of the convenings: seeing how well faculty and students could work together as colleagues.

As convening organizers we were also mindful that students often censor themselves, staying quiet in a room full of faculty members. We worked hard to make sure students took an active part in discussions. Each convening began with a dinner, and after dinner each student was asked to speak for a few minutes. Students introduced themselves and their other campus team members, and, as requested in advance, gave brief reports as representatives of their departments. Students were thus the first speakers, and this broke the ice. Each convening also included one timeblock in which students, faculty members, and observers each caucused as a group by role. In one memorable session both faculty members and students spent time lamenting that students lose their passion in the first year of graduate school. Both groups were reluctant to share this concern with the other, but when they did, it galvanized a shared commitment to addressing this problem, one faced by many departments.

The relationships formed at the meetings were marked by generosity. Members of the convening communities came from many different backgrounds, yet, without fail, connections developed between people who had no professional obligation to extend themselves to others. Faculty offered advice to graduate students from other programs, graduate students suggested ideas to each other for how to stay on track to completing their dissertations, and individuals were willing to take the lead on projects that probably wouldn't provide tangible rewards. This spirit of goodwill affects a group and makes a community a more positive and productive place, and it is worth cultivating it purposefully.

HIGH EXPECTATIONS. It is tempting to acknowledge the amount of work on every student's and faculty member's plate, and thus set low demands for preparation for a convening. But in fact, we set high expectations and asked each participant to complete several assignments in advance, which often involved consulting widely with the leadership team and other members of the department. We usually sent background readings as well, including a packet of the participants' biographical sketches to peruse on the plane. By asking a lot we sent the signal that this was a working meeting and everyone was expected to pull their weight. It was gratifying to see these expectations met every single time. Of course, we clearly explained what we were asking, and why. This meant that convenings truly were an opportunity to learn about departments' work, including their successes and setbacks, with other departments in a spirit of candor and the camaraderie of a shared mission. These meetings were also an opportunity to be accountable to other departments for actual progress made since the group last met, and to formulate action plans for the next year.

UNSTRUCTURED CONVERSATIONS. Last, but not least, the Carnegie convenings included the all-important social components. Although it can be easy to dismiss socializing as "touchy-feely engineering," building personal connections is a key to strengthening intellectual connections. The opening dinner always had carefully planned seating—mixing diners by role (student, faculty, observer, Carnegie staff), by campus, and mixing new and returning participants. The rest of the meals were informal events that only occasionally included short presentations during dessert. And every convening included a chance to walk in the adjacent Stanford foothills. A simple question over wine, a new idea generated during a walk: these are moments of intellectual engagement that can be planned but not scripted.

Researching

Carnegie's goal is to leave a legacy of deeper understanding of the practice of graduate education. And so our third role was as research partners exploring the process of change in graduate education. The research agenda was integral to the activities of department and the Foundation throughout the CID. We partnered with departments that were willing to examine what they do in a scholarly manner, and to examine, document, and understand exemplary practices that advance student formation. Sharing ideas, effective practices, work in progress, and the deliberation and implementation process among participating departments was an important part of the CID. As described earlier, the commitment to "make it public" in the interests of knowledge building and field building was an up-front obligation of participating in the CID.

Most research projects start with a review of the prior literature, and this was no exception. We summarized the studies and reports on doctoral education writ large (Carnegie Initiative on the Doctorate, 2001) and wrote literature reviews for each field that were shared with all of the participating departments. The CID was an action and research project, and our questions and methods evolved in light of what we learned. Our research methods were primarily observational and unobtrusive. Carnegie staff saw every event (site visits, meetings at disciplinary societies, convenings) as an opportunity for us to learn, enriching our thinking and collecting examples. We watched, listened, and learned as faculty and students told us about what was happening on their campuses.

Foundation staff conducted two surveys in all participating departments, one of graduate students (in 2004) and one of graduate faculty (in 2005). Like most of our activities, the surveys did double duty. Survey data were shared with participating departments to provide information about their students and their program. The surveys were not hypothesis-testing instruments; rather, they informed us at Carnegie about the impact of the initiative and broad matters of doctoral pedagogy. (The surveys are described in greater detail in Appendix C.)

A number of publications in disciplinary, campus, and national outlets have emerged from the CID, some written by Carnegie staff and others by departmental participants. This book, of course, is a culminating publication of the project.

Conclusion

Boiling down five years of work into a few pages tends to obscure the hard work and the hard thinking that went on in each participating department and behind the scenes of the CID. But we want to conclude by making clear that the structures and processes of the CID were intended to serve as a blueprint for how to organize a doctoral program. Two principles deserve to be articulated. First, our strategies were not set in stone. Even during the planning stage of the CID, we were sharing our ideas at disciplinary society meetings, and incorporating feedback into an ever-evolving game plan. Once we selected the participating departments, and got to know members of the leadership teams, the ways in which we communicated evolved. Newly emerging technological advances, notably the KEEP tool, allowed us to give up PowerPoint templates as a way for departments to share their work. By the same token, the premise of the CID is that doctoral programs should be continuously interrogated: Are we doing the best we can? Do changing circumstances demand new practices?

Second, we were creating our own intellectual community within the CID. In particular, the convenings were designed to provide a model for fostering intellectual community on campus. Of course an academic department is far more complex than a project meeting, but our participants often told us that our tactics were successful on campus as well. It therefore seems useful to look at CID convenings as an example of what is needed to create and sustain intellectual community. Because no one is expected to have all the answers, people can admit what they don't know. Hearing ideas from others, asking questions that might reveal one's own lack of knowledge, and getting excited about learning something new are all features of a vibrant intellectual community. The excitement generated by these kinds of teaching and learning exchanges is exactly what we hoped to foster in participants' home settings.

ENDNOTES

1. A summary of the studies and reports of the 1990s was prepared in the early months of the CID (Carnegie Initiative on the Doctorate, 2001).

2. The project director was senior scholar George E. Walker. Chris Golde was the research director. Senior scholar Laura Jones and research scholar Andrea Conklin Bueschel were also members of the CID team. Pat Hutchings joined the project during the year this book was written. Amita Chudgar and Kim Rapp were research assistants for the CID.

Sonia Gonzalez, Leslie Eustice, Ruby Kerawalla, Tasha Kalista, Emily
Stewart, and Lydia Baldwin were all administrative assistants during the
project.

3. The CID Advisory Committee was chaired by Donald Kennedy, president
emeritus and Bing Professor of Environmental Science and Policy emeritus,
Stanford University, and editor-in-chief of *Science* magazine. The other
members were Bruce Alberts, former president of the National Academy
of Sciences and professor of Biochemistry and Biophysics, University of
California, San Francisco David Damrosch, professor of English and Comparative Literature, Columbia University; Michael Feuer, executive director
of the Division of Behavioral and Social Sciences and Education, National
Research Council; Phillip Griffiths, professor of mathematics and former
director of the Institute for Advanced Study, Princeton University; Dudley
Herschbach, Baird Professor of Science in chemistry, Harvard University;
Stanley Katz, professor of Public and International Affairs and director
of the Center for Arts and Cultural Policy Studies at Princeton University;
Joshua Lederberg, Sackler Foundation Scholar and professor emeritus,
Rockefeller University; Kenneth Prewitt, Carnegie Professor of Public
Affairs, Columbia University; Robert Rosenzweig, president emeritus of the
Association of American Universities; Henry Rosovsky, Lewis P. and
Linda L. Geyser University Professor emeritus, Harvard University;
Lee S. Shulman, president of The Carnegie Foundation for the Advancement
of Teaching; and Debra W. Stewart, president of the Council of
Graduate Schools.

APPENDIX B: LIST OF PARTICIPATING DEPARTMENTS

Eighty-four departments and programs representing forty-four universities were selected to participate in the Carnegie Initiative on the Doctorate (CID). In the field of education some of the participants represent entire colleges of education. Originally, fifty were designated "partner departments" and thirty-four were called "allied departments." All departments received regular communications from the Foundation, and were included in many of the CID's activities, as detailed in Appendix A. In addition, representatives from partner departments were invited to attend the two rounds of disciplinary convenings in 2003 and 2004, and all partner departments were visited by a Carnegie staff member at least once. After fall 2004 we no longer distinguished between categories of departments, and began to refer to all eighty-four as "participating departments." All participating departments were able to apply to participate in the 2005 cross-disciplinary convenings. Departments originally designated allied departments are indicated with an asterisk.

Chemistry

Duke University, Department of Chemistry

Howard University, Department of Chemistry

* Northeastern University, Department of Chemistry and Chemical Biology

The Ohio State University, Department of Chemistry

* Stony Brook University, Department of Chemistry

University of Colorado at Boulder, Department of Chemistry and Biochemistry

University of Michigan, Department of Chemistry

* University of Oklahoma, Department of Chemistry and Biochemistry

University of Texas at Austin, Department of Chemistry and Biochemistry

University of Wisconsin-Madison, Department of Chemistry

* Virginia Polytechnic Institute and State University, Department of Chemistry

Education

Arizona State University, Division of Curriculum and Instruction

Indiana University, School of Education

Michigan State University, Division of Science and Mathematics Education

Michigan State University, Department of Teacher Education

The Ohio State University, College of Education

* Texas A&M University, Department of Educational Psychology

* University of California, Davis, School of Education

University of Colorado at Boulder, School of Education

* University of Georgia, Department of Educational Psychology and Instructional Technology

* University of Illinois at Urbana-Champaign, Department of Educational Psychology

* University of Iowa, Department of Psychological & Quantitative Foundations

University of Michigan, Educational Studies Program

University of North Carolina at Chapel Hill, School of Education

University of Southern California, Rossier School of Education

Washington State University, College of Education

English

Columbia University, Department of English and Comparative Literature

Duke University, Department of English

* Howard University, Department of English

Indiana University, Department of English

* Michigan State University, Department of English

The Ohio State University, Department of English

* Pennsylvania State University, Department of English

Texas A&M University, Department of English

* University of Georgia, Department of English

* University of Kentucky, Department of English

University of Michigan, Department of English

University of Pittsburgh, Department of English Language and Literature

* University of Rochester, Department of English

* University of Toronto, Department of English

* Washington University in St. Louis, Department of English

* Wayne State University, Department of English

History

Arizona State University, Department of History

Duke University, Department of History

* Howard University, Department of History

* Kent State University, Department of History

* Michigan State University, Department of History

The Ohio State University, Department of History

* Stony Brook University, Department of History

Texas A&M University, Department of History

University of Connecticut, Department of History

University of Illinois at Urbana-Champaign, Department of History

University of Kansas, Department of History

University of Minnesota, Department of History

* University of New Mexico, Department of History

University of Pittsburgh, Department of History

* University of Southern California, Department of History

University of Texas at Austin, Department of History

Mathematics

Duke University, Department of Mathematics

* Howard University, Department of Mathematics

* Kent State University, Department of Mathematical Sciences

The Ohio State University, Department of Mathematics

Stony Brook University, Mathematics Department & Institute for Mathematical Sciences

University of Illinois at Urbana-Champaign, Department of Mathematics

University of Michigan, Department of Mathematics

University of Nebraska-Lincoln, Department of Mathematics

* University of North Carolina at Chapel Hill, Department of Mathematics

University of Southern California, Department of Mathematics

* University of Utah, Department of Mathematics

Neuroscience

Boston University School of Medicine, Department of Anatomy and Neurobiology

* Dartmouth College, Neuroscience Center

Duke University, Department of Psychological and Brain Sciences

Georgetown University, Interdisciplinary Program in Neuroscience

Michigan State University, Neuroscience Program

The Ohio State University, Neuroscience Graduate Studies Program

* University of Alabama at Birmingham, Department of Neurobiology

University of Illinois at Urbana-Champaign, Neuroscience Program

* University of Louisville, Anatomical Sciences and Neurobiology

* University of Maryland, Baltimore, Program in Neuroscience

University of Minnesota, Graduate Program in Neuroscience

University of Pittsburgh, Center for Neuroscience (CNUP)

* University of Southern California, Neuroscience Graduate Program

* University of Vermont, Anatomy & Neurobiology (Biomedical Neuroscience)

University of Wisconsin-Madison, Neuroscience Training Program

APPENDIX C: OVERVIEW OF
THE SURVEYS

Carnegie staff administered two surveys, one of graduate students and one of graduate faculty, to CID participating departments. Both the surveys were exploratory in nature; they were efforts to better understand the contours of doctoral education and to provide useful information to CID staff and participating departments. (The survey instruments for the graduate student and faculty surveys are in Appendices D and E respectively.) It was not our intention to be able to make claims about the state of doctoral education generally or in each field specifically, nor was this an assessment of the particular programs; rather, these data are indicators of potential trouble spots. They suggest avenues for further investigation and highlight disciplinary differences and similarities. The responses to the open-ended questions, particularly the specific probes in the faculty survey, provide a window into practice and the rationale that underlies it. Survey data were shared with participating departments to provide information about their students, their faculty, and their program.

Graduate Student Survey

The Carnegie Graduate Student (GS) survey examined the relationship between student experiences in a doctoral program and the outcomes of doctoral education. It asked questions about students' preparation for the full range of responsibilities which may be expected of doctorate holders, including research, teaching, and the application of disciplinary knowledge and skills to practical problems in the world outside the university. The questions were intended to inquire about opportunities provided by the doctoral program and not to evaluate individual students' personal achievements. The student survey included questions about whether students have had specific experiences (in the areas of teaching, research, service, participation in the department and discipline) and the extent to which their experiences contributed to their knowledge, skills, and habits of mind. Other questions asked how students are integrated into the department's intellectual community; how students develop as researchers and scholars; the relationship of students with their advisors; clarity of formal requirements and informal expectations; and the participation of students in activities related to the CID.

Graduate Faculty Survey

The Carnegie Graduate Faculty (GF) survey was designed to explore graduate faculty members' perceptions, beliefs, and activities related to doctoral education and to advising and teaching doctoral students. The GF survey focused on the relationship between faculty practices and responsibilities in doctoral programs and the outcomes of doctoral education. The aim was to understand the role of faculty in doctoral education from the faculty point of view. It was not a survey about faculty time, faculty work, or other aspects of being a faculty member that are not directly related to graduate education. Some questions asked about philosophy and practice of teaching and advising. Others asked how faculty are integrated into the department's intellectual community; the role of faculty in developing students as researchers and scholars; the role of faculty in developing students as teachers; and the participation of faculty in activities related to the CID. The GF survey included several questions about the extent to which the respondents believe that their advisees engage in some of the experiences or achieve the outcomes probed in the GS survey.

Survey Administration

We endeavored to survey all doctoral students and tenure-track or tenured faculty (we assumed that most of these have the responsibility of "graduate faculty") in all CID participating departments. To preserve confidentiality and reduce workload, departments were simply asked to forward an e-mail with the URL of the survey to all possible respondents. Participation was voluntary; some departments did not forward the invitation to participate.

In the spring and summer of 2004, students were invited to complete the GS survey, and gift certificates were awarded to ten randomly selected respondents who provided their contact information at a second Web site. In all, 2,176 students from seventy-six departments participated in the survey. In the spring and summer of 2005, faculty members were invited to complete the GF survey, and gift certificates were also awarded to ten randomly selected respondents. A total of 668 faculty members from sixty-three departments participated in the survey. We do not know the response rates, because we do not know the total number of possible respondents. The number of respondents by discipline for both surveys is shown in Table C.1.

Data Analysis and Interpretation

Tables C.2 (students) and C.3 (faculty) describe the characteristics of the survey respondents. These data help situate our respondents relative to national profiles of students and faculty at doctoral-granting institutions, and to highlight some disciplinary differences.

In general, our analysis of quantitative items was limited to simple frequencies. One of the most interesting uses of the survey data was to confirm disciplinary differences about which we had anecdotal evidence. To be sure, there are many things about which there is general agreement among students or faculty, but when the differences are striking, we disaggregate the data we report. We only report data for "all students" or "all faculty" when the differences between fields are not significant, but remind readers that the disciplines are not equally represented in the survey sample. In many cases we only report the student data for those in the final stage of their program, working primarily on their dissertations; we call these students "dissertators."

Both of the GF and GS surveys included open-ended questions, often of the "please make additional comments" variety. We culled some of the comments from each survey to illustrate points throughout this manuscript. The GF survey also included more specific open-ended questions, and the responses were categorized and coded by at least two members of the team, who received input on categories from several other Carnegie Foundation scholars.

One of our goals for the GS survey was to develop the ability to measure stewardship; using factor analysis, we tested the conceptual robustness of our items. We feel reasonably confident that the student survey does so, but in order to be used as a diagnostic tool at the department level, or to measure change over time, it is important to have nearly census-like response rates (Golde and Rapp, 2006).

Table C.1. Number of Respondents for Carnegie Graduate Student and Graduate Faculty Surveys

	Graduate student survey (2004)			Graduate faculty survey (2005)		
Discipline	Number of departments represented	Total number of respondents	Respondents per department (min–max)	Number of departments represented	Total number of respondents	Respondents per department (min–max)
Chemistry	11	397	8–87	10	74	2–18
Education	11	538	28–105	12	126	1–30
English	14	409	8–58	10	121	1–21
History	15	293	9–41	11	120	2–17
Mathematics	11	282	2–86	8	78	2–18
Neuroscience	14	257	10–35	12	147	1–28
Total	76	2,176	—	63	668	—

Table C.2. Profile of Carnegie Graduate Student Survey Respondents

	Chemistry	Education	English	History	Mathematics	Neuroscience	Total
Number of respondents	397 (18.2% of total)	538 (24.7%)	409 (18.7%)	293 (13.5%)	282 (13.0%)	257 (11.8%)	2,176
Average age	27	36	30	34	26	28	31
Female	50.0%	72.9%	69.8%	47.5%	28.6%	57.0%	57.4%
U.S. citizen	75.0%	83.6%	84.6%	85.3%	58.8%	79.0%	78.9%
White (of U.S. citizens)	85.2%	79.6%	88.9%	80.8%	78.3%	74.3%	81.8%
Stage in program							
Course taker	9.8%	30.1%	19.2%	17.7%	20.2%	10.6%	19.1%
Pre-proposal	45.5%	40.9%	42.3%	29.4%	58.9%	53.5%	44.2%
Dissertator	44.7%	28.9%	38.6%	52.8%	21.0%	35.9%	36.6%
Expected total time to degree	5.2 years	5.0 years	5.8 years	6.2 years	5.4 years	5.1 years	5.4 years
Primary career goal							
Research-intensive faculty	17.2%	19.6%	35.9%	28.6%	39.9%	38.1%	28.2%
Teaching-intensive faculty	23.8%	33.0%	43.3%	45.4%	25.0%	13.9%	31.7%
Academic research (non-teaching)	4.4%	4.9%	1.8%	3.7%	6.5%	6.6%	4.4%
Business, government, or non-profit organization	36.1%	11.3%	1.8%	5.6%	10.9%	13.5%	13.4%

Table C.3. Profile of Carnegie Graduate Faculty Survey Respondents

	Chemistry	Education	English	History	Mathematics	Neuroscience	Total
Number of respondents	74 (11.1% of total)	126 (18.9%)	121 (18.1%)	120 (18.0%)	78 (11.7%)	147 (22.0%)	668
Female	19.4%	53.2%	45.8%	47.4%	8.3%	36.6%	38.4%
Tenure-track or tenured	98.6%	92.7%	100.0%	98.3%	93.6%	95.9%	96.5%
Year received doctorate							
1991–2004	31.5%	33.9%	35.3%	34.8%	17.9%	29.5%	31.1%
1981–1990	23.3%	22.3%	22.7%	21.7%	34.6%	34.2%	25.5%
1980 or earlier	45.2%	43.8%	42.0%	43.5%	47.4%	36.3%	42.3%
Employed four or more years at current institution	89.0%	81.1%	83.8%	84.5%	87.0%	80.0%	83.6%
Served as Chair, Director of Graduate Studies, or Dean	32.4%	54.8%	48.8%	44.2%	47.4%	36.1%	44.3%
Mean number of students currently advising							
Primary advisor/dissertation chair	5.27	4.39	2.51	2.49	1.56	1.56	2.94
Committee member	7.38	6.71	4.18	4.59	1.90	3.81	4.72
Pre-dissertation advisor	1.85	3.56	2.59	2.32	1.68	1.63	2.34
Total number of students served as primary advisor during career							
0	1.4%	5.7%	8.3%	11.2%	6.6%	4.2%	6.5%
1–5	12.9%	18.9%	29.2%	34.5%	50.0%	45.8%	32.6%
6–10	18.6%	18.9%	20.0%	21.6%	25.0%	27.1%	22.1%
11–15	17.1%	17.2%	11.7%	12.9%	9.2%	13.9%	13.7%
15+	50.0%	39.3%	30.8%	19.8%	9.2%	9.0%	25.2%

APPENDIX D: GRADUATE
STUDENT SURVEY

I. *Your Experiences as a Doctoral Student*

These activities might be required or optional parts of your program, and may have taken place in the summer or during a time when you were not formally enrolled. Please do not include activities from the time before you enrolled in this doctoral program. There are eleven questions in this section.

1. While pursuing doctoral studies, which of the following have you discussed with faculty or fellow doctoral students? (Check all that apply.)

   ____ I have discussed the historical progression of ideas and approaches in my discipline.

   ____ I have discussed controversies in my discipline.

   ____ I have discussed current issues of importance in my discipline.

   ____ I have discussed the contributions of my discipline to society.

   ____ I have discussed ethical dilemmas that might arise in research (e.g., intellectual property, plagiarism, confidentiality).

   ____ I have discussed ethical dilemmas that might arise in teaching (e.g., cheating, sexual harassment).

   ____ I have discussed ethical dilemmas that might arise in non-academic work settings (e.g., freedom of expression, intellectual property, issues of conscience, conflict of interest).

2. While pursuing doctoral studies, which of the following teaching activities have you engaged in? (Check all that apply.)

   ____ I attended a workshop or course on teaching in my discipline.

   ____ I attended a general workshop or course on teaching.

   ____ My teaching was observed by a faculty member or fellow doctoral student with the goal of providing me constructive feedback on my teaching.

____ I used the resources of the campus teaching and learning center.

____ I discussed teaching philosophy and strategies with a faculty member.

____ I discussed teaching philosophy and strategies with fellow graduate students.

3. While pursuing doctoral studies, which of these teaching activities have you performed? (Check all that apply.)

____ I led a discussion section or lab section.

____ I gave a lecture.

____ I prepared a syllabus.

____ I experimented with a variety of instructional strategies.

____ I designed assignments or examinations.

____ I evaluated and graded assignments or examinations.

____ I used information technology in teaching (e.g., PowerPoint, animations, digital video).

____ I defined learning objectives for my students.

____ I held office hours.

____ I developed a written teaching philosophy.

____ I had successive teaching opportunities in which I took increased responsibility (e.g., from grader to section leader to independent instructor; or from lab assistant to head lab manager to developing labs).

____ I was the primary instructor for an undergraduate course at my university.

____ I was the primary instructor for an undergraduate course at another college or university.

4. While pursuing doctoral studies, which of the following community service activities related to your discipline have you engaged in? (Check all that apply.)

____ I took part in civic or advocacy activities related to my discipline (e.g., writing legislation, writing an opinion piece, giving testimony).

____ I gave a formal talk about my research to an audience of people outside of my discipline (e.g., alumni, civic organizations).

____ I took part in an educational event aimed at the public (e.g., museum display, Brain Awareness Week, a public history project).

____ I took part in an educational event aimed for K–12 students or undergraduates (e.g., majors day, tutoring, literacy programs).

5. Prior to starting work on your dissertation, which of these research-related activities have you engaged in? (Check all that apply.)

____ I discussed what makes a good research question.

____ I critically evaluated or reviewed published work in my field.

____ I helped others develop a research or funding proposal.

____ I independently developed a proposal for a research grant or fellowship.

____ I analyzed and interpreted data (or text).

____ I wrote up research findings.

6. Have you started work (e.g., literature review, proposal development, data collection) on your dissertation?

____ Yes

____ No

7. While working on your dissertation, which of these research-related activities have you engaged in? (Check all that apply.)

____ I discussed what makes a good research question.

____ I critically evaluated or reviewed published work in my field.

____ I helped others develop a research or funding proposal.

____ I independently developed a proposal for a research grant or fellowship.

____ I analyzed and interpreted data (or text).

____ I wrote up research findings.

____ I haven't yet begun my dissertation research.

8. While pursuing doctoral studies, I engaged in collaborative intellectual work (research, teaching, outreach, writing) with colleagues in other disciplines:

____ Never

____ On two occasions or fewer

____ On three occasions or more

9. While pursuing doctoral studies, how many research presentations (including poster presentations) have you made at conferences? (Enter number below.)

____ On my campus

____ At regional or national meetings

10. While pursuing doctoral studies, how many research papers have you authored or co-authored (including pieces accepted for publication but not yet published)? _____

11. Please use this space to elaborate on your answer to any question in this section, or to tell us anything else you would like us to know about your experiences as a doctoral student. (Please limit your response to 250 words or less.)

II. *Your Experiences with Advising and Mentoring*

This section asks questions about the faculty members who are responsible for guiding you through your program. Your Primary Advisor is the faculty member formally serving as your academic advisor, dissertation chair, or research supervisor. If you have co-advisors, answer questions in reference to the one person with whom you work most closely. If you have no advisor, you can skip the question. There are four questions in this section.

12. Which of these behaviors describes your primary advisor:

	Not at all				To a great extent	
A. My advisor is available to me when I have questions related to my research.	1	2	3	4	5	N/A
B. My advisor gives me regular feedback on my research.	1	2	3	4	5	N/A
C. My advisor gives me regular feedback on my progress toward degree completion.	1	2	3	4	5	N/A
D. My advisor's feedback is valuable to me.	1	2	3	4	5	N/A
E. My advisor helps me develop professional relationships with others in the field.	1	2	3	4	5	N/A
F. My advisor advocates for me with others.	1	2	3	4	5	N/A
G. My advisor challenges me intellectually.	1	2	3	4	5	N/A
H. My advisor provides information about academic career paths open to me.	1	2	3	4	5	N/A
I. My advisor provides information about non-academic career paths open to me.	1	2	3	4	5	N/A
J. My advisor supports me in the career path of my choosing.	1	2	3	4	5	N/A
K. My advisor models good professional relationships.	1	2	3	4	5	N/A
L. My advisor clearly keeps my personal and professional interests in mind.	1	2	3	4	5	N/A

13. How many faculty members do you consider to be your advisors or mentors?

_____ None

_____ One

_____ Two

_____ Three

_____ Four or more

14. If there are people who consistently provide you with advice that you find helpful, who are they? (Check all that apply.)

_____ My primary or formal advisor

_____ Another faculty member (who is not my formal advisor)

_____ A doctoral student in my program

_____ A post-doctoral fellow

_____ My spouse or partner

_____ Another family member

_____ A friend (who is not listed above)

_____ No one

_____ Other (please specify)

15. Please use this space to elaborate on your answer to any question in this section, or to tell us anything else you would like us to know about your experiences with advising and mentoring. (Please limit your response to 250 words or less.)

III. Your Understanding of Your Doctoral Program

A doctoral program consists both of formal written requirements (e.g., courses, examinations, the dissertation, some number of terms one must be registered) and informal expectations (e.g., to participate in meetings or conferences, to advise younger students, to apply for outside fellowships). Some doctoral programs make the formal requirements and informal expectations very clear; in other cases they are less clearly understood. In this section we want to determine the degree of clarity in your program regarding the requirements and expectations you must fulfill in order to receive the PhD. There are four questions in this section.

16. How well do you know the formal requirements for successful completion of your program?

_____ I know the requirements well enough to explain them to someone else.

____ I know the requirements well enough to make it through the program but I could not fully explain them to someone else.

____ I have an incomplete understanding of the requirements.

____ I have no idea what the requirements are.

17. How well do you know the informal (or unspoken) expectations for successful completion of your program?

____ I know the expectations well enough to explain them to someone else.

____ I know the expectations well enough to make it through the program but I could not fully explain them to someone else.

____ I have an incomplete understanding of the expectations.

____ I have no idea what the expectations are.

18. Has the educational purpose of each of the following requirements or expectations been clearly conveyed to you? (Check N/A if not an expected part of your program.)

	Yes	No	N/A
A. Introductory first year overview course			
B. Cumulative exam(s) (usually in first two years, demonstrating subject mastery)			
C. Qualifying exam or process (the requirement for Advancement to Candidacy)			
D. The dissertation prospectus/proposal			
E. Oral presentation or defense of the dissertation			
F. Annual review of your progress			
G. Preparation of a research or funding proposal			
H. Development of a research program (a stream of research projects)			
I. Development of a career plan			

19. Please use this space to elaborate on your answer to any question, or to tell us anything else you would like us to know about your understanding of your doctoral program. (Please limit your response to 250 words or less.)

IV. Your Sense of Community

Departments and disciplines can contain communities of scholars: groups of colleagues who interact socially and intellectually. Participation in these communities includes formal interactions (in classrooms, seminars, labs and offices) and activities that are informal (for example, eating lunch together); and activities that may be primarily social in nature (potluck dinners, a softball team). Some of these interactions may take other forms than face-to-face exchanges (e.g., email, letters, telephone calls). This section has five questions.

20. While pursuing doctoral studies, which of the following activities related to participating in your departmental community have you engaged in? (Check all that apply.)

_____ I served on a departmental committee with faculty.

_____ I played a formal role in faculty hiring (e.g., served on a search committee, interviewed candidates).

_____ I played a formal role in graduate student admissions (e.g., served on an admissions committee, hosted potential students during campus visits).

_____ I participated in graduate student events (e.g., social events, orientation for new students, study groups).

_____ I organized graduate student events.

_____ I mentored other graduate students.

_____ I mentored undergraduate students.

_____ I gave or received feedback on ideas or work in progress to/from a fellow student.

_____ I am part of an intellectual network that goes beyond my immediate classmates and includes colleagues senior or junior to myself.

_____ I know a significant proportion of people in my department (faculty and students) outside my subfield.

21. While pursuing doctoral studies, which of the following activities related to participating in the broader disciplinary community have you engaged in? (Check all that apply.)

_____ I subscribed to a professional journal.

_____ I joined a professional association.

_____ I served on a committee for a professional association.

_____ I attended a regional or national professional meeting.

_____ I read professional journals regularly.

_____ I have given or received feedback on ideas or work in progress to/from a faculty member or researcher outside of my university.

_____ I have given or received feedback on ideas or work in progress to/from a student outside of my university.

_____ I am part of a professional network that extends beyond the boundaries of my department or university (e.g., keeping in touch with former classmates or colleagues, corresponding with colleagues at other institutions with similar interests).

22. In your doctoral program, to what extent do the following groups operate as intellectual and social communities?

	Not at all				To a great extent	
A. Cohorts of students (entering in the same year)	1	2	3	4	5	N/A
B. Cross-cohort groups of students	1	2	3	4	5	N/A
C. Lab groups	1	2	3	4	5	N/A
D. Subfields or areas of study	1	2	3	4	5	N/A
E. The department or program as a whole	1	2	3	4	5	N/A

23. To what extent do you participate in these communities?

	Not at all				To a great extent	
A. Student cohort	1	2	3	4	5	N/A
B. Cross-cohort group of students	1	2	3	4	5	N/A
C. Lab group	1	2	3	4	5	N/A
D. Subfield or area of study	1	2	3	4	5	N/A
E. The department or program as a whole	1	2	3	4	5	N/A

24. Please use this space to elaborate on your answer to any question, or to tell us anything else you would like us to know about your sense of belonging to a community. (Please limit your response to 250 words or less.)

V. Outcomes of Your Doctoral Program

At the end of your doctoral program, regardless of the career you pursue, you will be joining a disciplinary community. There are norms and standards for the knowledge, skills, and habits of mind you ought to learn and develop over the course of your doctoral studies. We want to understand how well you believe you have internalized them at this stage in your career. We also want to understand your overall assessment of your doctoral experiences to this point. There are eight questions in this section.

25. To what extent have your experiences in your doctoral program contributed to your knowledge, skills, and habits of mind in the following areas:

	Not at all				To a great extent	
A. I have a broad understanding of my discipline as a whole.	1	2	3	4	5	N/A
B. I have deep expertise in at least one specialized area of knowledge.	1	2	3	4	5	N/A
C. I am proficient in some research techniques commonly used within my discipline.	1	2	3	4	5	N/A
D. I am familiar with most of the research techniques used in my field.	1	2	3	4	5	N/A
E. I am aware of major issues and controversies in my discipline.	1	2	3	4	5	N/A
F. I am aware of major issues and controversies in my discipline about methodological approaches.	1	2	3	4	5	N/A
G. I have knowledge of the history of my discipline.	1	2	3	4	5	N/A
H. I can locate my work in the intellectual landscape of my discipline.	1	2	3	4	5	N/A
I. I understand how knowledge in my discipline is relevant to public issues.	1	2	3	4	5	N/A
J. I can work collaboratively with colleagues.	1	2	3	4	5	N/A
K. I am comfortable explaining basic concepts of my discipline to someone outside of it.	1	2	3	4	5	N/A
L. I can apply the ethical standards of practice in my discipline.	1	2	3	4	5	N/A
M. I can design AND teach a course in my field.	1	2	3	4	5	N/A
N. I can use a variety of instructional strategies when teaching.	1	2	3	4	5	N/A

(Continued)

	Not at all				To a great extent	
O. I can create a classroom climate inclusive of a diverse population of students and diverse learning styles.	1	2	3	4	5	N/A
P. I am able to communicate my ideas in oral forms expected by my discipline.	1	2	3	4	5	N/A
Q. I can state and defend a position to a group of colleagues that includes colleagues senior to me.	1	2	3	4	5	N/A
R. I can generate interesting questions that are worth investigating.	1	2	3	4	5	N/A
S. I can design research that meets the standards of credible work in my discipline.	1	2	3	4	5	N/A
T. I can design AND carry out a line of research or scholarship of my own devising.	1	2	3	4	5	N/A
U. I feel prepared to become a leader in my disciplinary community.	1	2	3	4	5	N/A
V. I can apply my skills and knowledge to important social issues.	1	2	3	4	5	N/A

26. Which three areas of development should your program pay more attention to? (Choose three.)

_____ A broad understanding of my discipline as a whole.

_____ Deep expertise in at least one specialized area of knowledge.

_____ Proficiency in some research techniques commonly used within my discipline.

_____ Familiarity with most of the research techniques used in my field.

_____ Awareness of major issues and controversies in my discipline.

_____ Knowledge of the history of my discipline.

_____ Locating my work in the intellectual landscape of my discipline.

_____ Understanding how knowledge in my discipline is relevant to public issues.

_____ Working collaboratively with colleagues.

_____ Confidence when explaining basic concepts of my discipline to someone outside of it.

_____ Ability to apply the ethical standards of practice in my discipline.

_____ Ability to design AND teach a course in my field.

_____ Using a variety of instructional strategies when teaching.

_____ Creating a classroom climate inclusive of a diverse population of students and diverse learning styles.

_____ Communicating my ideas in oral forms expected by my discipline.

_____ Stating and defending a position to a group of colleagues that includes colleagues senior to me.

_____ Generating interesting questions that are worth investigating.

_____ Designing research that meets the standards of credible work in my discipline.

_____ Designing AND carrying out a line of research or scholarship of my own devising.

_____ Participating as a member of the intellectual community of my department.

_____ Participating as a member of the intellectual community of my discipline.

27. If you could go back in time, knowing what you know now, would you enter doctoral studies again?

_____ Yes

_____ Maybe

_____ No

28. If you would choose to pursue the doctorate again, would you change your choice of the following:

	Yes	Maybe	No
A. Discipline			
B. Subfield or Area			
C. University			
D. Department			
E. Advisor			

29. At this point in your studies:

	Not at all				To a great extent	
A. How satisfied are you with the educational experiences you have had in this program?	1	2	3	4	5	N/A
B. How well prepared do you feel to begin a career in your discipline?	1	2	3	4	5	N/A

30. What is your primary career goal?

____ I would prefer a research-intensive faculty position.

____ I would prefer a teaching-intensive faculty position.

____ I would prefer a non-teaching academic research position.

____ I would prefer to work in business, government, or a non-profit organization.

____ I would prefer to be self-employed.

____ Undecided

____ Other (please specify)

31. How many faculty members in your department personify the principles and life you aspire to, regardless of your career goals?

____ None

____ One or two

____ Three or more

32. Please use this space to elaborate on your answer to any question, or to tell us anything else you would like us to know about the outcomes of your doctoral program. (Please limit your response to 250 words or less.)

VI. Your Program and the CID

We would like to know your impressions of how much influence participation in the CID (Carnegie Initiative on the Doctorate) has had in your department during the last year. There are four questions in this section.

33. Have you been invited to participate in activities related to your department's CID work?

_____ Yes

_____ Not sure

_____ No

34. Do you feel that your opinions and those of other doctoral students are influencing the decision-making process in your program's CID work? (Check N/A if you haven't participated or don't know.)

	Not at all				To a great extent	
To what extent?	1	2	3	4	5	N/A

35. Do the proposed changes to the doctoral program appear significant to you? (Check N/A if you haven't participated or don't know.)

	Not at all				To a great extent	
How significant?	1	2	3	4	5	N/A

36. Please use this space to elaborate on your answer to any question, or to tell us anything else you would like us to know about your program's participation in the Carnegie Initiative on the Doctorate. (Please limit your response to 250 words or less.)

VII. *Information About You*

37. What is your discipline?

_____ Chemistry

_____ Education

_____ English

_____ History

_____ Mathematics

_____ Neuroscience

38. What is your university? _____

39. How many years of doctoral study have you completed? _____

40. How many more years of doctoral study do you anticipate before earning your doctorate? _____

41. Which of these have you completed? (Check all that apply.)

____ Required courses

____ Qualifying exams

____ Advancement to candidacy

____ Approval of proposed dissertation project

____ Dissertation defense

____ None of the above

42. Sex:

____ Male

____ Female

43. Age:

44. Nationality:

____ U.S. citizen

____ Resident alien

____ Other (please specify)

45. Race/ethnicity: (If more than one apply, check all that apply.)

____ White, non-Hispanic

____ Black, non-Hispanic

____ Hispanic or Latino

____ Asian

____ Native Hawaiian or Other Pacific Islander

____ American Indian or Alaskan Native

APPENDIX E: GRADUATE FACULTY SURVEY

I. *Teaching and Advising Doctoral Students*

This section asks questions about your roles teaching and advising doctoral students. Several items focus on the role of the primary advisor, while others address teaching and advising more generally. There are five questions in this section.

1. When you teach graduate courses (courses in which a majority of students are pursuing a graduate degree), how frequently during class do you:

	Never				Nearly every class session	
A. Discuss the historical progression of ideas and approaches in the discipline.	1	2	3	4	5	N/A
B. Discuss the choices you made in constructing the course itself.	1	2	3	4	5	N/A
C. Discuss controversies in the discipline.	1	2	3	4	5	N/A
D. Discuss current issues of importance in the discipline.	1	2	3	4	5	N/A
E. Discuss the contributions of the discipline to society.	1	2	3	4	5	N/A
F. Discuss ethical dilemmas that might arise in research (e.g., intellectual property, plagiarism, confidentiality).	1	2	3	4	5	N/A
G. Discuss ethical dilemmas that might arise in teaching (e.g., cheating, sexual harassment).	1	2	3	4	5	N/A

(Continued)

	Never				Nearly every class session	
H. Discuss ethical dilemmas that might arise in work settings (e.g., freedom of expression, intellectual property, issues of conscience, conflict of interest).	1	2	3	4	5	N/A
I. Discuss what makes a good research question.	1	2	3	4	5	N/A
J. Ask students to critically evaluate or review published work in the discipline.	1	2	3	4	5	N/A

2. We understand there is variation among students and how one advises them.

   a. Please consider a typical student for whom you serve(d) as primary advisor (by "primary advisor" we mean serving as primary academic advisor, dissertation chair, or research supervisor), and estimate how often you:

	Never	Rarely			Nearly every class session	
A. Give feedback on progress toward degree completion.	1	2	3	4	5	N/A
B. Give feedback on their research.	1	2	3	4	5	N/A
C. Give feedback on their teaching.	1	2	3	4	5	N/A
D. Advocate for them with others.	1	2	3	4	5	N/A
E. Provide information about academic career paths open to them.	1	2	3	4	5	N/A
F. Provide information about non-academic career paths open to them.	1	2	3	4	5	N/A
G. Solicit their input on matters of teaching.	1	2	3	4	5	N/A
H. Solicit their input on matters of research.	1	2	3	4	5	N/A
I. Set mutual expectations of your mutual working relationship.	1	2	3	4	5	N/A
J. Assist them in developing a research program that will continue after PhD.	1	2	3	4	5	N/A

b. Please consider a typical student upon whose dissertation committee you serve(d) but are not primary advisor, and estimate how often you:

	Never	Rarely			Nearly every class session	
A. Give feedback on progress toward degree completion.	1	2	3	4	5	N/A
B. Give feedback on their research.	1	2	3	4	5	N/A
C. Give feedback on their teaching.	1	2	3	4	5	N/A
D. Advocate for them with others.	1	2	3	4	5	N/A
E. Provide information about academic career paths open to them.	1	2	3	4	5	N/A
F. Provide information about non-academic career paths open to them.	1	2	3	4	5	N/A
G. Solicit their input on matters of teaching.	1	2	3	4	5	N/A
H. Solicit their input on matters of research.	1	2	3	4	5	N/A
I. Set mutual expectations of your mutual working relationship.	1	2	3	4	5	N/A
J. Assist them in developing a research program that will continue after PhD.	1	2	3	4	5	N/A

3. How frequently do you typically meet outside of class with students for whom you are the primary advisor? Check the box that best applies for students at each stage.

a. First-year students

____ Once or twice a term (semester or quarter)

____ Once a month

____ Once a week

____ Two to three times a week

____ Daily

____ Not applicable

b. Students within a year of completing dissertation

____ Once or twice a term (semester or quarter)

____ Once a month

____ Once a week

____ Two to three times a week

____ Daily

____ Not applicable

4. Is there someone whose advising you try to emulate? (Check all that apply).

____ No one

____ My doctoral advisor

____ Another faculty member from graduate program or post-doc

____ A faculty member from undergraduate program

____ A colleague I worked with at this or another university

____ Someone else (please specify): _____

5. Please use this space to elaborate on your answer to any question in this section (teaching and advising doctoral students). (Please limit your response to 250 words.)

II. Student Outcomes

This section asks you to assess how proficient your students become as teachers, researchers, and members of the discipline as a result of their education in the doctoral program. There are seven questions in this section.

6. When serving as a primary advisor (primary academic advisor, dissertation chair, or research supervisor), how important is it to you to ensure that your doctoral advisees are effective teachers by the time they receive their doctorate?

Not at all				Very important	
1	2	3	4	5	N/A

7. Considering a typical student you advised (as primary advisor or dissertation committee member), how proficient were they at these aspects of teaching by the time they received the doctorate?

	Unable				Excellent		
A. Giving lectures	1	2	3	4	5	Don't Know	N/A
B. Knowing the history of the discipline	1	2	3	4	5	Don't Know	N/A
C. Leading discussions	1	2	3	4	5	Don't Know	N/A
D. Preparing a syllabus	1	2	3	4	5	Don't Know	N/A
E. Designing assignments or examinations	1	2	3	4	5	Don't Know	N/A
F. Evaluating assignments or examinations	1	2	3	4	5	Don't Know	N/A
G. Creating classroom climate inclusive of a diverse population of students and diverse learning styles	1	2	3	4	5	Don't Know	N/A
H. Defining learning objectives for students	1	2	3	4	5	Don't Know	N/A

8. Students learn to teach in a variety of ways, including taking courses on teaching in the discipline, getting feedback from teaching mentors, and taking increased responsibility for instructing a series of courses. For your students, what experiences and activities are most effective for learning to teach an undergraduate class? (Please limit your response to 250 words.)

9. Considering a typical student you advised (as primary advisor or dissertation committee member), how proficient were they at these aspects of research by the time they received the doctorate?

	Unable				Excellent		
A. Having a broad understanding of the discipline as a whole	1	2	3	4	5	Don't Know	N/A
B. Recognizing what makes a good research question	1	2	3	4	5	Don't Know	N/A
C. Asking a good research question	1	2	3	4	5	Don't Know	N/A
D. Choosing a manageable research problem or project	1	2	3	4	5	Don't Know	N/A
E. Critically evaluating or reviewing published work in the field	1	2	3	4	5	Don't Know	N/A
F. Proficiently employing research techniques	1	2	3	4	5	Don't Know	N/A

(*Continued*)

	Unable				Excellent		
G. Independently developing a proposal for a research grant or fellowship	1	2	3	4	5	Don't Know	N/A
H. Analyzing and interpreting data (or text) with support and guidance from faculty	1	2	3	4	5	Don't Know	N/A
I. Independently analyzing and interpreting data (or text)	1	2	3	4	5	Don't Know	N/A
J. Writing up research findings for publication	1	2	3	4	5	Don't Know	N/A
K. Working collaboratively with colleagues	1	2	3	4	5	Don't Know	N/A
L. Applying the ethical standards of practice in the discipline	1	2	3	4	5	Don't Know	N/A
M. Applying their skills and knowledge to important social issues	1	2	3	4	5	Don't Know	N/A

10. Students become proficient at aspects of research by participating in many activities and experiences, such as reading articles, working on a research team, and presenting research findings at meetings.

   a. For your students, what experiences and activities are most effective for learning to ask a good research question? (Please limit your response to 250 words.)

   b. For your students, what experiences and activities are most effective for learning to independently analyze and interpret data (or text)? (Please limit your response to 250 words.)

11. What are the most effective things you do as an advisor that lead to overall student success? Please include a definition of "overall student success." (Please limit your response to 250 words.)

12. Please use this space to elaborate on your answer to any question in this section (student outcomes). (Please limit your response to 250 words.)

III. Your Department and Doctoral Program

Departments and disciplines contain communities of scholars: groups of colleagues who interact socially and intellectually. Participation in these communities includes formal interactions (in classrooms, seminars, labs, and offices) and activities that are informal (eating lunch together); and activities that may be primarily social in nature (potluck dinners, a softball team). Some of these interactions may take other forms than face-to-face exchanges (email, letters, telephone calls). This section has five questions.

13. In the department/program, to what extent do the following groups operate as intellectual and social communities?

	Not at all				To a great extent	
A. Cohorts of students (entering in the same year)	1	2	3	4	5	N/A
B. Cross-cohort groups of students	1	2	3	4	5	N/A
C. Lab groups	1	2	3	4	5	N/A
D. Subfields or areas of study	1	2	3	4	5	N/A
E. The faculty of the department or program as a whole	1	2	3	4	5	N/A
F. The faculty and students of the department or program as a whole	1	2	3	4	5	N/A
G. Interdisciplinary research groups	1	2	3	4	5	N/A
H. Cohorts of students (entering in the same year)	1	2	3	4	5	N/A

14. To what extent do you participate in these communities?

	Not at all				To a great extent	
A. Lab groups	1	2	3	4	5	N/A
B. Subfields or areas of study	1	2	3	4	5	N/A
C. The faculty of the department or program as a whole	1	2	3	4	5	N/A
D. The faculty and students of the department or program as a whole	1	2	3	4	5	N/A
E. Interdisciplinary research groups	1	2	3	4	5	N/A

15. Faculty members set expectations for students in the doctoral program. Some are shared among faculty, and others are idiosyncratic to each faculty member. To what extent do faculty in your department have a shared understanding of:

	Extremely individually determined				Shared by all faculty	
A. Purpose of the doctoral program	1	2	3	4	5	N/A
B. The educational purpose of the qualifying exam	1	2	3	4	5	N/A
C. What constitutes an acceptable level of student performance on the qualifying exam	1	2	3	4	5	N/A
D. Responsibilities of primary advisors	1	2	3	4	5	N/A
E. Responsibilities of dissertation committee members who are not primary advisors	1	2	3	4	5	N/A
F. Standards of rigor and quality for the dissertation	1	2	3	4	5	N/A
G. Acceptable career paths of graduates	1	2	3	4	5	N/A

16. In your opinion, what are the features of a doctoral program and its community that are most effective for developing doctoral students as junior colleagues? To what extent do these regularly occur within your department or program? (Please limit your response to 250 words.)

17. Please use this space to elaborate on your answer to any question in this section (your department and doctoral program). (Please limit your response to 250 words.)

IV. Your Program and the CID

We would like to know your impressions of how much influence participation in the CID (Carnegie Initiative on the Doctorate) has had in your department during the last year. There are four questions in this section.

18. Have you been invited to participate in activities related to your department's CID work?

____ No

____ Not sure

____ Yes

19. Do you feel that your opinions and those of other faculty members are influencing the decision-making process in your program's CID work? (Check N/A if you haven't participated or don't know.)

	Not at all				To a great extent	
To what extent?	1	2	3	4	5	N/A

20. Do the proposed changes to the doctoral program appear significant to you? (Check N/A if you haven't participated or don't know.)

	Not at all				To a great extent	
How significant?	1	2	3	4	5	N/A

21. Please use this space to elaborate on your answer to any question in this section (your program and the CID). (Please limit your response to 250 words.)

V. Information About You

Please tell us a little more about yourself. You are of course free to skip any questions that you do not wish to answer. There are nine questions in this section.

22. What is your discipline?

_____ Chemistry

_____ Education

_____ English

_____ History

_____ Mathematics

_____ Neuroscience

23. What is your university?_____

24. In all, how many students have you served as primary advisor during your faculty career?

____ 0

____ 1–5

____ 6–10

____ 11–15

____ 15+

25. For how many doctoral students are you currently:

____ Primary advisor/ Dissertation chair

____ Member of dissertation committee, not chair

____ Pre-dissertation students for whom I am the advisor of record

26. Is your current appointment as a faculty member tenure-track or tenured?

____ Yes

____ No [If No, then go to end of survey.]

27. How many years have you been employed at this institution as a faculty member?

____ 0–3

____ 4+

28. During what time period were you awarded the doctorate?

____ 2001–2004

____ 1991–2000

____ 1981–1990

____ 1971–1980

____ 1970 or earlier

29. Have you ever served in any of the following administrative roles? (Check all that apply; include service at all institutions where you have been employed since the PhD.)

____ Chair of the department or program

____ Director of graduate studies

____ Member of graduate admissions committee

____ Member of graduate policy committee

____ Member of a faculty search committee

_____ Member of a faculty tenure and promotion committee

_____ Academic administrator (i.e., assistant or associate dean, dean)

_____ CID leadership team or committee

_____ None of the above

_____ Other (please specify)

30. Sex:

_____ Male

_____ Female

REFERENCES

American Chemical Society. *Graduate Education in Chemistry. The ACS Committee on Professional Training: Surveys of Programs and Participants.* Washington, D.C.: American Chemical Society, 2002.

Arenson, K. W. "Columbia Soothes the Dogs of War in Its English Dept." *New York Times,* Mar. 17, 2002.

Arizona State University. "Outstanding Graduate Mentors." http://graduate.asu.edu/outstandingmentors.html, n.d.

Association of American Universities. "The Seventh Annual Conference." *Journal of Proceedings and Addresses of the Conference.* Washington, D.C.: Association of American Universities, 1906(7).

Association of American Universities. *Committee on Graduate Education: Report and Recommendations.* Washington, D.C.: Association of American Universities, 1998a.

Association of American Universities. *Committee on Postdoctoral Education: Report and Recommendations.* Washington, D.C.: Association of American Universities, 1998b.

Association of American Universities. *Report of the Interdisciplinarity Task Force.* Washington, D.C.: Association of American Universities, 2005.

Atkinson, R., and Tuzin, D. "Equilibrium in the Research University." *Change,* 1992, 24(3), 20–29.

Austin, A. E. "Preparing the Next Generation of Faculty: Graduate School as Socialization to the Academic Career." *Journal of Higher Education,* 2002, 73(1), 94–122.

Bacchetti, R., and Ehrlich, T. (eds.). *Reconnecting Education & Foundations: Turning Good Intentions into Educational Capital.* San Francisco: Jossey-Bass, 2006.

Bargar, R. R., and Duncan, J. K. "Cultivating Creative Endeavor in Doctoral Research." *Journal of Higher Education,* 1982, 53(1), 1–31.

Becher, T., and Trowler, P. R. *Academic Tribes and Territories: Intellectual Enquiry and the Culture of Disciplines.* Buckingham: The Society for Research into Higher Education & Open University Press, 2001.

Bender, T. "Expanding the Domain of History." In C. M. Golde and G. E. Walker (eds.), *Envisioning the Future of Doctoral Education:*

Preparing Stewards of the Discipline. Carnegie Essays on the Doctorate.
(pp. 295–310). San Francisco: Jossey-Bass, 2006.

Bender, T., Katz, P. M., Palmer, C., and Committee on Graduate Education of the American Historical Association. *The Education of Historians for the Twenty-First Century.* Urbana: University of Illinois Press, 2004.

Berelson, B. *Graduate Education in the United States.* New York: McGraw-Hill, 1960.

Berliner, D. C. "Toward a Future as Rich as Our Past." In C. M. Golde and G. E. Walker (eds.), *Envisioning the Future of Doctoral Education: Preparing Stewards of the Discipline. Carnegie Essays on the Doctorate.* (pp. 268–289). San Francisco: Jossey-Bass, 2006.

Beyer, C. H., Gillmore, G. M., and Fisher, A. T. *Inside the Undergraduate Experience: The University of Washington's Study of Undergraduate Learning.* San Francisco: Jossey-Bass, 2007.

Board on Mathematical Sciences. *Renewing U.S. Mathematics: A Plan for the 1990s.* Washington, D.C.: National Academy Press, 1990.

Board on Mathematical Sciences. *Educating Mathematical Scientists: Doctoral Study and the Postdoctoral Experience in the United States.* Washington, D.C.: National Academy Press, 1992.

Boston University School of Medicine Department of Anatomy and Neurobiology. *GMS AN 805 Teaching in the Biomedical Sciences II—Practicum.* http://www.bu.edu/dbin/anatneuro/programs/courses/gms_an_804/overview.php, n.d.

Bousquet, M. "The Waste Product of Graduate Education. Toward a Dictatorship of the Flexible." *Social Text,* 2002, 20(1), 81–104.

Bowen, W. G., and Rudenstine, N. L. *In Pursuit of the PhD.* Princeton, N.J.: Princeton University Press, 1992.

Bowen, W. G., and Sosa, J. A. *Prospects for Faculty in the Arts and Sciences: A Study of Factors Affecting Demand and Supply, 1987–2012.* Princeton, N.J.: Princeton University Press, 1989.

Boyer, E. L. *Scholarship Reconsidered: Priorities of the Professoriate.* Princeton, N.J.: The Carnegie Foundation for the Advancement of Teaching, 1990.

Bransford, J. D., Brown, A. L., and Cocking, R. R. (eds.). *How People Learn: Brain, Mind, Experience, and School.* Washington, D.C.: National Research Council, 2000.

Breneman, D. W. *Graduate School Adjustments to the "New Depression" in Higher Education.* Washington, D.C.: National Academy of Sciences, 1975.

Brooks, P. "Graduate Learning as Apprenticeship." *The Chronicle of Higher Education,* Dec. 20, 1996, 43(17).

Brown, J. S. "New Learning Environments for the 21st Century: Exploring the Edge." *Change*, 2006, 38(5), 18–24.

Brown, J. S., Collins, A., and Duguid, P. "Situated Cognition and the Culture of Learning." *Educational Researcher*, 1989, 18(1), 35–42.

Brown, J. S., and Duguid, P. *The Social Life of Information.* Boston: Harvard Business School Press, 2000.

Brunette, L. "New Dual-Degree Program Meshes Neuroscience and Public Policy." *Quarterly: for Alumni and Friends of University of Wisconsin School of Medicine and Public Health*, 2006, 8(12), 30–31.

Bush, V. *Science, the Endless Frontier: A Report to the President.* Washington, D.C.: Office of Scientific Research and Development, 1945.

Carnegie Foundation for the Advancement of Teaching. *The Carnegie Classification of Institutions of Higher Education.* http://www.carnegiefoundation .org/classifications/index.asp, 2006.

Carnegie Initiative on the Doctorate. *Overview of Doctoral Education Studies and Reports: 1990–Present.* Stanford, Calif. Carnegie Foundation for the Advancement of Teaching, 2001.

Center for the Integration of Research Teaching and Learning. *The Pillars of CIRTL.* http://cirtl.wceruw.org/pillars.html, n.d.

Chan, T. F. "A Time for Change? The Mathematics Doctorate." In C. M. Golde and G. E. Walker (eds.), *Envisioning the Future of Doctoral Education: Preparing Stewards of the Discipline. Carnegie Essays on the Doctorate.* (pp. 120–134). San Francisco: Jossey-Bass, 2006.

Cherwitz, R. A., and Sullivan, C. A. "Intellectual Entrepreneurship: A Vision for Graduate Education." *Change*, 2002, 88(6), 23–27.

Choy, S. P., Cataldi, E. F., and Griffith, J. *Student Financing of Graduate and First-Professional Education, 2003–04: Profiles of Students in Selected Degree Programs and Part-Time Students* (NCES 2006–185). Washington, D.C.: National Center for Education Statistics, 2006.

Collaborative on Academic Careers in Higher Education. *New Study Indicates Faculty Treatment Matters More Than Compensation.* http://www.coache .org/reports/20060925.html, Sept. 26, 2006.

Collins, A., Brown, J. S., and Holum, A. "Cognitive Apprenticeship: Making Thinking Visible." *American Educator*, Winter, 1991.

Committee on Science Engineering and Public Policy. *Adviser, Teacher, Role Model, Friend: On Being a Mentor to Students in Science and Engineering.* Washington, D.C.: National Academy Press, 1997.

Council of Graduate Schools. *Research Student and Supervisor. An Approach to Good Supervisory Practice.* Washington, D.C.: Council of Graduate Schools, 1990.

Council of Graduate Schools. *Ph.D. Completion and Attrition: Policy, Numbers, Leadership and Next Steps*. Washington, D.C.: Council of Graduate Schools, 2004.

Council of Graduate Schools. *The Doctor of Philosophy Degree*. Washington, D.C.: Council of Graduate Schools, 2005.

Council of Graduate Schools. *Graduate Education: The Backbone of American Competitiveness and Innovation*. Washington, D.C.: Council of Graduate Schools, 2007.

Cronon, W. "Getting Ready to Do History." In C. M. Golde and G. E. Walker (eds.), *Envisioning the Future of Doctoral Education: Preparing Stewards of the Discipline. Carnegie Essays on the Doctorate*. (pp. 327–349). San Francisco: Jossey-Bass, 2006.

Cuban, L. *How Scholars Trumped Teachers: Change Without Reform in University Curriculum, Teaching, and Research, 1890–1990*. New York: Teachers College Press, 1999.

Cyr, T., and Muth, R. "Portfolios in Doctoral Education." In P. L. Maki and N. Borkowski (eds.), *The Assessment of Doctoral Education*. (pp. 215–237). Sterling, Va.: Stylus Publishing, 2006.

Damrosch, D. "Vectors of Change." In C. M. Golde and G. E. Walker (eds.), *Envisioning the Future of Doctoral Education: Preparing Stewards of the Discipline. Carnegie Essays on the Doctorate*. (pp. 34–45). San Francisco: Jossey-Bass, 2006.

Davidson, C. N. "What If Scholars in the Humanities Worked Together, in a Lab?" *The Chronicle of Higher Education*. The Chronicle Review, May 28, 1999, 45(38), p. B4.

Department of English and Comparative Literature. *Revisions to the Graduate Program*. http://www.columbia.edu/cu/english/grad_revisions.htm, May 15, 2004.

Donald, J. G. *Learning to Think: Disciplinary Perspectives*. San Francisco: Jossey-Bass, 2002.

Dreyfus, H. L., Dreyfus, S. E., and Athanasiou, T. *Mind over Machine: The Power of Human Intuition and Expertise in the Era of the Computer*. New York: Free Press, 1986.

Edwards, M. *Studies in American Graduate Education*. New York: The Carnegie Foundation for the Advancement of Teaching, 1944.

Eells, W. C. "Earned Doctorates in American Institutions of Higher Education, 1861–1955." *Higher Education*, 1956, XII(7), 109–114.

Ehrenberg, R., and others. *Inside the Black Box of Doctoral Education: What Program Characteristics Influence Doctoral Students' Attrition and Graduation Probabilities?* Ithaca, N.Y.: Cornell Higher Education Research Institute, 2005.

Eley, A. R., and Jennings, R. *Effective Postgraduate Supervision. Improving the Student/Supervisor Relationship.* Berkshire, England: Open University Press, 2005.

Elkana, Y. "Unmasking Uncertainties and Embracing Contradictions: Graduate Education in the Sciences." In C. M. Golde and G. E. Walker (eds.), *Envisioning the Future of Doctoral Education: Preparing Stewards of the Discipline. Carnegie Essays on the Doctorate.* (pp. 65–96). San Francisco: Jossey-Bass, 2006.

Everts, S. "Evolving the Doctorate: Carnegie Initiative Inspires Reshaping of Ph.D. Programs to Fit Modern Times." *Chemical & Engineering News,* Sept. 4, 2006, pp. 89–95.

Flexner, A. "Medical Education in the United States and Canada." *The Flexner Report (Bulletin No. 4).* New York: The Carnegie Foundation for the Advancement of Teaching, 1910.

Foster, C. R., Dahill, L. E., Goleman, L. A., and Tolentino, B. W. *Educating Clergy: Teaching Practices and Pastoral Imagination.* San Francisco: Jossey-Bass, 2006.

Geiger, R. L. *To Advance Knowledge: The Growth of American Research Universities, 1900–1940.* New York: Oxford University Press, 1986.

Glazer, J. *A Teaching Doctorate? The Doctor of Arts Degree, Then and Now.* Washington, D.C.: American Association for Higher Education, 1993.

Goldberger, M., Maher, B. A., and Flattau, P. E. (eds.). *Research-Doctorate Programs in the United States: Continuity and Change.* Washington, D.C.: National Academy Press, 1995.

Golde, C. M. "The Role of the Department and Discipline in Doctoral Student Attrition: Lessons from Four Departments." *Journal of Higher Education,* 2005, 76(6), 669–700.

Golde, C. M., and Dore, T. M. *At Cross Purposes: What the Experiences of Doctoral Students Reveal About Doctoral Education.* Philadelphia: A Report for the Pew Charitable Trusts, 2001. http://www.phd-survey.org/report.htm

Golde, C. M., Jones, L., Bueschel, A. C., and Walker, G. E. "The Challenges of Doctoral Program Assessment: Lessons from the Carnegie Initiative on the Doctorate." In P. L. Maki and N. Borkowski (eds.), *The Assessment of Doctoral Education.* (pp. 53–82). Sterling, Va.: Stylus Publishing, 2006.

Golde, C. M., and Rapp, K. "Assessing the Aims and Strategies of Doctoral Education in Six Disciplines." Paper presented at the annual conference of the American Educational Research Association, San Francisco, April 10, 2006.

Golde, C. M., and Walker, G. E. (eds.). *Envisioning the Future of Doctoral Education: Preparing Stewards of the Discipline. Carnegie Essays on the Doctorate.* San Francisco: Jossey-Bass, 2006.

Graduate School, University of Washington. *How to Mentor Graduate Students: A Faculty Guide.* The Graduate School, University of Washington, 2005a. http://www.grad.washington.edu/mentoring/GradFacultyMentor.pdf

Graduate School, University of Washington. *How to Obtain the Mentoring You Need: A Graduate Student Guide.* The Graduate School, University of Washington, 2005b. http://www.grad.washington.edu/mentoring/ GradStudentMentor.pdf

Graff, G. *Beyond the Culture Wars: How Teaching the Conflicts Can Revitalize American Education.* New York: Norton, 1992.

Graff, G. *Clueless in Academe: How Schooling Obscures the Life of the Mind.* New Haven: Yale University Press, 2003.

Graff, G. "Toward a New Consensus: The Ph.D. in English." In C. M. Golde and G. E. Walker (eds.), *Envisioning the Future of Doctoral Education: Preparing Stewards of the Discipline. Carnegie Essays on the Doctorate.* (pp. 370–389). San Francisco: Jossey-Bass, 2006.

Gross, R. A. "The Adviser-Advisee Relationship." *The Chronicle of Higher Education Careers,* http://chronicle.com/jobs/2002/02/2002022802c.htm, Feb. 28, 2002.

Grossman, P., and others. *Unpacking Practice: The Teaching of Practice in the Preparation of Clergy, Teachers, and Clinical Psychologists.* Paper presented at the American Educational Research Association, Montréal, Canada, Apr., 2005.

Hall, D. "Collegiality and Graduate School Training." *Inside Higher Ed,* http:// insidehighered.com/workplace/2006/01/24/hall, Jan. 24, 2006.

Hall, Z. W. "Maintaining Vitality Through Change." In C. M. Golde and G. E. Walker (eds.), *Envisioning the Future of Doctoral Education: Preparing Stewards of the Discipline.* Carnegie Essays on the Doctorate. (pp. 211–225). San Francisco: Jossey-Bass, 2006.

Handelsman, J., Pfund, C., Lauffer, S. M., and Pribbenow, C. M. *Entering Mentoring. A Seminar to Train a New Generation of Scientists.* Madison: University of Wisconsin Press, 2005.

Harmon, L. *A Century of Doctorates: Data Analysis of Growth and Change. Report for the National Research Council.* Washington, D.C.: National Academy Press, 1978.

Hartnett, R. T. "Environments for Advanced Learning." In J. Katz and R. T. Hartnett (eds.), *Scholars in the Making: The Development of Graduate and Professional Students.* (pp. 49–84). Cambridge: Ballinger Publishing, 1976.

Harvard University. *The Graduate School of Arts and Sciences: History and Organization.* http://www.hugsas.harvard.edu/publications/handbook/ history.html, n.d.

Heiss, A. M. "Berkeley Doctoral Students Appraise Their Academic Programs." *Educational Record,* Winter, 1967, 30–44.

Heiss, A. M. *Challenges to Graduate Schools.* San Francisco: Jossey-Bass, 1970.

Hoffer, T. B., and others. *Doctorate Recipients from United States Universities: Summary Report 2000.* Chicago: National Opinion Research Center, 2001.

Hoffer, T. B., and others. *Doctorate Recipients from United States Universities: Summary Report 2004.* Chicago: National Opinion Research Center, 2005.

Hoffer, T. B., and others. *Doctorate Recipients from United States Universities: Summary Report 2005.* Chicago: National Opinion Research Center, 2006.

Huber, M. T., and Hutchings, P. *Integrative Learning: Mapping the Terrain.* Washington, D.C.: Association of American Colleges and Universities, 2004.

Huber, M. T., and Hutchings, P. *The Advancement of Learning: Building the Teaching Commons.* San Francisco: Jossey-Bass, 2005.

Hurtado, A. L. "Intellectual Entrepreneurship: Improving Education and Increasing Diversity." *Change,* 2007, 93(1), 48–50.

Hutchings, P., and Clarke, S. E. "The Scholarship of Teaching and Learning: Contributing to Reform in Graduate Education." In D. Wulff and A. Austin (eds.), *Paths to the Professoriate.* (pp. 161–176). San Francisco Jossey-Bass, 2004.

Indiana University Department of English CID Committee. *Integrated Portfolio Draft June 04.* Unpublished memorandum, Indiana University Department of English, 2004.

James, W. "The Ph.D. Octopus." *Harvard Monthly,* Mar., 1903, 149–157.

Jaschik, S. "Making Grad School 'Family Friendly.'" *Inside Higher Education.* http://insidehighered.com/news/2007/04/04/family, April 4, 2004.

Kamler, B., and Thomson, P. *Helping Doctoral Students Write: Pedagogies for Supervision.* New York: Routledge, 2006.

Katz, J., and Hartnett, R. T. (eds.). *Scholars in the Making: The Development of Graduate and Professional Students.* Cambridge: Ballinger, 1976.

Kunstler, B. *Hothouse Effect: Intensify Creativity in Your Organization Using Secrets from History's Most Innovative Communities.* Saranac Lake, NY: AMACOM, 2004.

Laurence, D. "Employment of 1996–97 English Ph.Ds: A Report on the MLA's Census of Ph.D. Placement." *ADE Bulletin,* Winter, 1998(121), 58–69.

Laurence, D. "The Latest Forecast." *ADE Bulletin,* Spring, 2002(131), 14–19.

Levin, E. *Portfolio Exam Proposal.* Unpublished memorandum, University of Kansas, n.d.

Loehle, C. "A Guide to Increased Creativity in Research—Inspiration or Perspiration?" *Bioscience,* 1990, 40(2), 123–129.

Lovitts, B. E. *Leaving the Ivory Tower. The Causes and Consequences of Departure from Doctoral Study.* New York: Rowman and Littlefield, 2001.

Lovitts, B. E. "Being a Good Course-Taker Is Not Enough: A Theoretical Perspective on the Transition to Independent Research." *Studies in Higher Education,* 2005a, 30(2), 137–154.

Lovitts, B. E. "How to Grade a Dissertation." *Academe,* 2005b, 91(6), 18–23.

Lovitts, B. E. *Making the Implicit Explicit: Creating Performance Expectations for the Dissertation.* Sterling, Va.: Stylus, 2007.

Lunsford, A. A. "Rethinking the Ph.D. in English." In C. M. Golde and G. E. Walker (eds.), *Envisioning the Future of Doctoral Education: Preparing Stewards of the Discipline. Carnegie Essays on the Doctorate.* (pp. 357–369). San Francisco: Jossey-Bass, 2006.

Lunsford, A. A., Moglen, H., and Slevin, J. F. (eds.). *The Future of Doctoral Studies in English.* New York: Modern Language Association of America, 1989.

Maki, P. L., and Borkowski, N. (eds.). *The Assessment of Doctoral Education. Emerging Criteria and New Models for Improving Outcomes.* Sterling, Va.: Stylus, 2006.

Mathae, K. B., and Birzer, C. L. *Reinvigorating the Humanities: Enhancing Research and Education on Campus and Beyond.* Washington, D.C.: Association of American Universities, 2004.

Mayhew, L. B., and Ford, P. J. *Reform in Graduate and Professional Education.* San Francisco: Jossey-Bass, 1974.

MLA Committee on the Status of Graduate Students in the Profession. *Annual Report 2000–01.* New York: Modern Language Association, 2001.

MLA Executive Council Task Force on Graduate Education. "Conference on the Future of Doctoral Education." *PMLA,* 1999, 115(5), 1136–1278.

Modern Language Association. *Final Report of the MLA Committee on Professional Employment* (http://www.mla.org/reports/contents.htm). Washington, D.C.: Modern Language Association, 1998.

Modern Language Association. *Initial Employment Placements of 2000–01 Doctorate Recipients from U.S. Universities.* Unpublished data, Modern Language Association, 2003.

Mullen, C. A. *A Graduate Student Guide: Making the Most of Mentoring.* New York: Rowman and Littlefield, 2006.

Nathan, R. *My Freshman Year: What a Professor Learned by Becoming a Student.* Ithaca, N.Y.: Cornell University Press, 2005.

National Board on Graduate Education. *Graduate Education: Purposes, Problems and Potential (No. 1).* Washington, D.C.: National Board on Graduate Education, 1972.

National Board on Graduate Education. *Doctorate Manpower Forecasts and Policy (No. 2)*. Washington, D.C.: National Board on Graduate Education, 1973.

National Board on Graduate Education. *Federal Policy Alternatives Toward Graduate Education (No. 3)*. Washington, D.C.: National Board on Graduate Education, 1974.

National Board on Graduate Education. *Outlook and Opportunities for Graduate Education (No. 6)*. Washington, D.C.: National Board on Graduate Education, 1975a.

National Board on Graduate Education. *Science Development, University Development, and the Federal Government (No. 4)*. Washington, D.C.: National Board on Graduate Education, 1975b.

National Board on Graduate Education. *Minority Group Participation in Graduate Education (No. 5)*. Washington, D.C.: National Board on Graduate Education, 1976.

National Center for Education Statistics. *Digest of Education Statistics: 2005*. http://nces.ed.gov/programs/digest/d05/, 2005.

National Research Council. *Renewing U.S. Mathematics: Critical Resource for the Future*. Washington, D.C.: National Academy Press, 1984.

National Science Foundation. *Grants for Vertical Integration of Research and Education in the Mathematical Sciences (VIGRE). Program Solicitation*. Arlington, Va.: National Science Foundation, 1997.

National Science Foundation. *Postdoctoral Appointments: Roles and Opportunities*. Arlington, Va.: National Science Foundation (Division of Chemistry and the Office of Multidisciplinary Activities), 2003.

Nerad, M. "Ph.D.'s—Ten Years Later." Paper presented at the Re-envisioning the Ph.D. Conference, University of Washington, Apr. 14, 2000.

Nerad, M., and Cerny, J. "From Rumors to Facts: Career Outcomes of English Ph.D.'s: Results from the Ph.D.'s—Ten Years Later Study." *Council of Graduate Schools Communicator*, 1999, XXXII(7), 1–11.

Nettles, M. T., and Millet, C. M. *Three Magic Letters: Getting to Ph.D.* Baltimore, Md.: The Johns Hopkins University Press, 2006.

New York University. *The Graduate Forum*. http://www.nyu.edu/graduate.forum/, May 2004.

Nyquist, J. D., and others. "On the Road to Becoming a Professor: The Graduate Student Experience." *Change*, 1999, 31(3), 18–27.

Nyquist, J. D., and Woodford, B. J. Seven Propositions from 2000 Conference. Seattle: University of Washington, 2000.

Nyquist, J. D., and Wulff, D. *Working Effectively with Graduate Assistants*. Newbury Park, Calif.: Sage, 1995.

O'Meara, K., and Rice, R. E. *Faculty Priorities Reconsidered: Rewarding Multiple Forms of Scholarship*. San Francisco: Jossey-Bass, 2005.

Oakeshott, M. "The Voice of Poetry in the Conversation of Mankind." In M. Oakeshott (ed.), *Rationalism in Politics and Other Essays*. London: Methuen & Co. Ltd., 1962.

Odom, W. *Report of the Senior Assessment Panel of the International Assessment of the U.S. Mathematical Sciences*. Arlington, Va.: National Science Foundation, 1998.

Olson, G. A., and Drew, J. "(Re) Reenvisioning the Dissertation in English Studies." *College English*, 1998, 61(1), 56–66.

Paulovich, A. "Creativity and Graduate Education." *Molecular Biology of the Cell*, 1993, 4, 565–568.

Pelikan, J. J. *Scholarship and Its Survival: Questions on the Idea of Graduate Education*. Princeton, N.J.: Carnegie Foundation for the Advancement of Teaching, 1983.

Pelikan, J. J. *The Idea of the University: A Reexamination*. New Haven, Conn.: Yale University Press, 1992.

Pirrung, M. C. *Analysis of 2003 Graduate Student Survey*. Unpublished report, Duke University Department of Chemistry, 2003.

Preparing Future Faculty National Office. *PFF Web*. http://preparing-faculty.org, n.d.

Prewitt, K. "Who Should Do What: Implications for Institutional and National Leaders." In C. M. Golde and G. E. Walker (eds.), *Envisioning the Future of Doctoral Education: Preparing Stewards of the Discipline. Carnegie Essays on the Doctorate*. (pp. 23–33). San Francisco: Jossey-Bass, 2006.

Pyter, L. M., and others. *Mapping Neuroscience at Ohio State University: Graphic Representations of Program and Individual Scientific Breadth and Depth*. Conference poster. Presented at the Society for Neuroscience, Washington, D.C., Nov. 12–16, 2005.

Rudolph, F. *The American College and University: A History*. New York: Vintage Books, 1962.

Ryan, W. C. *Studies in Early Graduate Education: The Johns Hopkins, Clark University, the University of Chicago. (Bulletin No. 30)*. New York: The Carnegie Foundation for the Advancement of Teaching, 1939.

Savage, H. J. *Fruit of an Impulse: Forty-Five Years of The Carnegie Foundation, 1905–1950*. New York: Harcourt Brace, 1953.

Shulman, L. S. "From Minsk to Pinsk: Why a Scholarship of Teaching and Learning?" *The Journal of the Scholarship of Teaching and Learning*, 2000, 1, 48–52.

Shulman, L. S. *Report of the President (Report to the Board of Trustees)*. Stanford, Calif.: The Carnegie Foundation for the Advancement of Teaching, 2002.

Shulman, L. S. "Signature Pedagogies in the Professions." *Daedalus,* 2005, 134(3), 52–59.

Shulman, L. S., Golde, C. M., Bueschel, A. C., and Garabedian, K. J. "Reclaiming Education's Doctorates: A Critique and a Proposal." *Educational Researcher,* 2006, 35(3), 25–32.

Speicher, A. L. *The Association of American Universities: A Century of Service to Higher Education.* http://www.aau.edu/aau/Begin.html, n.d.

Stanford Research Communication. *About Our Program.* http://www.stanford .edu/group/i-rite/about.html, Apr. 5, 2007.

Stanford University Commission on Graduate Education. *Report of the Commission on Graduate Education.* Stanford, Calif.: Stanford University, 2005.

Stimpson, C. R. "General Education for Graduate Education." *The Chronicle of Higher Education,* November 1, 2002, p. B7.

Stimpson, C. R. "Words and Responsibilities: Graduate Education and the Humanities." In C. M. Golde and G. E. Walker (eds.), *Envisioning the Future of Doctoral Education: Preparing Stewards of the Discipline. Carnegie Essays on the Doctorate.* (pp. 390–418). San Francisco: Jossey-Bass, 2006.

Storr, R. F. *The Beginning of the Future.* New York: McGraw-Hill, 1973.

Sullivan, W. M. *Work and Integrity: The Crisis and Promise of Professionalism in America.* San Francisco: Jossey-Bass, 2005.

Sullivan, W. M., and others. *Educating Lawyers: Preparation for the Profession of Law.* San Francisco: Jossey-Bass, 2007.

Suzzallo, H. "Discussion of Graduate Work in American Universities." *Transactions and Proceedings of the National Association of State Universities in the United States of America,* 1927, 25, 83–99.

Taylor, C. "Heeding the Voices of Graduate Students and Postdocs." In C. M. Golde and G. E. Walker (eds.), *Envisioning the Future of Doctoral Education. Preparing Stewards of the Discipline. Carnegie Essays on the Doctorate.* (pp. 46–61). San Francisco: Jossey-Bass, 2006.

Tepper, S. J. "Taking the Measure of the Creative Campus." *Peer Review,* 2001, 8(2), 4–7.

Thelin, J. *A History of American Higher Education.* Baltimore: The Johns Hopkins University Press, 2004.

Thurgood, L., Golladay, M. J., and Hill, S.T. *U.S. Doctorates in the 20th Century (Special Report).* Washington, D.C.: National Science Foundation, 2006.

Tinto, V. "Appendix B: Toward a Theory of Doctoral Persistence." In *Leaving College: Rethinking the Causes and Cures of Student Attrition.* 2nd ed. (pp. 230–243). Chicago: University of Chicago Press, 1993.

Traweek, S. *Beamtimes and Lifetimes: The World of High Energy Physicists,*
    Cambridge, Mass.: Harvard University Press, 1988.

Tronsgard, D. T. "A Common-Sense Approach to the Dissertation: Should the
    Graduate Schools Take a Fresh Look at This Traditional Requirement."
    The Journal of Higher Education, 1963, 34(9), 491–495.

University of Chicago. *Graduate Workshops in the Humanities and Social
    Sciences.* http://cas.uchicago.edu/, n.d.

University of Michigan Department of Chemistry. *Chemical Sciences at the
    Interface of Education.* http://www.umich.edu/~csie/, Sept. 9, 2001.

van Gog, T., Ericsson, K. A., Rikers, R.M.J.P., and Paas, F. "Instructional
    Design for Advanced Learners: Establishing Connections Between the
    Theoretical Frameworks of Cognitive Load and Deliberate Practice."
    Educational Technology Research and Development, 2005, 53(3), 73–81.

Wenger, E. "Communities of Practice: The Social Fabric of a Learning
    Organization." *Healthcare Forum Journal,* 1996, 3(3), 149–164.

Wilson, E. O. "Back from Chaos." *The Atlantic Monthly,* 1998, 281(3), 41–62.

Wineburg, S. S. *Historical Thinking and Other Unnatural Acts: Charting the
    Future of Teaching the Past.* Philadelphia: Temple University Press, 2001.

Woodrow Wilson National Fellowship Foundation. *The Responsive Ph.D.:
    Innovations in U.S. Doctoral Education.* Princeton, N.J.: The Woodrow
    Wilson National Fellowship Foundation, 2005.

INDEX

A

Abzug, R., 32
Accreditors, 149
Adjunct faculty, 27
Administrator reform role, 146–147
American Chemical Society, 30
American Historical Association, 15, 121–122
Apprenticeship: advising agreement example, 104e–105e; conceptual underpinnings of, 109–110; defining features of, 91–103; making it work, 115–116; master-apprentice origins of, 89–90; positive versus negative forms of, 90–91; principles of effective pedagogy, 110–114; as signature pedagogy, 14, 117n.3; strategies for fostering humane qualities of, 103–109; terminology related to, 117n.5–118n.5. *See also* Faculty; Mentoring; Students
Apprenticeship features: collective responsibility as, 97–98; intentionality as, 91–94; multiple relationships as, 94–96; recognition as, 98–100, 102; respect, trust, reciprocity as, 102–103
Apprenticeship strategies: clear communication as, 103–104; knowing each other as, 013; providing regular feedback as, 104, 106–107; taking time as, 107–109
Arac, J., 6, 7
Arenson, K. W., 6
Arizona State University, 72, 100
Assessment: CID framework for guiding, 13; as doctoral education challenge, 156–157; portfolios used for, 156; of program effectiveness, 156–157

Association of American Colleges & Universities (AAC&U), 29, 137
Association of American Universities (AAU), 15, 22, 23, 27, 153
At Cross Purposes report, 86n.4
Austin, A. E., 132

B

Bacchetti, R., 149
Bargar, R. R., 61, 152
Bender, T., 10, 15, 122
Berelson, B., 21, 24, 34, 36
Berliner, D. C., 72
Beyer, C. H., 157
Birzer, C. L., 15
Boston University (BU), 98
Boston University School of Medicine, 70–71
Bousquet, M., 35
Bowen, W. G., 26, 29, 30
Boyer, E. L., 9
Bransford, J. D., 85, 103
Breneman, D. W., 24
Brooks, P., 89
Brown, A. L., 85
Brown, J. S., 92, 94, 109, 110, 123, 130, 133, 155
Bruner, J., 133
Brunette, L., 74
Bush, V., 23

C

Carnegie Foundation for the Advancement of Teaching: Flexner Report (1910) of, 62; graduate education study by, 28e–29e; reform role played by, 27. *See also* CID (Carnegie Initiative on the Doctorate)

Michigan State University, 65, 81, 99e
Multigenerational intellectual commu-
nity, 125–126
Muth, R., 55, 156

N

National Academy of Sciences, 100
National Board on Graduate Education
(NBGE), 23, 24, 25, 27, 38n.4
National Communication Association, 79
National Defense Education Act
(NDEA) [1957], 23
National Institutes of Health, 23
National Science Foundation (NSF), 9,
15, 23, 27, 74
National Security Agency, 46
Nerad, M., 27, 157
New York Times, 6
New York University Graduate Forum,
83–84
New York University Graduate School
of Arts and Sciences, 83
No Child Left Behind, 53
Nyquist, J. D., 29, 157

O

Oakeshott, M., 128
Office of Graduate Education (American
Chemical Society), 30
Ohio State University Neuroscience
Program, 51, 52e
Olson, G. A., 80

P

Paas, F., 85
Palmer, C., 15
PART principles, 13
Paulovich, A., 152
Pedagogy of research: early link between
doctoral education and, 23–24; as
emerging doctoral education challenge, 151–152; examining current
state of, 4–5; new approaches to,
13–14; student progressive development and, 63–66. *See also* University
research
Peer Review (journal), 34
Pelikan, J. J., 28–29

PhDs. *See* Doctorates (PhDs)
Preparing Future Faculty National
Office, 29, 138
Preparing Future Faculty (PFF) initiative
(1993), 29, 137, 139
Prewitt, K., 19, 141, 158
Professional identity, 71–74, 155–156
Professional portfolio: integrative
learning through, 78–79; qualifying
examinations replaced by, 54–56;
student assessment using, 156
Progress and Professional Grids (Univer-
sity of Kansas), 55–56
*Prospects for Faculty in the Arts and
Sciences* (Bowen and Sosa), 29
Public History Alumni Database
(Arizona State University), 73
Purposefulness principle, 13
Pyter, L. M., 51

Q

Qualifying examination: deliberations
over purpose of, 53; examining functions of, 41–42; mixed understanding of, 42; professional portfolio as
replacing, 54–56; shared understanding perceived by faculty, 42–43t. *See
also* Doctoral requirements

R

Racial/ethnic differences, 26fig
Reenvisioning the PhD project, 29–30
Reflection: CID framework for guiding,
13; portfolios as facilitating, 156;
providing time for, 130
REGS (Research Experiences for
Graduate Students), 66
Research. *See* Pedagogy of research;
University research
Respect: as apprenticeship feature,
102–103; as intellectual community
characteristic, 126–127
Rikers, R.M.J.P., 85
Rogers, W., 1, 2
Rosovky, H., 16
Rudenstine, N. L., 26, 30
Rudolph, F., 21, 22
Ryan, W. C., 28

S

Savage, H. J., 28

Scaffolding, 91–92

"Schemas," 85

Scholar formation: intellectual community theme of, 10–11, 120–139, 142; scholarly integration theme of, 9–10, 74–81, 142; stewardship theme of, 11–13, 142, 156–157. *See also* Doctoral education

Scholarship: integration theme of, 9–10, 74–81, 142; intellectual community theme of, 10–11, 120–139, 142; stewardship theme of, 11–13, 142, 156–157; tension between disciplinary and interdisciplinary, 153; traditional focus on teaching and learning, 157–158

Scholarship and its Survival: Questions on the Idea of Graduate Education (Pelikan), 28e

Scholarship Reconsidered: Priorities of the Professoriate (Boyer), 9

Science, the Endless Frontier (Bush), 23

Servicemen's Readjustment Act (1944)s, 23

Sharing ideas, 129

Shulman, L. S., 41, 43, 57, 81, 143

Signature pedagogy, 14, 117n.3. *See also* Apprenticeship

"Slowdown point," 54

Social event activities, 130

The Social Life of Information (Brown and Duguid), 123

Society for Neuroscience meeting (2005), 51

Sosa, J. A., 29

Stanford University Commission on Graduate Education, 71

Stanford University I-RITE program, 79

STEM (science, technology, engineering, and mathematics), 9–10

Stewardship: assessing program effectiveness as heart of, 156–157; as scholarship theme, 11–13, 142

Stimpson, C. R., 11, 61, 153

Storr, R. F., 22

Student progressive development: doctoral program models for, 62; formation of researchers, 63–66;

forming professional identity as part of, 71–74; forming teachers through experience, 66–71

Students: advising agreement between faculty and, 104e–105e; as agents of change and improvement, 35; allowing them to risk and fail, 129–130; challenge related to changing identities of, 155–156; collaborative learning by, 81–84; community service participation by, 74, 75t; conflict avoidance costs for, 45; demographics of doctoral recipients, 26t; doctoral education reform role of, 144–145; engaging fully in department life, 128; faculty reports on frequency of meetings with, 108fig; integrative learning by, 74–81; mentoring relationships and, 94–96, 101e; portfolios used to assess, 156; professional development of, 62–74; professional identity developed by, 71–74, 155–156; reflections on purpose of programs by, 45–47; reporting participation in engaged discipline activities in, 138fig; "slowdown point" for, 54; understanding of qualifying exam by, 41–42; vocational aspirations/concerns of, 35–37. *See also* Apprenticeship; Faculty

Studies in American Graduate Education (Carnegie Foundation), 28e

Studies in Early Graduate Education: The Johns Hopkins, Clark University, the University of Chicago (Carnegie Foundation), 28e

Sullivan, C. A., 73e

Sullivan, W. M., 109, 110

Suzzallo, H., 28

Sweeder, R., 81

T

TA training, 70

Taylor, C., 158

Teaching: progressive teacher formation, 66–71; traditional scholarship of, 157–158; Vesalius Program emphasis on, 70–71, 113–114

"Teaching commons" notion, 129